Enduring
Change
in Eating
Disorders

Other books by H. Charles Fishman

Family Therapy Techniques, co-author Salvador Minuchin
Evolving Models of Family Change, co-author Bernice Rosman
Treating Troubled Adolescents
Intensive Structural Therapy

Enduring Change in Eating Disorders

Interventions with long-term results

Foreword by Salvador Minuchin

H. Charles Fishman, M.D.

BRUNNER-ROUTLEDGE
NEW YORK AND HOVE

Information contained in this book accurately conveys the spirit of the author's work as a therapist, but all names, characteristics, and identifying details of the case histories in the book have been changed.

Published in 2004 by
Brunner-Routledge
29 West 35th Street
New York, NY 10001
www.brunner-routledge.com

Published in Great Britain by
Brunner-Routledge
27 Church Road
Hove, East Sussex
BN3 2FA
www.brunner-routledge.co.uk

Cover design: Polly Joseph, Auckland, New Zealand
Author photo: Jason Dorday, Auckland, New Zealand

Brunner-Routledge is an imprint of the Taylor & Francis Group.
Printed in the United States of America on acid-free paper.

10 9 8 7 6 5 4 3 2 1

Library of Congress Cataloging-in-Publication Data

Fishman, H. Charles (Herman Charles), date
    Enduring change in eating disorders : interventions with long-term
results / H. Charles Fishman.
        p. cm.
Includes bibliographical references and index.
    ISBN 0-415-94459-7 (hbk.)
    1. Eating disorders. 2. Eating disorders—Treatment. I. Title.
    RC552.E18F54 2004
    616.85'260651—dc22
                                        2003022220

To Salvador Minuchin, MD, and
in memory of Bernice Rosman, PhD
and Lester Baker, MD
For their contributions
to the treatment of eating disorders

And to Tana, Anu and Zev

Contents

Acknowledgments

There are many people to acknowledge in the creation of this book. First and foremost are the consumers and their families who willingly responded to my invitation to a follow-up interview. Their generosity is especially admirable, since I often asked them to revisit a difficult period in their lives. The follow-up interviews were intended to be informational, not therapeutic. Unlike in the treatment, I was careful not to be challenging; I only accepted information that was forthcoming. The last thing I wanted to do was to unstabilize things for these fine, caring families.

The work of Salvador Minuchin, Bernice Rosman, and Lester Baker (*Psychosomatic Families*) was paradigmatic for the therapy presented in this book. These pioneers deserve far greater acknowledgment beyond this volume.

My dear friend Braulio Montalvo was a vast source of wisdom and encouragement during the writing of this book. Braulio's suggestions on the transcripts of the treatment and the follow-up added invaluable wisdom and clarity. I also want to thank Salvador Minuchin for his comments on the draft of the book and his support for this project. A few weeks after orthopedic surgery, Sal climbed out of his sickbed to pen the Foreword. Nina Gunsenhauser, my long time editor, has again been instrumental in the development of this book. Nina's clarity of language and logic are invaluable. Nina delayed her retirement to help with this book—for this favor I am all the more grateful.

I also want to thank Cecile Herscovici from Buenos Aires who was a valuable resource of ideas and support for this book. I want to acknowledge Dr. Frank Thomas for his comments and his help in obtaining follow-up information for one of the cases.

Clare Docherty, my research assistant, was invaluable in terms of organizing the references. Clare's organizational skills and good cheer were extremely instrumental in bringing this volume to fruition. I would also like to acknowledge Kara Bettigole, who also helped with the references and always added an incisive view.

I also want to thank George Zimmar (editor) as well as Shannon Vargo at Taylor & Francis for their expert support in the development of this book. It was a pleasure working with them and their very professional organization.

Finally, I am forever fortunate for the love and support of my wife Tana, and our two terrific children, Anu and Zev.

Foreword

I will never forget her. Ann was 16 years old, with a long Modigliani neck, prominent cheekbones like Katharine Hepburn, and the mysterious, dark, longing eyes that starvation seems to favor. She had been transferred to Children's Hospital in Philadelphia from another hospital where, for the last 2 months she had refused to eat and first had been fed through a tube inserted through her nostrils into her stomach; her life now was maintained by intravenous feeding.

Ann's parents, her two younger siblings, the ward nurse, the pediatrician, and I surrounded her bed. Ann's smile was contagious. She was friendly, connected, and clearly wanted to be liked. The pediatrician was optimistic, and so was I. We had been there before, and had been successful. This pediatric ward specialized in eating disorders, and the staff was trained in the behavioral procedures that seemed to be effective in working with such patients during hospitalization.

The family was anxious to help. They had come from a nearby town and were staying in a nearby hotel. We had the first session around the bed, the pediatrician and myself exploring our territory. We were friendly and curious, joining with the family members to create an atmosphere of hope, but at 4 A.M., I received a call from the hospital. Ann was in a coma. An hour later, we congregated again around her bed, but Ann was not there. She remained in a coma and died the next day. Her face still haunts me, but she was the only patient who died during the period of our research project, in which we successfully treated over 50 patients, with a follow-up of 1 to 7 years.

Dr. Fishman's book is timely. It comes at a time when the therapeutic field has moved back toward working with the isolated individual and is preoccupied with a search for quick results through medication. In this book, instead, we see the importance of clinical thinking and, even more unusual, the value of long-term follow-ups to determine what went well in therapy, and where therapy failed the patient. Dr. Fishman talks about more than 100 patients, with a follow-up of up to 20 years. The author is honest and courageous, and the reader is invited into the sessions to see the struggles and the moments of "aha!" when a particular intervention creates the necessary tension to produce change. Fortunately for us, we can also observe the moments when family members correct the therapist or, in the follow-up many years later, invite him to reflect on the road not taken.

For me, the book brought back memories of my practice with anorexic patients. I relived the frustration of working with families caught in compulsive interpersonal circles that reduce the members to narrow renditions of themselves. Frequently, competent and sometimes brilliant people spend a large part of their lives counting calories.

The lunch sessions, which Dr. Fishman has conducted more of than any other practitioner, evolved not as part of a theoretical exploration but out of the frustration of our frequent failures at the initial stage of therapy. We had observed that families whose members were engaged and cooperative, nonetheless remained stuck in their usual patterns of relating, and the patient did not improve. Out of this observation, and following inductive pathways, we designed techniques directed to challenging dysfunctional patterns. Mistrusting words or stories, we were looking at what family members were doing to each other. The sessions became the stage on which the therapist could observe the dance of life. Instead of asking family members to describe the daily drama that revolved around eating, we invited the family to eat with the therapist—a procedure that subjected the therapist to the high emotionality of this routine encounter. This procedure became the "lunch session," a technique that was strenuous, primitive, unaesthetic, sometimes ugly, but surprisingly effective.

The intent behind the lunch session technique was to move the patient from monologue to dialogue; the obsessive-compulsive behavior of the eating disorder patient was pushed out, changing from an internal experience to the sphere of interpersonal polemic. We thought that, in her struggle for control, the patient was hurting herself, and we put the parents in the position of control, inviting them to save their daughter. This process required more than words and more than dialogue; it required the intensity of the struggle.

The way in which patients, family members, and therapists interact around the routine of lunch becomes visible in the segments that Dr. Fishman has selected. Of course, it becomes evident through the follow-ups that this initial technique is not a magic bullet for eating disorders, and the author describes the specificity with which he responds to individual needs. Among his innovations is the use of training in martial arts as a way of exploring self-control. During the follow-ups, as Dr. Fishman invites family members to reflect on their past experience it becomes evident that therapy does not immunize for life, but it is also clear that engaging the family in the process of healing builds bridges for further growth.

The cases presented are heterogeneous, underlining the fact that there is no formulaic approach to eating disorders, but the book is a necessary wake up call for the mental health profession. This is a period in which we are lured toward the simplistic search for the chemical compound to tame life. It is necessary, therefore, to reinforce the importance of seeing the person in his or her social context, developing therapeutic strategies based on grounded observation, stressing the significance of continuity in care, and recognizing the value of tracing the consequences of our interventions over the long term.

This is the book of a clinician who believes in his craft. We can see him observing, reflecting, worrying, doubting, pushing, rejoicing. He is the image of the kind of commitment that is necessary to succeed with some of the most difficult and resistant patients who come to us for help.

Salvador Minuchin

Introduction

If one was to pluck the tender shoot of the flax
From where will the bellbird sing its song?
Ask me, "What is the most important thing in the world?"
I will reply, "It is people, it is people, it is people!"
—Maori Proverb

In the early 1970s, three girls in their early teens with uncontrollable juvenile onset diabetes mellitus became an enormous challenge to the diabeticians at the Children's Hospital of Philadelphia. The girls' diabetes was so uncontrollable that on any given day one of the three girls was an inpatient. The treatment team searched for causes. Finding no biological cause, they delved into possible psychological factors. Individual counseling made no difference. The girls' diabetes continued to surge out of control. Likewise, counseling sessions with the mother and father brought no relief.

The cases were referred to Salvador Minuchin, MD, Bernice Rosman, PhD, and Lester Baker, MD, (1978), a team of clinicians at the Philadelphia Child Guidance Clinic (PCGC). The team was investigating psychosomatic illness and made an interesting observation: The girls' diabetes spiraled out of control in only one context—at home. Whereas ordinarily they would require 20 to 30 units of insulin per day, at certain times, at home, they would require as much as 500 units. These exacerbations would then lead to hospitalization. The team posited that family interactional patterns might be leading to these exacerbations. They postulated and tested a model they called the "psychosomatic family," whose characteristics are rigidity, triangulation, diffusion of conflict, and overprotectiveness.

While I was a general psychiatry resident at University of Pennsylvania, I heard (erroneous) tales that the doctors at PCGC were "curing" diabetes. What they were doing, however, was no mean feat in itself: finding a way to tame the stress in families so that the child's disease did not exacerbate.

At that point in my career, I was a refugee from philosophy, which I had studied in college. I fled philosophy because of the absence of data; everybody had their favorite theory, tenaciously argued with, at times, fervent religiosity. So I enrolled in medical school. There I was introduced to the beautiful scientific tradition that is evidence based and truly life saving. The medical profession relies on objective data. Each morning during rounds, the doctors would review lab results that gave concrete evidence that told them whether what they were doing was effective. Either way, the data led the way.

I specialized in psychiatry because that is where my real interests lie. But before I knew it, I was back in the realm of the subjective. In the world of psychotherapy theories were abundant, but there were no objective data to direct and track one's psychotherapy. I was looking for a model of psychotherapy that was based on grounded observation, and that was the beauty of the psychosomatic family model—treatment was directed according to clear, observable interactional patterns!

I learned the psychosomatic family model and added my own perspective to fit the more complex family systems. Intensive structural therapy (IST), a modification of structural family therapy that directs the therapist to work with and include the more complex social systems of today and that incorporates the concept of the homeostatic maintainer, helps the therapist to direct therapy more incisively. The model proved powerful in terms of producing objective changes. It was the rare anorexic child whose eating disorder did not ameliorate within a few months. But stability resulting from restructuring the family took longer—4 to 6 months—and at times took considerably longer. I often asked myself, did the changes last for the long haul? That would make it a truly effective treatment if it could offer that kind of change.

IST is the treatment model used in all of the cases reviewed in this book. I am going to discuss long-term follow-up, sometimes as long as 20 years. Most of the cases are successes, but a chapter on dysfunctional systems provides valuable lessons and caveats to the clinician.

Unfortunately, the original model developed by Minuchin and his colleagues has almost disappeared, but for a very few exceptions. As we move into the new millennium, eating disorders such as anorexia, bulimia, and, to a lesser extent, compulsive overeating continue to be widespread and troubling, not only in the United States but internationally. Eating disorders are unique in that they are diseases that appear to be entirely brought about by the social context. Indeed, in eating disorders the data confirm that it is the social context that is responsible for the expression and maintenance of the symptomatology.

The focus on the social context is not currently a trendy position. Indeed, we have entered the "century of the brain," and neuroscience has become an immensely exciting area, just as biology as a whole becomes increasingly promising. Whereas 40 years ago the United States was intent on exploring the frontiers of outer space, today it is not the vast skies that capture the human imagination so much as a journey much closer to home: the human genome project.

Our fascination with the biological has profoundly influenced the treatment of eating disorders. From this perspective, problems are seen as residing solely in the biology of the sufferer. As former U.S. Surgeon General Louis Satcher represented this position, scientific materialism "says that the bases of mental illness are chemical changes in the brain and, therefore physical changes, changes in the basic cells of the brain. That's why I hold that there's no longer any justification for the distinction that we've made between 'mind and body' or 'mental and physical illnesses.' Mental illnesses are physical illnesses. They're related to physical changes in the brain" (Frattaroli, 2001, p. 7). One cannot argue that this position of scientific materialism is not valid on prima facie evidence. Clearly there must be biochemical correlates to consciousness, luridly demonstrated by the positron emission therapy (PET) scans. This argument supports pharmacological interventions for the treatment of problems that are situated in biochemical processes such as the infectious disease model.

However, I see this as reductionist—and even dangerous. This biological model does not fit for the eating disorders anorexia nervosa and bulimia nervosa, which are socially maintained problems that indeed are "diseases of the well fed": They are primarily found in a significant number of countries that have sizable middle classes. It is safe to say that eating disorders such as anorexia and bulimia are culturally bound syndromes (Gordon, 2001). Researchers have found that the more industrialized the society becomes, the higher the incidence of eating disorders (Anderson, 2001). Chapter 2 will document that these diseases are found in countries that have well-established upper middle classes; indeed, to the extent that countries become more middle class, the incidence of the diseases increases.

That the brain is the site of consciousness is well established. No one would argue against the statement that every successful intervention has an effect on the biology of the brain. The relevant question is, what is the theory of change that leads to the most profound changes, with the greatest alacrity, with maintenance for the longest length of time? As clinicians, we are in the business of change. Indeed, I believe we have the moral obligation to use the most effective treatment available for the individual who is seeking help for the amelioration of her or his suffering.

Some psychiatric problems such as schizophrenia and manic-depressive disease clearly have well-documented biological correlates (Torrey, Bowler, & Taylor, 1994). Eating disorders have no similar documentation. This book is based on the premise that, for the viability and effectiveness of treatment, the client's social system must be *central* to the intervention. I am not going to argue the social basis of eating disorders, and I recognize that there are times when adjunctive biological treatments such as medication are helpful.

The stories of therapy in this volume focus on the social context of the client. These are, if you will, the tales told after many years, sometimes decades after the families were in therapy. What are the enduring changes? What are the surprises? What are the tenets that are held dearly by eating disorder sufferers, their families, and clinicians, in spite of best intentions that have boomeranged? For example, a standard intervention like group therapy may not be valuable for eating disorder patients. As one patient said, "The worst thing you can do for an eating disorder patient is to put her into a group. She just becomes too competitive—who can be the best [most symptomatic] anorexic."

In the psychotherapy world, dearly held theories hold the essentiality of early experience as causative to the later development of symptoms such as eating disorders. There is also a hierarchy of experiences such as sexual abuse that are believed to be more predictive of future development of eating disorder symptoms. This is a controversial area, and opinions and studies differ as to whether sexual abuse is a specific or nonspecific risk factor (Fallon & Wonderlich, 1997). As this is a practical book, I have no intention of wading in those waters. What follows is a treatment model that, regardless of theories of etiology, focuses on transforming the contemporary context and thus the eating disorder.

Another theoretical basis of this book is the sufferer's contemporary context, that the people and social forces in their life are maintaining their eating disorder. I am not speaking about etiology, but rather of the interactional patterns that lead to the expression of symptoms and their maintenance. Even though I cannot see the initial cause, the interpersonal sequences can be witnessed. And when they change, the symptoms cease. Here, we will we see that the cessation of symptomatology extends over many years, even decades.

Mine is not a mainstream position, but when you consider the theory of evolution, it is common sense. Over the eons when we were evolving from our progenitors, those who looked over their shoulders were sensitive to their contexts—they had a better chance of making it to the point of reproducing. I can't imagine that we could have helped our genetic competitiveness by focusing on our childhoods. Such a preoccupation with early experience is an artifact of the leisure of middle-class comfort, and a Victorian desire to make psychology more "scientific." When we focus only on the past, we are assuming, in ways, a politically conservative position—we let the immediate contemporary context off the hook, if you will. Inattention to the real tensions in our lives is a *de facto* means of acceptance. We must deal in good faith with our relationships: In eating disorders, the reader will see that it is diminishing conflict avoidance and enabling the emergence of conflict in therapy that transforms families and systems and frees the sufferer from the eating disorder.

Another great challenge in the world of psychotherapy is the unit of intervention we choose. I remember how my first teacher of family therapy, Jay Haley, would address this question when it came up—which was very often. He would lounge back, propping his bad leg on a chair, and ask, his blue eyes and Western drawl confronting us, "The major question is what is your unit of intervention? Is it one, two, or three people? It is best to look at a problem as a problem of three people;" for example, this is often the mother, father, and the triangulated child. Most psychotherapy is focused on the individual, but we evolve in families. We survive in families. In fact, without families, our young could not survive. Our offspring depend on the family not just for a few months or years, but for at least a decade. Nobel prize winner Jean Monod has spoken about the primacy of families, positing that we very probably have a genetic hardwiring to live as part of a family (as cited in Howard, 1978). Of course, modern day families are not the traditional two-parent, biological families of previous generations. Instead, the young person tends to be connected emotionally to a caregiver regardless of any biological connection.

I see this book as being in the tradition of qualitative research, and offer a series of stories of the treatment and follow-up of individuals and their families. What can we learn from these individuals' experiences? Does their information enable us to better understand and treat these fierce problems? As the clinician in these cases, on reflection I find that I did some things pretty well. Other times, things did not turn out so well, and I believe I think the chapter on dysfunctional systems is perhaps the most useful one in the book.

I feel a certain passion for working with eating disorder patients and for reintroducing the essentiality of the psychosomatic family model to the world of treatment for these problems. As I complete this book in early 2004, I am struck by the mainstream's inattention to this work. People worldwide are suffering unnecessarily from eating disorders when their problems could be treated in a relatively straightforward manner. Recently, I learned of a 16-year-old girl with anorexia who had been in a psychiatric hospital for nine months. Why don't they send her home? I asked. "Because she doesn't eat at home," I was told. Ironically, I received an e-mail soon after from Bonnie (one of the first anorexics I treated, whose follow-up and treatment is found in chapter 5) who asked me if I could help the daughter of a friend of hers. This girl was 16 years old and had had anorexia for 6 months. She had been placed in a daily treatment program, was forced to withdraw from school, yet despite this intervention she continued to lose weight. I sought unsuccessfully to find a therapist who used the psychosomatic treatment model.

The psychosomatic family and the psychotherapy interventions based upon it are valuable additions to an eating disorder clinician's arsenal of treatment. A corollary to the psychosomatic model, the intensive structural therapy model, is also tested in the pages of this book. This model, which will be described later, is derived from the early work done by Minuchin and Rosman at the Wildwyck School for Boys.

Although this book is a qualitative assessment of the effectiveness of the IST model, it is not qualitatively objective. Indeed, these are some of the more representative cases I could find. I cannot say that all the patients I've treated over the years have done as well as these cases. I also cannot say that they *didn't* do as well over the years. I have included here representatives of families that I could find. There are important lessons to be learned, I believe, from these follow-ups. Not the least of the lessons is the reassurance that this model of treatment is effective. The structural changes obtained in the therapy hold, and the dependent variable, the symptoms, remains ameliorated. It is a unique privilege to be able to talk to a patient many years after treatment has ended and learn that what we attempted hit its mark, which is change over time.

I believe this book is all the more important because, 25 years after the publication of *Psychosomatic Families*, the model is still only a footnote to existing treatments across the world for these very dangerous problems. I personally am aware of innumerable inpatient and outpatient programs treating anorexia that do not address the heart of the problem, the family interactional problem. There is some hope—the work of Maudsley Hospital in England, the University of Chicago, and Stanford University are continuing this model's tradition with good results. This will be described at greater length in chapter 3.

THE CONTENTS OF THIS BOOK

Chapter 1 is an overall introduction to the problem of eating disorders. It examines exactly what the phenomenon is: the incidence, prevalence, and the medical consequences to the sufferer for anorexia nervosa, bulimia nervosa, and compulsive overeating.

Chapter 2 asks the question, can the disorder be treated? It is essentially a review of the research, especially the evidence-based research for all three eating disorders. The chapter ends with a description of the psychosomatic family model, addressing some of the criticisms.

Chapter 3 deals with the central concepts of this therapy: grounded observation, the essentiality of dealing with the family's immediate social context, and the use of the identification of the homeostatic maintainer, which is essential for assessing the system. The chapter then presents segments of the therapy of a woman and her family. The woman's anorexia began 40 years prior to the follow-up interview, and I treated her 20 years ago. This case is included to demonstrate the power of using observation interactional patterns to direct therapy. This chapter ends with a recent follow-up of the therapy.

Chapter 4 deals with the basic tenets of intensive structural therapy, the basis of the treatment. I then present the case of a woman with profound bulimia whom I saw in consultation. This is one of the two cases in the book that has a relatively short follow-up, less than two years. During the course of the interview this chronically bulimic woman and her family underwent dramatic change.

Chapter 5 deals with the area of younger anorexics. This treatment model is based on the family therapy lunch session, in which the family has lunch at the beginning of therapy. This situation provides an opportunity to observe the eating behavior, creating a therapeutic crisis where the parents feed their child. This is a challenge to the system, by getting the parents, who customarily triangulate the child and undermine each other, to change this behavior as they get their child to eat. I present some segments of treatment with Bonnie, whom I worked with for a few months, and a 20-year follow-up of her care. She had no additional psychotherapy after that first course of treatment in which her anorexia ceased within a few months.

Chapter 6 continues with the topic of the younger anorexic. The specific focus is the second part of the paradigm, a behavioral paradigm after the lunch session. In this, the youngster has to have bed rest enforced by the parents or other people close to the family. This again is a way of stabilizing the new structure, in which the parental figures no longer triangulate the child. To the extent that this structure is effective, the eating disorder ameliorates. In a family with two twin girls who were sequentially anorexic the first daughter was hospitalized psychiatrically for about three months. There was a behavioral paradigm where the only time the child could see the parents was when the child ate. This proved to be profoundly traumatic for the entire family. The family was then referred to me, and I treated the other twin who had become anorexic. The major thrust of my therapy, however, was stabilizing the family system. The mother had been profoundly sexually abused as a child, was chronically suicidal, and was homicidal toward her abusing father. This chapter presents a 6-year follow-up.

Chapter 7 focuses on the bed rest paradigm. This was an 11-year-old girl who had been anorexic for 2 years. She had an indwelling tube down her throat into her stomach through which she was fed. The family lived far from Philadelphia, and I could find no therapist in the area, so I asked them to come to Philadelphia and stay at the Ronald McDonald House. I did the lunch session with the family. At the end of the fifth hour, my wife, Dr. Tana Fishman, who is a family practitioner, came down to my office on the first floor of my home and took the tube out. This chapter presents a 7-year follow-up. In essence, the family became the doctors in enforcing the protocol very successfully. This chapter provides a 4-year follow-up.

Chapter 8 talks about the treatment of a 19-year-old boy whose bulimia was so severe that his potassium dropped to near-fatal levels. I worked with the family for about three months. This was a 7-year follow-up with this dramatic case.

Chapter 9 deals with compulsive overeating. This woman self-referred to treatment after she saw the changes in her friend who had been treated for her bulimia (Joy, chapter 10). The complex problem of compulsive overeating is more difficult to treat because of the biological components of this disorder. This chapter provides the IST treatment as well as a 7-year follow-up. It deals with the different causes of this problem and the important similarities of all the treatments.

Chapter 10 deals with a woman who had been bulimic and chronically suicidal for 20 years. She had had numerous hospitalizations and was on high levels of psychotropic medications. The 7-year follow-up demonstrates dramatic lessons as far as I'm concerned on the treatment of individuals with chronic eating disorders in a context that is often referred to as borderline.

Chapter 11 deals with the problematic systems where therapy does not go well. In my experience, this is a systemic phenomenon that is not determined on the basis of the chronicity or severity but instead by the treatment that is provided, especially the congruence of the therapeutic system.

Chapter 12 deals with overall significance of the model in terms of the use of this model as well as policy issues. Finally, because this is a book focused on psychotherapy, I discuss what I see as the major challenge in the field, that psychotherapy is being marginalized. In my estimation, the biomedical model may be leading to a dangerous dehumanization of treatment. More importantly, we are losing, in many ways, the humanity in what had been humanistic tradition. The overall message of this book is that psychotherapy can be immensely powerful, and that, from the perspective of a biopsychosocial model, medications should be seen only as an adjunct. Our challenge is to see the individual in context and to transform the individual and his or her system accordingly.

One final minor concern is the quandary of terminology. "Consumer," the most customary term used today, feels a bit commercial and has connotations that I'm not comfortable with in the healing world. "Client" may be a good term, but it comes out a bit legal. The best term would be the Maori word *whaiora* (*wh* is pronounced as *f*), which means a person seeking wellness; unfortunately, that term would make this book hopelessly arcane and pedantic for an American readership. So I'm going to alternate between patient and client, and use consumer in the appropriate contexts as well. But I find the very best term to be "once an eating disorder sufferer, but no longer!"

CHAPTER 1

The Nature
of Eating Disorders

Eating disorders are ironically cruel problems, in which one of the most pleasurable, eminently life-sustaining functions has gone awry. They are terrible problems in their consequences. Although anorexia nervosa (AN) has a much lower incidence in the population in comparison with other psychiatric diseases such as depression and schizophrenia (American Psychiatric Association, 2000; Murphy et al., 2000), it is most likely to prove fatal (Vitiello & Lederhendler, 2000). These problems are recalcitrant in terms of treatment, tending to become chronic and resistant. The cause of these disorders is not entirely known, but it is the premise of this book that they are maintained by the patient's social context. A brief look at their occurrence in history supports this premise.

A SHORT HISTORY OF EATING DISORDERS

It is thought that Gull (1873) and Laségue (1873), almost simultaneously, were the first to describe anorexia. The first case mentioned in medical literature may have been over 300 years ago, however, in Morton's 1689 report of "nervous consumption." Even earlier references from the Middle Ages report evidence of syndromes that strongly resemble anorexia. Bell, in his book *Holy Anorexia* (1985), relates the disease to religious impulses of medieval nuns, who believed starvation to be a form of purification. Parry-Jones (1991) describes references in the literature as far back as ancient Greece and Rome to food refusal as well as gorging followed by vomiting.

In her book *Fasting Girls* (2000), Joan Jacobs Brumberg details the origins and history of anorexia nervosa alongside the sociocultural influences that have shaped it into what has become, in modern times, an increasingly pervasive disease. Between the thirteenth and the sixteenth centuries, fasting was common among women, and prolonged fasting was thought to be a "female miracle." Saint Catherine of Siena claimed she was "incapable of eating normal earthly fare" (p. 43), and her daily intake of food consisted of a handful of herbs; if she was made to eat other food, she would force a stick down her throat to bring it back up. As food abstinence became extremely common among women of the High Middle Ages, medical science expanded on the religious theme by coining the terms *inedia prodigiosa* (a great starvation) and *anorexia mirabilis* (miraculously inspired loss of appetite). During the early modern period, under the influence of the Protestant Reformation, abstinence from eating was seen as the work of the Devil rather than of God; however, where Catholicism was still widespread, "miraculous maids" were supposedly surviving on as little as the smell of a rose: "The symbolic diet of the maiden underscored her purity" (p. 49).

Though Brumberg sees the routes to anorexia mirabilis and anorexia nervosa as quite different, the former does aid our understanding of the modern-day disease, for both reflect important values or beliefs of their times. "In the earlier era, control of appetite was linked to piety and belief; through fasting, the medieval ascetic strove for perfection in the eyes of her God. In the modern period, female control of appetite is embedded in patterns of class, gender, and family relations established in the nineteenth century; the modern anorexic strives for perfection in terms of society's ideal of physical, rather than spiritual, beauty" (p. 48).

By the turn of the 20th century, the importance placed on being thin had become a widespread phenomenon. As early as 1905, Albutt wrote, "Many young women, as their frames develop, fall into a panic fear of obesity, and not only cut down on their food, but swallow vinegar and other alleged antidotes to fatness" (quoted in Brumberg, 2000, p. 184). Furthermore, middle-class girls made efforts to obtain a small, slim body in order to be recognized as distinct from working and rural youth.

Brumberg points out that even as early as the 1870s Laségue recognized the role that the family environment played in anorexia. Although his contemporary Gull focused on identifying the disease in medical terms, Laségue described the relations between his anorexic adolescent patients and their families. In Brumberg's words,

> Among the bourgeoisie, adolescent girls who refused to eat had the power to disrupt their families. A girl who declined the food provided by her family became the focus of conversation and concern; her appetite, her diet, and her body became a preoccupation in the child-centered family. . . . Laségue's attention to his patients' relations with her family and friends confirmed what Gull's work only suggested: that anorexic women came from families willing and able to expend emotional and financial resources on them. Laségue was the first nineteenth-century physician to suggest

that food refusal constituted a form of intrafamilial conflict between the maturing girl and her parents. (p. 126)

In one sense, Laségue was the world's first family therapist.

EATING DISORDERS DESCRIBED

Increasingly, the literature on various diseases describes spectrums within a given disease, and with eating disorders this has certainly been the case. As with anything else in nature, there is variability, and varying degrees of pathologic presentation are to be expected, while the overall patterns of these diseases remain the same. In my experience, although there is some latitude regarding the presentation, these problems yield to the psychosomatic family model conceptualization as well as to the treatment interventions described in this book. Of course, the caveat is that my experience is with severe cases; one cannot be certain that these interventions would work with mild or subclinical cases.

The diagnostic signs of anorexia nervosa have been well established. As described in the *Diagnostic and Statistical Manual of Mental Disorders, 4th Edition (DSM-IV),* AN is "characterized by a refusal to maintain a minimally normal body weight" (p. 583). A person may be one of two subtypes: restricting food intake or binge eating followed by purging (either vomiting or use of laxatives) and must meet the following diagnostic criteria (p. 589):

- weigh less than 85% of expected weight for height and age
- fear becoming fat
- manifest disturbance in body image or deny seriousness of weight loss
- in postmenarcheal females, miss three consecutive periods

Similarly, in the *International Classification of Diseases, 10th edition (ICD-10)* (p. 31), the World Health Organization states that a diagnosis of AN includes all of the following criteria (p. 177):

- body weight at least 15% lower than expected, or body mass index (BMI) 17.5 or less
- self-induced weight loss
- body image distortion from dread of fatness
- widespread endocrine disorder—amenorrhea in women, and loss of sexual interest and/or potency in men
- with prepubertal onset, delay or arrest of pubertal events

As with most other psychiatric syndromes, there is a spectrum of severity of anorexic presentations. Cecile Herscovici (2002) has described three types (p. 135):

- imitative anorectics, who "have had a healthy development in a favorable family context, go onto an 'innocent' diet with the goal of looking better and then become trapped in the biological vulnerabilities to food restriction and the psychopathology of starvation. Many of these cases remit spontaneously or with little therapeutic effort, if detected early. These are the ones that prove most amenable to self-help and psychoeducational strategies."
- those for whom the disorder evolves in the context of a dysfunctional family, whose "members are immersed in the tension derived from unresolved issues of the past. Often their equilibrium is threatened by the exogamy inherent in adolescence. They will benefit most from family therapy."
- those with an eating disorder in the context of a dysfunctional family system where the patient has experienced a pervasive developmental impairment resulting in a personality problem and reflecting a disorder of the self. Some of the cases in this book demonstrate that the intensive structured therapy (IST) approach addresses these lacunae by transforming the patient's present system and accessing additional contexts, such as vocation, to augment deficits.

The term "bulimia nervosa" (BN) was introduced in 1979 by Russell, who described it as an "ominous variant of anorexia nervosa." According to *DSM-IV* (p. 594), bulimia nervosa is "characterized by repeated episodes of binge eating followed by inappropriate compensatory behaviors." Again, two subtypes are possible, according to the compensatory behavior: purging (by vomiting or use of laxatives, diuretics, or enemas) and nonpurging (such as fasting or excessive exercise). The following diagnostic criteria must be met:

- recurrent episodes of binge eating
- recurrent inappropriate compensatory behavior
- occurrence of this behavior at least twice a week for 3 months
- self-evaluation unduly influenced by body shape and weight
- occurrence of behavior not exclusively during an episode of AN

The *ICD-10* (pp. 178–179) states that BN is "characterized by repeated bouts of overeating and an excessive preoccupation with the control of body weight" and lists the following diagnostic criteria:

- persistent preoccupation with eating and an irresistible craving for food
- attempts to counteract the "fattening" effects of food through behaviors such as self-induced vomiting
- sharply defined weight threshold well below a healthy weight range, because of a morbid dread of fatness

ICD-10 also mentions that BN "may be viewed as a sequel to persistent AN." This view is supported by a follow-up study of 41 AN patients; 20 years later, 15% of the group had developed BN (Ratnasuriya et al., 1991).

Binge eating disorder (also known as compulsive overeating) was first described in 1992 (Spitzer et al.) and is newly recognized in *DSM-IV*, classified under "Eating Disorders Not Otherwise Specified." It is characterized by "recurrent episodes of binge eating in the absence of regular use of inappropriate compensatory behaviors characteristic of BN" (p. 595). *ICD-10* classifies overeating as an eating disorder only when it occurs along with other psychological disturbances. Furthermore, obesity, as a cause of psychological disturbance, is not coded under the eating disorders category. In binge eating disorder (BED), eating binges are much like those of BN, but the "hallmark feature distinguishing BN and BED is inappropriate compensatory behavior subsequent to binge eating [in BN]" (Pike et al., 2001, p. 1459).

In terms of treatment, chapter 9 will detail my approach to this problem, focusing on the psychosomatic family characteristics, IST, and the patient's broader social context. My review of the literature supports the difficulty in treating this problem: for example, Walsh and Devlin (1998) mention that with clinical trials a distinction needs to be made between obese binge eaters and nonobese binge eaters. Devlin, Yanovski, and Wilson's (2000) review states that appetite suppressant medications clearly promote weight loss but their use in suppressing binge eating has yet to be studied specifically. Similarly, in obese BED patients, psychotherapy (particularly cognitive behavioral therapy and interpersonal therapy) is effective in normalizing eating and reducing distress, but is not associated with significant weight loss. *Devlin* (1996) also mentions another area that needs to be addressed, other than normalizing eating and improving physical health, which is enhancement of a patient's acceptance of his or her body image. This issue of self-esteem is crucial when exploring the sociocultural factors that contribute to the existence of this disorder.

Clearly the social context is significant in terms of etiology. Fairburn et al. (1998) found those with BED were more exposed to negative comments from family members about shape, weight, and eating.

SHORT-TERM AND LONG-TERM
HEALTH CONSEQUENCES OF EATING DISORDERS

The medical consequences of AN are many and varied. Individuals differ in the sequelae they present, but as Goldbloom and Kennedy (1995) expressed it most succinctly, "no organ system is spared" (p. 269). The effects of anorectic behavior include:

- amenorrhea (a mandatory diagnostic criterion in females in *DSM-IV*)
- fainting, fatigue, and muscle weakness
- discoloration of skin
- hair loss and growth of lanugo (downy layer of hair) over body
- abnormally slow heart rate and low blood pressure, leading to risk of heart failure
- reduction in bone density leading to osteoporosis
- severe dehydration and risk of kidney failure
- structural abnormalities of the brain
- gastrointestinal difficulties

Specific medical complications for adolescents include:

- changes in growth hormone, resulting in significant growth retardation
- pubertal delay or interruption
- peak bone mass interruption

Indeed, the sequelae years later include profound problems resulting from the behavioral manifestations, such as the debilitating condition osteoporosis. Chronic ED sufferers may die because of lack of calcium and electrolyte imbalances that create abnormal heart rhythm patterns (Noordenbos et al., 2002). Many long-term patients have been found to be susceptible to alcohol and/or drug addiction (see, for example, Lammers, 1995 and Homgren et al., 1983 cited in Noordenbos et al., 2002).

The health consequences of bulimic behavior are as severe in both the short and long term as those of anorexia. They include:

- dehydration, resulting in loss of potassium and sodium
- electrolyte imbalances that can lead to irregular heartbeats and even to heart failure
- a risk of gastric rupture
- inflammation and possible rupture of esophagus
- tooth decay and staining

- chronic irregular bowel movements and constipation
- peptic ulcers and/or pancreatitis
- neuroendocrine and metabolic abnormalities

For a fuller description of the sequelae of BN, see Halmi (1995). Daluiski et al. also mentions the likelihood that the BN patient will manifest a characteristic sign called Russel's sign: calluses on the hand indicative of the act of stimulating a gag reflex.

A risk factor for BED is obesity (Devlin et al., 2000), and therefore the disorder entails some of the health risks associated with clinical obesity. According to the National Eating Disorders Association (2002), these include

- high blood pressure
- high cholesterol levels
- heart disease from high triglyceride levels
- secondary diabetes
- gallbladder disease

The BED and obesity populations are not necessarily contiguous, however. While BED is most commonly found in the obese population, it is not exclusively found there (de Zwaan, 2001). Moreover, Fairburn et al. (1998) put the percentage of the obese population that suffers from frequent bouts of binge eating at about 25%. Therefore a distinction between obese binge eaters and nonobese binge eaters needs to be made in clinical trials, according to Walsh and Devlin (1998).

EPIDEMIOLOGY OF EATING DISORDERS

Although the incidence of eating disorders is relatively low, the tenacity of these problems and the health dangers they pose make them major mental health problems. It is significant, therefore, that as more of the world becomes westernized and increasingly middle class, the incidence of these diseases is increasing (Gordon, 2001).

The sentinel study of the incidence and prevalence of AN, to my knowledge, is the work of Lucas and colleagues (1991). Their study of 181 patients (166 females and 15 males) in Rochester, Minnesota, spanned 50 years. They noted that AN is 9 to 10 times more common in girls, with prevalence rates of approximately 0.27% for females and 0.02% for males. They also found an overall incidence rate per 100,000 person-years of 14.6 for females and 1.8 for males. During the years of the study, the overall incidence rate for female adolescents and young adults (15 to 24 years old) has increased. More specifically, the incidence rate for females 10 to 19 years old decreased from 16.6 in the 1935–1939 period to 7.0 in the 1950–1954 period but then increased to 26.3 in the 1980–1984 period.

Commenting on this study, Gordon (2000) calculated, "If [Lucas's] study can be extrapolated to the US . . . using 1980 census figures, then the number of anorexic women residing in the United States would be roughly 300,000" (p. 70). Of course, that was in 1980, and I have not found studies to support or disqualify this figure.

DSM-IV notes that females have a lifetime prevalence rate of 0.5% and males one-tenth that rate. In Gordon's view, the prevalence per 100,000 population in terms of overall incidence is misleading; what is most relevant is the incidence in the at-risk population. According to *DSM-IV*, over 90% of AN cases occur in females, and as the *ICD-10* notes, these are most commonly adolescent girls and young women. Gidwani and Rome (1997) set this figure for girls and women at 95%. Gordon also points out that AN affects a population that is otherwise relatively healthy and thus has a much greater health significance because it is so chronic, debilitating, and potentially lethal.

The overall prevalence rate for BN is 1% to 3% (Johnson et al., 1996). *DSM-IV* gives the rate for females as 1% to 3% and for males one-tenth of that (0.1% to 0.3%). According to both *DSM-IV* and *ICD-10,* the gender distribution of BN is similar to that of AN, with 90 percent of the cases occurring in females. Gidwani and Rome (1997) set that figure at 80% and note that the onset of BN tends to occur later, in women aged 17 to 25 years.

Binge eating disorder is thought to be the most common eating disorder, with a prevalence rate of 2% to 5% of the population (Johnson et al., 1996). It is also more evenly distributed over gender and age groups than are AN and BN (Walsh & Devlin, 1998).

Pike et al. (2001) found interesting cultural differences. Black women are as much at risk for developing BED as white women, but among those with BED, black women were much less concerned about body weight, shape, and eating, and therefore at less risk of developing BN.

There are studies, less well substantiated, suggesting that the incidence of eating disorders is much higher than the figures described in the previous paragraphs. Naomi Wolf, for example, states in *The Beauty Myth* (2002) that the rate of bulimia among college girls is about 60%. There is no way of knowing how many cases of the less severe phenomena there are. It may be that we as professionals see only the extreme cases and that subclinical cases of eating disorders appear transiently in people's lives, even as discrete episodes that spontaneously remit.

COMORBIDITY

The most common disorders to co-vary with EDs are depression, obsessive-compulsive disorder (OCD), anxiety disorders, and various personality disorders (Johnson et al., 1996). A meta-analytic review (Rosenvinge et al., 2000) found a higher proportion of personality disorders in ED patients than in controls, and BN patients were more likely to have concurrent cluster B personality disorder and borderline disorder than were AN patients.

DSM-IV lists as the most common comorbid conditions with AN:

- depressive symptoms, which can develop into major depressive disorder
- obsessive compulsive behaviors, which can develop into OCD (this diagnosis is given only if not related to food, weight, or body shape)
- personality disorders
- alcohol/drug abuse (more common with the binge eating/purging type of AN)
- higher frequency of suicide attempts and borderline personality disorder (comorbid with binge eating/purging type) (pp. 585–586)

Lock et al. (2001) mention that with AN there is considerable evidence suggesting that the disorder often co-occurs with other psychiatric disorders. Depression is a common comorbid diagnosis (O'Brien & Vincent, 2003). Lock et al. (2001) go on to say that with persistent AN there is a high incidence of anxiety disorders (Smith et al., 1993). Herzog and colleagues (1992) found a moderate overlap between avoidant personality disorder and AN in adults; it is not clear to what extent this overlap occurs with children and adolescents. Finally, OCD seems to be common with AN; one study found a comorbidity rate of 35% (Rastam, 1992, cited in Steiner & Lock, 1998).

The comorbidity studies in essence seek to reduce anorexia to a subset of obsessive-compulsive disease. That approach would have value, as I see it, if there were an exemplary treatment for obsessive compulsives, such as a demonstrably effective medication, that ameliorated the anorexia as well as it relieved the obsessive-compulsive disorder. One article by Kim found conflicting results that did suggest that fluoxetine may be an option as part of a maintenance program with obsessive-compulsive disorder and AN, but further studies need to be done with a larger sample size (Kim, 2003).

The most common comorbid conditions with BN are, according to *DSM-IV*:

- depressive (more common with purging type) and mood disorders, which usually begin at the same time as the BN
- anxiety disorders
- substance abuse/dependence, mainly alcohol or stimulants, with a lifetime prevalence of 30%
- personality disorders, in particular borderline personality disorder (p. 591)

In a comparison of AN and BN sufferers, Fairburn and colleagues (1999) found that there was more parental psychiatric disorder—high rates of depression, alcoholism, and drug abuse—during childhood for BN patients. In a study of BN patients, Braun and colleagues (1994) found that 26% had been diagnosed with a cluster B personality disorder and 19% with borderline personality disorder.

In a study by Yanovski et al. (1993) of obese female and male patients, those with binge eating disorder had higher lifetime prevalence rates of BN, major depression, panic disorder, borderline personality disorder, and avoidant personality disorder than non-BED controls. Similarly, a community-based study (Telch & Stice, 1998) using only female subjects found greater lifetime prevalence rates of major depression in BED subjects (49%) compared to overweight, non-eating-disordered controls (28%). However, no significant difference was found between the two groups for lifetime prevalence rates of BN, panic disorder, borderline personality disorder, or avoidant personality disorder.

That there tends to be a comorbidity involving depression and substance abuse underscores the fact that psychiatric diseases are not discrete entities like diphtheria and congestive heart failure. In the area of psychiatric diseases, with the stress that they create in people's lives, it is the rare person who expresses a completely unitary symptomatology.

As I have suggested earlier, I find the focus on comorbidity of little value, and even counterproductive, in the treatment of eating disorders. In my view, it draws attention away from the essential component in these individual problems, which is the contextual difficulties, and frequently adds a complement of medications that do not address the central eating problem but may add new side effects. Psychiatric diagnoses, unlike diagnoses in physical medicine, are in many cases imprecise. In spite of the efforts of the framers of *DSM-IV*, it is not uncommon for a patient to be given different diagnoses by different diagnosticians simultaneously.

My major concern with the comorbidity focus is that psychiatrists and psychologists may see depression or OCD as the *primary* problem. These may be components of behaviors that the patient is manifesting, but the essential issue is the eating disorder, which is, after all, often the most dangerous of the psychiatric diseases. Also, it is the eating disorder that will readily yield to the contextual therapy described in this book, so the wrong emphasis can result in a lost opportunity. Indeed, while one cannot deny an inevitable circularity of causation, in my experience these comorbid diagnoses tend to be secondary emotional reactions to the profound emotional consequences of an eating disorder. From a practical viewpoint, when the eating disorder ameliorates, the secondary diagnosis diminishes. Indeed, the compulsion in anorexia to starve oneself is profound, but it vanishes with this treatment. Absent the treatment, the patient has no conscious control of this compulsion. The wrong emphasis—treating the compulsion first and not the eating disorder—is like treating the fever in bacterial pneumonia first and not using antibiotics to address the cause. I acknowledge this position may be contrary to some of the prevailing beliefs and literature in the field. However, in my experience, if one focuses on the contextual dysfunction in the individual's life, the other issues, such as depression, remit. I see these dynamics as the *key* issue that maintains the symptoms.

A key point is that, with the focus on the diagnosis, the patient can go into a self-deprecating, self-devaluating downward spiral. The comorbidity emphasis can make the patient impotent throughout the course of therapy and delay motivation to be liberated from the disease, creating significant harm.

MORTALITY, MORBIDITY, AND CHRONICITY

Anorexia nervosa is notoriously difficult to treat and may become chronic. In about 20% of cases, the patient develops a chronic illness, defined as having the disorder for 10 years or more (Steinhausen, 1991). Longer duration makes improvement or recovery more difficult, but even Gull (1873) commented that "none of these cases, however exhausted, are really hopeless as long as life exists." In one 20-year follow-up study of 41 AN patients (Ratnasuriya et al., 1991), 17.5% of the patients had died and 20% had a chronic course; but 32.5% had an "intermediate" outcome, and 30% had recovered. It is not unusual for chronic sufferers of AN to recover after 15 years or more. Moreover, as Noordenbos and colleagues (2002) aptly note in their study of 41 patients who had had an ED for 10 years or more, "even though complete recovery may be far away, [small] improvement in the quality of the lives of patients with long-term ED's is very important" (p. 27). Nonetheless, the chronicity of AN has major long-term consequences. Over and above the serious debilitation of the disease itself, as Ratnasuriya and colleagues (1991) note, there is a high level of dysfunction in daily life. They found that one-third of the patients still alive at 20-year follow-up were socially isolated and restricted and very dependent on the family of origin. Thus, there are not only physiological but social sequelae that in many ways appear to be the most debilitating.

Bulimia nervosa has somewhat lower mortality rates than anorexia and overall more favorable outcomes. A meta-analysis (Keel & Mitchell, 1997) found 50% of BN patients to have a favorable outcome. Of those who did not recover, 20% continued to meet full criteria for BN. In a 6-year follow-up study of BN patients, 60% were rated as "good," 29% as "intermediate," and 10% as "poor," with 1% deceased (Fichter & Quad-flieg, 1997). Another study, a 10-year follow-up of 50 patients, found that 52% of the patients traced had fully recovered, 39% experienced some symptoms, and 9% continued to suffer from BN (Collings & King, 1994). The investigators noted, however, that it might have been advantageous to assess outcome at regular intervals throughout the 10-year period to gain a better picture of the cycle of improvements and relapses. In another 10-year follow-up study, Keel and colleagues (1999) mention that although many women with BN improve over time, a large number continue to suffer from threshold and subthreshold eating disorders.

ETIOLOGY OF EATING DISORDERS

The work that is described in this book is based on general systems theory. In that model, the focus is not on ascertaining the cause of a problem but on determining what in the current system is maintaining it. This approach represents a paradigm shift from most areas of medicine, where the search for the cause leads to amelioration of the problem. In the therapy described here, the cause is irrelevant; we can transform these cases of eating disorders by working with the patient's contemporaries, the influential people in the person's social system.

In any case, the causes of eating disorders continue to elude researchers, though there seems to be strong evidence of an interaction between sociocultural and biological influences. The cultural etiology model of AN is a popular one, with feminists being the most outspoken supporters. Brumberg (2000) notes that instead of "casting the behavior as pathological . . . they seek to demonstrate that these disorders are an inevitable consequence of a misogynistic society that demeans women" (p. 35). Susie Orbach asserts that noneating and overeating are forms of "protest against the way in which women are regarded in our society as objects of adornment and pleasure" (quoted in Brumberg, p. 291).

One major theory held over the years has posited that eating disorders result from a history of sexual abuse. A number of studies (e.g., Horesh et al., 1995, 1996) have found, however, that although sexual abuse is more common in ED populations than among healthy controls, it is not more common when ED groups are compared with groups of patients with other psychiatric disorders. A review by Pope and Hudson (1992) criticized the very methodology in the studies that associated sexual abuse with BN, finding that when the inadequacies in these studies are corrected for, the high rate of sexual abuse among BN patients is comparable with the rate in the general population.

The role of genetics in ED is not clear, but there are studies pointing to a genetic predisposition to the expression of these symptoms. An interesting review of these studies (Gorwood, et al., 1998) reports, for example, that first-degree relatives of ED patients have a 6% lifetime risk for developing an ED, compared with a 1% risk among controls. The twin studies may shed some light on this question. Bulik et al. (2000) found that bulimia nervosa is familial; the study reveals significant contributions of additive genetic effects and of unique environmental factors in disposition to bulimia. They go on to say that the contribution of shared environments is less clear. They confirm that they found a 17% to 46% variance in anorexia and bulimia, which can be accounted for by nonshared environmental factors; however, studies examining these influences are scarce. Initial data indicate that differential paternal relationships, body weight teasing, peer group experiences, and life events may account for the development of eating pathology in one sibling versus another (Klump et al., 2002). Finally, Fairburn, Cowan, and Harrison (1999) conclude that the findings of twin studies are inconsistent and difficult to interpret. From the perspective of the model presented in this book, genetics would appear to be a likely risk factor. The percentage of ED patients in the general population is low, while psychosomatic family organization is by no means rare and the social pressure on women to diet is huge. It is not unreasonable to speculate that genetic vulnerability is a necessary factor for the expression of full-blown disease.

Whatever the role of genetics, it is clear that eating disorders are diseases of westernized civilization. There has been a tremendous amount written about culture and ED, but to my mind the most impressive connection is the fact that eating disorders emerge as a country becomes more middle class. Richard Gordon cites several examples in his article "Eating Disorders East and West" (2001). In South Korea, prior to 1991 a psychiatrist named Kim Joon Ki had seen only one patient with an ED, but by 1997 he had seen over 200, about evenly split between anorexics and bulimics. As Gordon points out, these changes were concurrent with "the forces of industrialization, urbanization, consumerism and democratization" that produced "rapid cultural transition" (p. 8). Even countries like India with their profound economic deprivation are starting to manifest eating disorders. This phenomenon is again co-occurring with the rapid commercial and industrial development and the emergence of high technology.

One poignant example of westernization and attitudes regarding weight are found in the work of Anne Becker. A psychiatrist and anthropologist, Becker (1995) first conducted research in Fiji in the early 1990s. She found a higher percentage of Fijian women were overweight when compared to their Western counterparts. She found the Fijian woman accepting of overweight status. "Meals are characterized by an abundance of food and often a variety of dishes. Most women rest after a meal, and after a large Sunday dinner it is not unusual to observe young women unfastening their skirt waist bands when uncomfortably full. . . . One informant, remarked that regardless of how overweight people are, "they don't care about their weight'" (p. 54). According to Gordon (2000), when Becker returned to Fiji in 1998, these attitudes had undergone dramatic change. At this point, there were large numbers of women, especially teenage girls, who manifested unhappiness with their body size and were actively dieting. Over the time that elapsed between Becker's two visits, there had been a crucial change introduced into Fijian culture: the introduction of television (Gordon, 2000, p. 136).

One aspect of Western culture that is consistently pointed to as a risk factor for EDs is the cultural value that thinness is beautiful. Young people exposed to Western movies, television, and advertising are bombarded with images of slim, even skinny, girls and women presented as ideals of female beauty. This issue, however, brings up the old causation questions of necessary and sufficient. The pressures, especially on young women, to be thin are ubiquitous, yet diseases such as anorexia and bulimia are relatively rare. Clearly there are other risk factors that determine the expression of these symptoms.

To explore what these factors might be, let us consider first in what sense eating disorders are culturally based. Richard Gordon, in his excellent book *Eating Disorders: Anatomy of a Social Epidemic* (2000), draws on the work of George Devereux (p. 8) to describe culturally based diseases in terms of a number of characteristics. Of these, three seem particularly salient in describing ED in relation to the culture. First, the symptoms of the disease are direct extensions and exaggerations of normal behaviors that are highly valued. Second, the disorder is a highly patterned and widely imitated model of expressing distress. Third, the pattern of misconduct is seen as irrational, deviant, and crazy; "because the disorder draws upon valued behaviors but on the other hand is an expression of deviance, it elicits highly ambivalent responses from others: awe, respect, perhaps, but also punitive and controlling reactions to deviance" (p. 8).

Certainly eating disorders fit these criteria. In anorexia, there is a clear extrapolation between the normal functional behaviors and these symptoms going awry as the compulsion takes over. Frequently described as going on a diet, a common everyday behavior, the compulsion leads to a life-threatening problem. Nonetheless it is ironically a parody of the values of our culture. I often have people who know my specialty say to me, "I would like to have just a touch of anorexia." Moreover, as will be seen in the cases in this book, eating disorders are highly patterned behavior, carried to such extremes that the patients, at times, appear almost literally at the edge of life. What these people cannot do, once the compulsion has taken over, is what is so easy—sometimes too easy—to everyone else, and that is eat. (This inability to eat has always added to the almost poetic fascination that this disease has.) The usefulness of the response to anorexia is, of course, seen in self-starvation as a traditional template for civil disobedience.

What is interesting for our purposes is to look at these characteristics on the micro level—that is, the level of the family. How do the symptoms relate to the culture of the family? Specifically, let us consider the selection of anorexia as a symptom from the perspective of the family.

On a micro-systemic level, the value system of the family supports the emergence and maintenance of the ED. It is the rare ED family, in my experience, that is not involved with food. For example, the parents may be gourmet cooks, dieters, or vegetarians. In fact, the father of the youngest anorexic I have treated was a cookie manufacturer. In every family's life there is a constant flow of experiences that have differing levels of importance to the family members. Sometimes children misbehave, sometimes they have problems in school, and sometimes they do not eat. From this random flow of events, certain experiences have higher valences than others to the family. Those that are more important to the values of the family will be focused on. When that family is a psychosomatic system—a system that will be described in detail in the chapter that follows—the act of focusing can serve to decrease tension in the family, especially between parental figures. In a food-oriented psychosomatic family, focusing on a child who has stopped eating stabilizes the system, which in turn reinforces the anorexic behavior.

This chapter has briefly described the phenomena of eating disorders and their main characteristics. Although this information is important, the major issue is to help liberate those who are suffering from these terrible problems. The next chapter discusses the domain of treatment—what has been done and what the evidence-based literature tells us is effective. Chapters 3 and 4 then describe a model of therapy that underlies what is for the most part a very successful treatment of eating disorders.

CHAPTER 2

Can Eating Disorders Be Treated?

It is such a terrible disease because you watch
your child deliberately hurting herself, and obviously
suffering, and yet you are unable to help her.
—Hilde Bruch, *The Golden Cage*

Eating disorders (ED) are notoriously difficult to treat. As the previous chapter indicated, across the developed world there are large numbers of people, especially women, who are suffering from these disorders. In many cases they are receiving treatment that is not proving effective. How does one define effectiveness when it comes to treatment of ED? There is considerable research evaluating various approaches to therapy on the basis of follow-ups 6 weeks or even 6 months after the conclusion of therapy. The question is, do the changes hold in the long term?

It is the long-term outcomes of the intensive structural therapy (IST) approach that this book is designed to describe. My experience with hundreds of cases has been that the changes made in therapy not only have been effective in ameliorating the ED but have been maintained. Follow-ups as long as 20 years after the conclusion of therapy have found that the patient has had no reappearance of the ED symptoms in all that time. These are qualitative data from only one clinician; nevertheless, there are important lessons learned.

This chapter begins with a brief review of the various types of therapy that are currently in use, looking first at therapies that address the individual patient and then moving to the more contextual therapies. It will conclude with an introduction to IST with eating disorder patients. In the next chapter, the model will be illustrated by a summary of treatment in a case with a patient who had been anorexic for 20 years before treatment and had remained asymptomatic in the 20 years following treatment.

In researching the various models of therapy, I have sought evidence-based medicine and meta-articles reviewing the quantitative data. From a generic perspective, I encountered a number of difficulties with this literature:

1. Males are generally not included.
2. Adult samples are not necessarily generalizable to adolescent populations.
3. Clinical academic research samples tend to be at the more severe end of the spectrum rather than community samples.
4. Many of the studies deal with small and thus questionable sample sizes. This problem, of course, is due to the relatively small ED population.
5. Definitions of "remission" and "recovery" tend to vary from one study to another, and although patients may be considered "recovered," symptoms such as weight loss/gain may continue to fluctuate.
6. Finding patients for follow-up many years after treatment can be a problem.
7. In comparison with bulimia nervosa (BN), relatively few randomized controlled studies have looked at psychological treatments for anorexia nervosa (AN).

Some treatments have little research evidence but are interesting and important because they address the phenomenological experiences of the patients with eating disorders. They are therefore relevant and will be mentioned briefly.

INPATIENT HOSPITALIZATION

Inpatient hospitalization is a site for treatment rather than a model of treatment, but it deserves mention here because it was formerly the treatment of choice for AN patients, because weight gain, the primary treatment imperative, has been considered to be more likely in the hospital setting (Piran et al., 1989). In the last 10 years, the role of the hospital has changed dramatically. At one time eating disorder patients were hospitalized for weeks, months, or even years to address anorexia. Today, in the U.S., hospitalization is usually secondary to profound medical instability—the pediatrician or internist prescribes inpatient care or a hospital's specialized program—but for the most part hospital stays tend to be short term. Not only is hospitalization a more expensive treatment option, but, more importantly, the gains made in treatment are difficult to maintain after discharge (Eckert et al., 1995; Lay et al., 2002). Maintaining good long-term outcomes and preventing relapse are challenging issues; these patients tend to have a persistent, intense fear of becoming fat and may rapidly start losing any weight gains when external controls are reduced. A study of inpatient weight gain in AN adolescents showed that patients with a short duration of weight stabilization during treatment were more likely to be readmitted within a short period of time (Lay et al., 2002). In fact, it is unclear whether major risks and vulnerabilities for reoccurrence ever resolve completely (Herzog et al., 1993; Steiner & Lock, 1998). According to Dare and Eisler (1997), the treatment paradigms in many psychiatric inpatient programs appear to be punitive. "The patient is kept on a strict regimen of bed rest and restriction of visitors and occupation, with privileges being allowed as a result of the weight increase" (p. 322). In other words, long-term amelioration is difficult and unlikely when treatment is hospital-based only: the patient's context must be involved and the professionals must create an organized system of care. Improvement can be made difficult via hospitalization because the patient's outside context, especially the family, is usually not central to the treatment. In fact, the very act of hospitalization removes the pressure on the family to address the patient's difficulties. Change is now considered to reside in the domain of doctors and nurses. Indeed, even when family therapy is offered, and it usually is, the family involvement is considered ancillary—in fact, marginal—rather than central to the professionals' theory of change.

The crucial issue is not necessarily the site of the treatment but whether the social context is closely involved in the treatment. Hospitalization can be essential if the patient is so medically unstable that it would be dangerous for her to be in the community. The site of the treatment is secondary to the fundamental tenet that the treatment must be focused on the patient's context and be embedded in an organized continuum of care. In many ways, the most crucial issue is what happens after hospitalization is over.

The excellent results of Strober et al. (1997) found nearly 76% of the cohort of previously hospitalized patients met the criteria for full recovery. The investigators suggested that the intensive treatment received by these patients may be responsible for the lower levels of morbidity and mortality when considered in relation to other reports in the follow-up literature (p. 339). The patients had the benefit of early intensive treatment, which continued after hospital discharge for most. I would suggest it is the system of care after hospitalization that is significantly responsible for the good outcomes.

PSYCHODYNAMIC THERAPIES

A valuable resource for the understanding of the psychodynamic approach is the work of Cecile Herscovici (2002). According to Herscovici, traditional psychoanalytic thinking places the core of a problem within the individual and his or her unique personal history. Infancy and early experience are considered particularly important in predisposing the person to symptoms that some psychoanalytic theorists see as serving powerful unmet needs and unfulfilled wishes. Psychoanalytic treatment therefore is directed at looking for the symbolic *meaning* of the symptoms to understand what is motivating the disordered behavior.

Contemporary psychoanalysis deals with eating disorders in the context of personal relationships as well as the organization of the self. The emphasis is still on the patient's unique history and finding a safe haven in which to process that history to claim a more thorough understanding of the antecedents of the ED symptoms. Psychodynamic theories strive to integrate insights from one of the four traditional models: analytic, interpersonal, object relations, and self-psychology (Herscovici, 2002). Garner and Needleman (1997) also note that there "has been considerable movement among dynamically oriented writers towards integrating psychodynamic therapy with active symptom management principles in treating eating disorders" (p. 59).

There is a paucity of controlled studies examining psychodynamic treatments of eating disorders. Garner et al. (1993) compared supportive-expressive psychotherapy with cognitive behavioral therapy (CBT, to be discussed later in the chapter) in BN patients. The two treatments were equally effective in reducing binge eating, but the psychodynamic therapy was inferior to CBT on other core measures and associated psychopathology. A randomized controlled trial (Treasure et al., 1995) found no difference in outcome between cognitive-analytic and educational behavioral therapy, though there were gains from both treatments. Hamburg (1996) maintains that some AN patients do benefit from long-term psychoanalytic psychotherapy. Evidence-based support for this assertion comes from the controlled study mentioned earlier (Dare et al., 2001) comparing outpatient psychotherapy treatments. AN patients in both psychoanalytic psychotherapy and family therapy were significantly superior to controls in producing weight gain at 1-year follow-up.

FEMINIST THERAPIES

Cecile Herscovici's (2002) work is also valuable in terms of feminist therapy of ED. It provides a superb overview of the feminist perspective on ED and highlights some worthwhile literature in the area. In this perspective, ED is a response to cultural stereotypes and practices that devalue women as well as to social pressures to conform to certain ideals of appearance. Feminists find clear confirmation of this view in the preponderance of girls and women in the ED population (discussed in the previous chapter). Indeed, they see anorexia, bulimia, and compulsive overeating as logical, initially sane responses to the social order: "The anorexic refuses to let the official cycle master her: By starving, she masters it. . . . Eating disorders are often interpreted as symptomatic of a neurotic need for control. But surely it is a sign of mental health to try to control something that is trying to control you. . . ." (Herscovici, 2002, p. 198).

Feminist therapists emphasize sharing control of the therapeutic process in a partnership with the patient and her family rather than a hierarchical relationship (Madanes, 1981, as cited in Lock et al., 2001). In the feminist model of family therapy, therapists focus on gender-related issues in family life, working to build a positive image of gender differences and sense of self-worth, enhancing autonomy, and encouraging the patient to assume responsibility for her own health and well-being (Herscovici, 2002, p. 30).

Though there is little evidence-based data to support the feminist model, some studies have highlighted important connections between body image identities—influenced by current sociocultural ideals—and the existence of eating disorders. One study of 71 college women, aged 17 to 22, who completed a number of questionnaires and scales found that feminist values, such as commitment to nonsexist roles and personal empowerment, negatively correlated with body dissatisfaction, bulimic symptoms, and feelings of ineffectiveness (Snyder & Hasbrouck, 1996).

The problem with the feminist work so far is that there appears to be no data that suggest these ideas can be incorporated into treatment per se. The identification of sexism in society is an essential backdrop to the understanding of the cultural underpinning of these diseases. The pressure on girls and women to be seen as sexual objects may indeed foster a young girl's belief that attractive (read "thin") is better. This understanding does not, however, necessarily lead to amelioration of the problem. Sexism is endemic in society, and although an understanding of it certainly enlightens one's understanding of ED, this understanding apparently has not thus far led to separating the woman from the problem.

Clearly, however, there is a commonality between the tenets of this book and the feminist critique. The feminists see the political context as central to the understanding of these diseases. There is, of course, an unfortunate linearity to this position: Society is doing these things to the women, and they are the passive victims. But the feminist critiques provide an invaluable contextual understanding to these problems; eating disorders are not written off as if they were an individual problem of the woman, as if she were living all alone in the woods! The matrix between the feminist model and IST crosses at the experience of conflict avoidance: What Brumberg (2000) calls "the appetite as voice" and the IST tenet that conflict avoidance leads to the manifestation of the eating disorder. The family-based model of IST operationalizes the phenomenological experience from one of helplessness or at the best passive-aggressiveness to a proactive challenge to the people in their context who are causing stress.

GROUP THERAPIES

Group therapy has been very popular as a form of treatment for EDs since the early 1980s with many different approaches currently available: psychodynamic/interpersonal, cognitive behavioral, behavioral, psychoeducational, addiction oriented (such as 12-step programs), intensive short term, single issue (e.g., body image), and self-help (see Polivy & Federoff, 1997, for a description of each of these approaches and an overview of relevant literature). A group therapy setting allows for exchange of information, whereby participants are encouraged to share their feelings and experiences with regard to food, weight, and body shape and to explore the relationships among eating, body image, and interpersonal relationships. Though the specific goals of each group therapy can vary, most goals are based on enhancing self-esteem and assertiveness and providing members with coping skills and social and emotional support.

In 12-step programs, eating disorders are conceptualized as addictions comparable to alcoholism and drug addiction. Addiction models generally promote abstinence as their main goal. The APA Practice Guidelines (2000) express concern that well-intentioned nonprofessionals may therefore offer misleading advice in such programs. Groups such as Overeaters Anonymous, as additions to other initial treatments, have been helpful for some BN patients in preventing relapse.

Most studies of group therapy have looked at BN where it appears to be effacacious (Polivy & Federoff, 1997; Rosenvinge, 1990; Zimpfer, 1990). Although these programs could perhaps provide benefits as supplements to more conventional ED treatments such as cognitive behavioral therapy (CBT) or family therapy, few systematic studies have been published regarding their efficacy specifically for AN.

One interesting study (Geist et al., 2000) compared family group psychoeducation in a group of 25 hospitalized female adolescents. After a 4-month period of treatment, the family group psychoeducation, although less expensive than family therapy, proved equally effective in weight restoration to the medically compromised AN patients, but no significant change in psychological functioning by the patients or their families was reported in either group.

A major problem with group treatments is that they tend to have high attrition rates (Fairburn & Cooper, 1993). In fact, my patient Joy, described in a later chapter, found them counterproductive. A veteran of eating disorder groups, she reported that members become competitive and their symptoms are exacerbated: "Put me in a room full of bulimics and I'll be throwing up by the next night. It's a control issue. If a person with bulimia can do it better than the person over here can, they will try, because that is their personality, to have more control." This may be one reason for the high attrition rate.

COGNITIVE BEHAVIORAL THERAPY

Cognitive behavioral therapy (CBT) is the only model other than family therapy that has a significant evidence-based literature to document its effectiveness with eating disorders. CBT addresses behaviors and cognitions specific to the ED. Its aim is to alter abnormal attitudes about body shape and weight, and replace dysfunctional dieting with normal eating habits. It also attempts to develop coping skills for resisting binge eating and purging (Wilson & Fairburn, 1993).

One of the most important contributions of CBT is its development of a treatment manual (Fairburn, 1985), which has been expanded (Fairburn, Marcus, & Wilson, 1993). The goals of manual-based CBT—namely, eliminating dysfunctional patterns of eating—are similar to those of nutritional counseling for eating disorders. With behavioral therapy, on the other hand, the cognitive element—attitudes and concerns regarding body weight and shape—are omitted; treatment is focused solely on altering eating behaviors. For example, the goal for those with anorexia is weight gain.

Of the various eating disorders, CBT has been most intensively studied with BN; there have been relatively few controlled studies looking at CBT with AN. Moreover, the APA Practice Guideline (2000) mentions that "there is no clear evidence that any specific form of psychotherapy is superior for all [AN] patients" (p. 2). However, as a result of the encouraging results with BN, CBT has also been applied to BED, where it has shown moderate effectiveness but is no more effective than any other treatment (Ricca et al., 2000; Wilson, 1999).

A meta-analysis of CBT with BN found that it is effective in producing "a substantial reduction of bulimic behaviors and cognitive distortions or attitudes," although the authors could not conclude which of the various components of CBT are most effective (Lewandowski et al., 1997, p. 713). A review by Peterson and Mitchell (1999) showed that indeed CBT has been found to be the most effective, or certainly an equally effective, form of psychotherapy for BN. Wilson (1996) asserts that on average 50% of patients treated with CBT recover. In a randomized controlled trial, Bulik et al. (1999) found that lesser severity of BN is associated with a more rapid response to CBT.

A review by Anderson and Maloney (2001), however, found that most studies provide outcome data on binge eating, purgative behavior, and concern with shape and weight, while fewer provide data on restraint and self-esteem. They also mention that use of different outcome measures, such as self-reports versus standardized rating scales, can produce discrepancies in efficacy estimates of CBT.

Similarly, a very recent systematic review looking at psychotherapy for BN and binging mentioned that, although there is a small body of evidence supporting CBT, most of the studies used evaluated patients with the purging type of BN. Also, the quality of the trials administered varies, and sample sizes tend to be rather small; therefore, the validity of any findings remains questionable (Hay & Bacaltchuk, 2002).

Clearly, CBT weighs in as a well-documented treatment model; it is especially well supported in relation to adult bulimia. There seem to be no evidence-based studies with sufficient subject numbers comparing CBT with family therapy in the eating disorders area. It is interesting to note, however, that Blouin (1994) found family environment to be the *only* significant predictor of a reduction in binge-eating and bulimic conditions—supporting family-orientated therapy as an essential part of treatment for ED.

MEDICATIONS

For the clinician who focuses his or her work on creating contextual change, the use of medications represents a major clash of paradigms. From a true biopsychosocial model there should be no clash, because one covers the biological aspects and the other covers the psychosocial side. In reality there is always a tension. Why can't they be seen as complementary techniques working toward the same goal? The major problem, I believe, is that the two models are based on conflicting fundamental theories of change. The medical model seeks fundamental change within the individual brain chemistry of the eating disorders patient; the systems therapist seeks fundamental change within the patient's social context. These two perspectives present contradictory responses. Of course, I must emphasize that I know of no treatment protocol that advocates using medication alone, without a complementary psychosocial intervention. And there are times when the contextual therapist must use medications to support change.

The literature on medications is voluminous, so the discussion here will be limited to some of the more salient studies supporting psychopharmacologic interventions for eating disorders.

Studies have found various medications, mainly antidepressants such as the SSRI (selective serotonin reuptake inhibitor) fluoxetine, or Prozac®, to be effective agents for short-term clinical improvement, and at times remission, in patients with BN (Goldstein et al., 1995; Hsu et al., 1991). A rigorous review (Morgan, 2002) incorporating 16 randomized trials with a total of 1,300 bulimia patients and a follow-up of 4 weeks or more, found that, in the short term, antidepressants were more effective than placebo for improving remission (i.e., complete reduction in binge or purge episodes) at a mean follow-up of 8 weeks, and clinical improvement (i.e., 50% or more reduction in binge or purge episodes) at a mean follow-up of 9 weeks.

Numerous clinicians question whether the results secondary to the SSRIs are long-standing. They believe the salutary effect may be short term and a result of the anorexigenic side effect of the SSRIs, an effect that tends to wear off after a couple of months. An interesting review of the psychopharmacotherapy literature for EDs found the following:

> There have been several studies on the combination of psychotherapy and fluoxetine for the treatment of patients with bulimia nervosa (Beaumont, Russell & Toyz, 1997; Fichter et al., 1991; Goldbloom et al., 1997; Walsh et al., 1997). With the exception of 1 study (Goldbloom et al., 1997), all trials were placebo-controlled. The results are somewhat inconsistent—in 2 studies, no difference was found between cognitive behavioural therapy and nutritional counselling and other psychotherapeutic interventions were superior to medication alone (Beaumont, Russell, & Touyz, 1997; Walsh et al., 1997). However, in the latter study, after 20 weeks, there were no differences in outcome measures between the group who had received fluoxetine and those who had received placebo or cognitive behavioural therapy. (Kruger & Kennedy, 2000)

Placebo as good as the other treatments? Interesting!

The picture may be even less clear with AN; even after the encouraging achievement of weight restoration, patients often relapse (Kaye et al., 1999). Vitiello and Lederhendler (2000) state that no specific drug interventions have proved efficacious in the long-term outcome of AN. Where AN is concerned, according to Johnson, Tsoh, and Varnado (1996), "the literature clearly indicates that current medications do not promote weight gain nor influence the core characteristics of the disorder" (p. 472) such as body image disturbance. At the present time studies provide only preliminary evidence, as research in this area is limited by the difficulty of finding sufficient numbers of AN patients and by other clinical and methodological difficulties in studying the disorder (Krueger & Kennedy, 2000).

As Garfinkel and Walsh (1997) note, the numerous possible side effects as well as some patients' personal aversion to using medication means that dropout rates in most studies tend to be high. Similarly, when maintenance medication is required in therapy, side effects may oblige some patients to withdraw from treatment.

The Cochrane Library, the gold standard of evidence-based medicine, has done some interesting reviews in the area of eating disorders. One review (Bacaltchuk & Hay, 2003) included 16 trials with the major categories of antidepressants versus placebo for people with bulimia nervosa. The categories were tricyclic antidepressants, MAO inhibitors, and the SSRI fluoxetine. The studies found that the patients treated with antidepressants, especially the tricyclic antidepressants, were more likely to interrupt treatment prematurely because of adverse effects. It was not true of the fluoxetine, suggesting that this may be a more acceptable treatment, presumably because of fewer side effects. As the APA Practice Guideline (2000) notes, "[t]o date, the only medication approved by the Food and Drug Administration for bulimia nervosa is fluoxetine" (p. 17).

The APA Practice Guideline (2000) recommends that antidepressants be considered as a treatment option for patients with AN if associated comorbid problems exist, such as depression, or after the primary goal of weight restoration has been achieved. Similarly, with BN, Fairburn and Cooper (1993) point out that benefits gained from drug treatments tend to be lost once the drugs are discontinued, so they suggest that antidepressants be prescribed only for patients exhibiting a comorbid depressive disorder. But though AN patients frequently exhibit symptoms of mood disturbance and obsessive-compulsive disorders (OCD), and antidepressant medications (in particular SSRIs like fluoxetine) tend to be effective with these disorders, Attia et al. (1998) found that no additional benefit was gained from using fluoxetine with a structured inpatient program. As I discussed in the first chapter, it can be problematic for the treatment process to add a comorbid diagnosis.

Perhaps the most important question for the purposes of this book has to do with the efficacy of psychopharmacologic versus psychotherapeutic treatments for eating disorders. The Cochrane Library has done a systematic review of all randomized controlled trials comparing antidepressants with psychological approaches and comparing their combination with each single approach in the treatment of bulimia (Bacaltchuk, Hay, & Trefiglio, 2003). Five trials were included in comparison one (antidepressants versus psychological treatments), five in comparison two (antidepressants versus the combination), and seven in comparison three (psychological treatments versus the combination). In comparison one, remission rates were 20% for single antidepressants and 39% for single psychotherapy; dropout rates were higher for antidepressants than for psychotherapy. Comparison two found remission rates of 42% for the combination of medications and psychotherapy and 23% for antidepressants alone. Comparison three showed a 36% pooled remission rate for psychological approaches compared with 49% for the combination. Dropout rates, however, were higher for the combination than for the psychological treatments alone, suggesting that adding medications with their side effects made staying in the therapy less attractive. One might speculate that perhaps patients were not getting the alleviation of their symptoms that would have encouraged them to tolerate the side effects.

Clearly, this evidence suggests that the combination of psychotherapy with antidepressants may be useful. Other studies, however, have found varied results. Though a Johnson, Tsoh, and Varnado (1996) review found that for the majority of BN patients medication must be combined with CBT to be effective, a Peterson and Mitchell (1999) review states that there is only modest evidence for this, as the results from comparison studies are inconsistent. Indeed, the clinician must be aware that, given that fact, it may not be worth the risk of premature dropping out.

Psychotropic medications continue to be an extremely controversial area. Recent challenges to antidepressants in particular question their effectiveness (Kirsch et al., 2002) and their tendency to "blame the body" (Ross & Pam, 1995, p. 3), relieving everyone, including the patient, of accountability for his or her behavior. This indeed is one of the most problematic issues of biological psychiatry: Does it negate personal responsibility? It gives a conflicting message to the family of the AN/BN patient. Is their family member, and are they themselves, responsible and even accountable for making profound changes, or is it a biological dysfunction that is responsible, making patience all that is needed? In my estimation this dichotomy is a little extreme. In my experience, medications can facilitate the clinical work for some people.

INTERPERSONAL THERAPY:
A TRANSITIONAL MODEL

As we move away from the more individually oriented therapies, the bridge into my approach is interpersonal therapy (IPT). IPT, a time-limited treatment, is based on the ideas of Harry Stack Sullivan in the interpersonal school. It deals with current rather than past interpersonal relationships (Sadock & Sadock, 2003). It is essentially an individual psychotherapy that focuses on the individual's contemporary social context. With the latter, it is akin to family therapy. But because the family is not inculded in IPT, it is profoundly different.

As Jay Haley (personal communication 1970) would say in our training seminars, "It's important to be aware when you look at a problem whether you are seeing it as a problem of one person, a problem of two, or a problem of three people." How the clinician conceptualizes the problem has profound consequences for the outcome. IPT moves from the model of one person to an interpersonal context in which the unit is more than one. It is in this sense that IPT is a bridge to family therapy approaches, which not only see a problem as at least three people, but also have a specific valence to the system of the family. The family, of course, is not just one of many contexts; for children and adolescents, it is the defining context, and it continues to be profoundly influential as they go through life.

With IPT, the goal of therapy is to improve the current interpersonal context in which disordered eating occurs. It therefore targets personal stress and difficulties in interpersonal relationships, rather than the ED itself. Controlled trials evaluating IPT have found it to be very useful with BN, and it has also been successful in short-term reduction of binge eating episodes in binge eating disorders (Wilfley & Cohen, 1997). IPT has not, however, been studied systematically with adolescent populations (Steiner & Lock, 1998).

One study (Fairburn et al., 1996) evaluating the effectiveness of CBT, behavioral therapy, and focal IPT in BN patients found focal IPT led to a lower rate of total *DSM-IV* eating disorders than did behavioral therapy: 28% versus 86%. Those in the focal IPT group were twice as likely (and those who received CBT were more than three times as likely) to be in remission than those who received behavioral therapy. Wilson (1996) has suggested that IPT is an appealing option for BN patients who are considered CBT nonresponders.

FAMILY THERAPY

Family therapy is a systems theory-based model that addresses a patient's problems by seeking to transform that person's context. The problem is seen as residing not in the individual and not in a problem of communication but in the organization of the patient's social context. After a thorough assessment of the biopsychosocial elements, the clinician addresses the context that is responsible for maintaining the present dysfunctional homeostasis that is leading to the symptom.

There are numerous models of family therapy. The best description of these systems, I think, is that of Douglas Sprenkel (personal communication), who classifies schools by the periodicity of the sequences. The therapy of Murray Bowen, for example, deals with transgenerational sequences, so the patterns are repeated over many years. Jay Haley's problem-solving therapy uses patterns that are repetitive over months. In *Leaving Home* (1980) he gives a classic description of families with a young person with schizophrenia: The parents begin to fight. The child becomes symptomatic.

As the parents focus on the hospitalized youngster, the stress between them is deflected. When the child is returned home, some months later, the conflict between the parents exacerbates, and the child becomes symptomatic again. In contrast to both of these models, in structural family therapy the sequences emerge within a short period, directly in the treatment room.

The importance of the role family therapy plays when treating patients with anorexia is emphasized by Dare and Eisler (1997), who see the disorder as paradigmatic for family therapy, "in much the same way that hysteria served as a paradigm for psychoanalysis and phobias served for behavior therapy" (p. 308). I agree that family therapy in many ways is perfectly suited for the treatment of AN. Anorexia is a disorder that is profoundly influenced and indeed maintained by the social context. Family therapy, a technology for transforming that context, is perfectly suited for the task of liberating individuals from the grasp of the disease, as a number of controlled studies have shown.

Perhaps the most widely documented research on the efficacy of family therapy for treating ED is the series of studies carried out by the group at the Maudsley Hospital in London. Their original study (Russell et al., 1987) compared family therapy in AN patients, in which the family was encouraged to take charge of the patient's eating, with individual therapy. Outcomes at 1-year follow-up showed family therapy to be superior for younger patients (those under 19 years of age) with a short history of the disorder (less than 3 years), while individual therapy was more effective with older patients (Dare et al., 1990). It was also found that dropout rates in the family therapy group (but not in the individual therapy group) were greater among patients whose families had high levels of expressed emotion. For BN patients included in the study, outcome tended to be poor regardless of treatment modality. At 5-year follow-up (Eisler et al., 1997), it was found that these results held.

In an expanded version of the first study, family therapy was again found to be more effective than either individual supportive therapy or individual psychodynamic therapy, even for adults with AN, particularly if the illness had started during adolescence (Russell et al., 1992).

Other studies have had similar findings. Robin et al. (1994) found, in a randomized controlled trial, that family systems therapy was more efficacious than ego-oriented individual therapy for increased body mass index (BMI) in anorexic adolescents, and the same result was elicited at 1-year follow-up (Robin et al., 1999). Although individual therapy proved equally effective in the follow-up study, adolescents regained healthy functioning faster with family therapy.

Another, earlier relevant study looked at the 1-year follow-up of 90 adolescents who had been randomly allocated to one of four treatment groups: inpatient, individual and family outpatient, group therapy outpatient, or "no treatment"/one-time counseling session assessment control (Crisp et al., 1991). They found that the outpatient treatments were just as effective as the inpatient treatment, with no benefit found for controls. This finding was also upheld at 2-year follow-up (Gowers et al., 1994). The investigators pointed out, however, that, although these studies demonstrate some support for family therapy, therapy was combined with individual therapy. Therefore, it is difficult to compare it directly with other family therapy studies.

Similarly, a review of seven studies of AN and BN children and adolescents assessed the efficacy of various treatments including family therapy and/or IPT, CBT, multimodal inpatient therapy, concurrent group therapy or counseling for patients and parents, and behavior therapy. Prolonged weight gain and improvement in psychological adjustment were more often found with outpatient family therapy or family-based treatment programs involving concurrent therapy for parents and adolescents (Mitchell & Carr, 2000).

The Geist et al. (2000) article challenges the IST model of family therapy for the treatment of eating disorders, showing that psychoeducation for the family (a less intensive form of treatment) may be equally effective. The study, using 25 newly diagnosed, medically compromised female adolescents with AN who required hospitalization, compared family therapy and family group psychoeducation. Weight restoration was achieved following the 4-month period of treatment in both groups; group averages ranged from 75% to 77% of ideal body weight before treatment and from 91% to 96% after. No significant change, however, was reported in psychological functioning by either adolescents or parents.

One significant aspect of this family therapy research is that on the whole it focuses on adolescents. Benefits with adult patients have been much less apparent, as the Russell et al. (1987) study showed. In a recent randomized controlled trial (Dare et al., 2001), however, 84 adult patients with AN were placed into either focal psychoanalytic psychotherapy, cognitive-analytic therapy (CAT), family therapy, or a low-contact, "routine" treatment control group. The researchers found that psychoanalytic psychotherapy and family therapy were significantly superior to the control treatment after 1 year. The CAT group tended to show benefits, but the difference between the routine control group and CAT was not statistically significant. The overall outcome found the following: "This was a group of patients with a relatively poor prognosis (late age of onset, long duration of illness, history of unsuccessful treatment) but the majority engaged well in out-patient treatment. However, overall, more than two-thirds remained abnormally underweight at the end of treatment" (Dare et al., 2001, p. 220). This finding supports the established fact that longer duration of illness and later age of onset make obtaining a good outcome in treatment more difficult.

For some clinicians, the idea of family therapy with adolescents may conflict with adolescent developmental needs. The *Treatment Manual for Anorexia Nervosa* (Lock et al., 2001) recognizes that this approach may appear "counterintuitive to some clinicians who emphasize the adolescent's need for autonomy and self-control, which is indeed an expected part of adolescent development" (p. 11). In view of the fact that family-based approaches seem to be superior to individual approaches where adolescents are concerned, however, the authors maintain that families are a crucial resource to assist in getting the regressed, out-of-control AN adolescent back on track. Once the youngster's symptoms have remitted, the natural processes of adolescent individuation can be resumed.

The Psychosomatic Family Model

Some of the earliest work in family therapy with ED patients was the research carried out in the 1970s at the Philadelphia Child Guidance Clinic (PCGC), on which the clinical work reported in this book is based. As was described in the introduction to this book, the researchers at the Clinic developed the concept of the psychosomatic family, which is characterized by interactional patterns such as conflict avoidance, rigidity, and overprotectiveness. In their work with anorectic patients, they postulated that it was these dysfunctional patterns, observable in the therapy room, that caused the symptoms to emerge. Therapy was directed to challenging the family to change these patterns, which have been enabling the family to avoid conflict by focusing on a symptomatic member whose illness provided a distraction.

The results of their work were published in their seminal book, *Psychosomatic Families: Treating Anorexia in Context* (Minuchin, Rosman, & Baker, 1978). In the original psychosomatic project, follow-ups conducted over 2 to 7 years of the sample of 53 anorexic adolescents (median age 14) found 86% asymptomatic with good psychosocial functioning. A study by Martin (1985) conducted with AN adolescents in Toronto and followed up at 5 years used a similar approach to treatment and found the same degree of success in outcome. Although the effectiveness of the psychosomatic model has clearly been replicated, I am not aware of an evidence-based study with controls that has explicitly tested it.

The psychosomatic family model has come under some criticism, specifically from Dare and Eisler (1997), who found that some of the techniques aimed at transforming habitual patterns of conflict avoidance are unnecessary and at times counterproductive, especially in the early stages of treatment with families where conflicts are associated with feelings of guilt and blame; therefore, the techniques should be used cautiously. I agree with Dare and Eisler in their call for caution; the techniques employed in the cases in this book are extremely powerful and should be used only by well-trained therapists who have the close collaboration of a medical colleague. My experience in hundreds of sessions, however, does not bear out their concerns about guilt and blame. In my goal-directed therapy, I explicitly address issues such as guilt and blame only when the content has been presented in such a way that it is keeping the system stuck. The work is directed toward liberating parents to do what has made sense to them but they have been hampered in doing by the professionals: acting to get their child to eat. Rather than feeling guilty, they are relieved to be able to do something that is clearly effective, not just stand by and watch their child starve.

The blame and guilt that Dare and Eisler identify may in part be a result of what the therapists are asking for and expecting to see. That is always a danger as therapists in their questioning elicit certain responses. I have not focused on them or queried them routinely, and I have rarely seen them in my work. What I have seen is a profound sense of change, and at times loss, for the family. There is a different relationship, and family members may miss the extreme closeness of the enmeshment. Especially in the case of adolescents, the transformation means that they move on; liberated from the position of being stuck in the family, they differentiate, separating to a greater or lesser degree. In the case described in chapter 5, for example, the mother was left feeling deprived of her daughter's closeness.

Intensive Structural Therapy

Intensive structural therapy, the model on which the cases in this book are based, grew directly out of the psychosomatic family model. In 1981, I co-authored *Family Therapy Techniques* with Salvador Minuchin. Over the years, I came to see a need for the structural family therapy (SFT) model to be broadened to address resources in the patient's contemporary context. In addition, I became aware of an important facet of systems—that there are forces that maintain the problematic status quo. I call this assessment tool the homeostatic maintainer (HM). The use of the HM concept allows the clinician to direct treatment more incisively. The next two chapters describe and illustrate how IST is used with youngsters and adults suffering with eating disorders.

Before we go to the model, I would like to suggest that the quote that began this chapter, the words of Hilde Bruch, speaks of the powerlessness of the families in most models of treatment. As you will see in the pages ahead, the family is not a corollary to the treatment. Indeed, the family, in many ways, *is* the treatment delivery system itself.

CHAPTER 3

Intensive Structural Therapy:
Basic Concepts

> You know that after the therapy that we did
> the anorexia has never returned.
> —Herb, referring to his wife's anorexia
> that had begun 40 years before.

The intensive structural therapy (IST) model is described in detail in my 1993 volume, *Intensive Structural Therapy: Treating Families in Their Social Context*. The brief summary that follows is designed simply to introduce the basic concepts that were elaborated in that earlier book and, more importantly, are used in the cases described in this book.

THE IMPORTANCE OF THE SOCIAL CONTEXT

Intensive structural therapy has in common with all family therapies the principle that patients are seen in their social context. This approach is a profound shift from therapies in which the problem is seen as residing within the individual. The primary context that is focused on is the family—the nuclear family and often the extended family—particularly for the adolescent anorectics and bulimics described in most of the chapters in this book. The significant context includes all the people who are influential in the person's life; for older patients, it is common to involve such contexts as friends, co-workers, and social agencies in the therapy.

Interactional Patterns

Unlike most family therapy models, IST follows the psychosomatic family model in focusing on specific interactional patterns that can be observed and addressed in the treatment room. The specific interactional patterns that characterize the psychosomatic families of eating-disorder (ED) patients are enmeshment, overprotectiveness, rigidity, and conflict avoidance, which may take the form of conflict diffusion or triangulation. *Enmeshment* is inappropriate closeness between family members gauged against a backdrop of their developmental stage. For example, the closeness between a parent and a 4-year-old should be much different when the child is 14. *Overprotectiveness* results when members of the family feel a tremendous responsibility for protecting the family members. *Rigidity* in families means being heavily committed to maintaining the status quo and therefore having difficulty with inevitable periods of change and growth. *Triangulation* is often a crucial dynamic in understanding ED; when conflict starts to arise, a third person, often the symptomatic child, is recruited to activate to diffuse the conflict, and, in doing so, the symptoms exacerbate and the conflict diminishes. In my experience with ED patients, *conflict avoidance* is a central characteristic that keeps these systems stuck. Empirically, I have found a continuum: To the extent that there is conflict avoidance, the symptomatology is manifested; to the extent that conflict is addressed, the symptoms are controlled.

The Homeostatic Maintainer

IST also differs from other family therapy models in using the concept of the *homeostatic maintainer* in assessing the family system. In the 1970s, Mara Selvini Palazzolli and her colleagues at the Center for the Study of the Family in Milan did pioneering work with anorexia and family therapy. Their Milan systems therapy is unique in its description of the family as a rigidly organized homeostatic mechanism that remains resistant to change from any external factors. The therapist remains neutral, encouraging the family to become observers and challengers of their own treatment process.

Selvini Palazzoli depended heavily on the concept of family homeostasis but did not use the concept of the homeostatic maintainer. In her major work *Self-Starvation: From the Intrapsychic to the Transpersonal Approach to Anorexia Nervosa* (1974), she pioneered the concept of homeostatic systems in understanding anorexia: "I am absolutely convinced that mental 'symptoms' arise in rigid homeostatic systems, and that they are the more intense the more secret is the cold war waged by the sub-system (parent-child coalitions) (p. 239)."

Her concept differs from the one used in the psychosomatic model and in my work. I do not see the problem as "wars" between family members, which imply conscious battles or even antipathy. Instead, I see the homeostasis of the system being maintained by the emergence of the symptom.

Nor do I see this as a conscious process—I often refer to it in my own mind as the "sixth sense," a controlling force that affects us in systems but that we are not overtly conscious of.

As Selvini Palazzoli describes the process, "In other words psychiatric 'symptoms' tend to develop in family systems threatened with collapse; in such systems they play the same part as submission rites play in the animal kingdom: they help to ward off aggression from one's own kind. There is just this tragic difference: the specific human rite, called 'illness' acquires its normative function from the very malfunction it is trying to eliminate" (p. 239). In many ways this is what I have observed as manifested and maintained by specific interactional patterns. What is different in the IST model is the specific pinpointing of homeostatic maintainers, the forces that are leading to the maintenance of the status quo of these systems.

The term *homeostasis* has had bad press in the last number of years, as connoting a linear process. I believe that family therapy orthodoxy has often led to paralysis in therapy. Everything in life is circular or linear, depending on how one analyzes the periodicity of the sequences. In my experience, the reality is that certain forces and individuals in systems are more influential than others in keeping the systems stuck. I have found that identification of this mechanism serves to direct therapy, as it provides a clear roadmap for the clinician. The next chapter discusses in more detail how the concept is used in the model of treatment.

Grounded Observation

The use of grounded observation is a key feature of both psychosomatic family theory and IST. By grounded observation I mean theory that is based on direct observation of data. An anecdote from the work of the Philadelphia Child Guidance Clinic will illustrate the power of this concept and its use as a tool in therapy.

During the 1970s, when the researchers at the clinic were actively treating many anorexics, a 13-year-old girl was referred from the adjacent children's hospital. She had been steadily losing weight, and when her doctors could find no medical reason, they concluded she must be anorexic. The medical psychosomatic team at PCGC did a family task test to see whether her family displayed the characteristic patterns of the psychosomatic family, such as enmeshment and conflict avoidance. These patterns were not manifested by the family. The researchers reported that they found no psychological grounds for the child's continuing loss of weight. The doctors at children's hospital redoubled their diagnostic efforts and found that the girl had a pineal tumor.

That's almost science! Rarely in our fuzzy field of mental health are assessments made on such objective data. Grounded theory, originally described by Barney Glaser and Anselm Strauss (1967), mandates "the discovery of theory from data" (p. 1) in doing social research. Ian Dey, in his important book *Grounding Grounded Theory* (1999), compares this approach to the work of physicist Richard Feynman, who, he says, "believed in the accumulated wisdom of science, but never took it on trust" (p. xii). Similarly, in psychiatry it is necessary to find objective ways of getting data, not relying on what we are told in the therapy room. People say things for a variety of reasons, not the least of which is to please the clinician.

In the area of mental health there are legions of theories and descriptions, but few that are based on direct observation of process that emerges from, at the very least, a semiobjective manner. Although there is very good documentation in the area of bipolar disorders (*DSM-IV*, pp. 173–178, 180–183) and well-defined subtypes of schizophrenia (*DSM-IV*, pp. 149–150), these data are, for the most part, based on subjective reporting and not interactional patterns *with the clinician decentralized*. Over the years, grounded theory has diverged into hotly contested versions, but for the purposes of this book I use my own version of grounded observation. That is, the theory has emanated from the observations of the clinical process as it unfolds in the clinical session. Whereas the fields of psychiatry and psychology often depend on intangible data such as subjective affect for assessment and treatment intervention, the data that emerge in a family session are more objective, observable interactional patterns that the therapist can use as a guide to questioning and intervention. As long as the clinician remains decentralized and the family (members and other influential members of the system) talks and responds to each other, the patterns that emerge are for the most part below the level of consciousness and therefore approximate what occurs at home. (I say "for the most part" because the presence of the therapist must constrain the family to some extent; but patterns in enmeshed families have their own compelling authority that produces patterned responses.)

The concept of grounded observation is central to my practices and to the work described in the remainder of this book. Before going on to the specifics of the model and the cases that follow, it is worthwhile to examine closely some brief portions of a case transcript to bring out this essential technique. The case is one that I have previously reported in detail in *Treating Troubled Adolescents* (Fishman, 1988). In the segments that follow, I focus specifically on how I use grounded theory with the psychosomatic family patterns. In addition, since I treated the family in 1980, I have had the rare opportunity of reporting 20-year follow-up on a course of psychotherapy; after 8 months of weekly outpatient treatment, the symptomatic behavior had ceased, and the eating disorder had not recurred.

DOROTHY: THE "WORLD'S OLDEST ANOREXIC"

Dorothy was 42 years old when I saw her. Dorothy presented with an eating disorder that, in addition to self-starvation, included taking laxatives—as many as one or two boxes of laxatives per day. A number of times, she was rushed to the emergency room in metabolic crisis. Her family consisted of her husband, Herb; her parents; and her two children, at the time aged 12 and 16. All of them were tied in a classic psychosomatic family system of enmeshment, overprotectiveness, rigidity, and conflict avoidance.

Patterns with the Parents

When Dorothy called to make a first appointment, I asked something generic about her issues. In response, she blurted out, "My parents are driving me crazy." The first session, therefore, involved Dorothy and her parents and her husband. One issue that arose was a habitual pattern on her parents' part of coming for brunch every Sunday without ever telling her when they would arrive; Dorothy and her family felt like hostages but had never expressed their annoyance. An agreement was reached that the parents would call and arrange a time, but at the second session patterns of extreme conflict avoidance, rigidity, and enmeshment emerged. Following are short excerpts from that session.

Dr. Fishman: [entering] How is everybody?

When using grounded observation, it is essential for the clinician to be decentralized so that the naturalistic patterns of the family emerge. As we begin this session, I very neutrally try to leave the door open for the patterns to emerge.

Father: Good. How've you been?

Mother: Great.

Dorothy: Except for me, I'm never great. They [referring to her parents] think this is very easy, but I say it isn't easy for me [laughs].

Everyone in the room is tense, and Dorothy diffuses the tension by identifying herself as having a problem. This is a microcosm of the pattern that leads to her symptoms: At moments of stress and potential conflict, she becomes symptomatic by gorging herself with laxatives. This time, while less intense—she is only complaining that she is "not okay"—it is the same pattern. By presenting herself as having a problem, she draws the attention to herself, thereby diffusing the tension in the room between the other members of the family.

I must emphasize that the obvious relevance of these patterns is an extrapolation to the home setting. At home as in the therapy room, Dorothy acts as the homeostatic maintainer; she activates whenever conflict emerges. The result is that the system does not change. When Dorothy gets upset with her parents and her husband, she does not deal with the conflict. Instead, she becomes symptomatic.

Dr. Fishman: How come?

Dorothy: This is the *worst* thing I have ever done.

Dr. Fishman: It is?

What Dorothy is referring to is bringing her parents in for a therapy session the previous week. This speaks to the rigidity, the overprotectiveness, and the conflict avoidance of the system. Here she is, a woman well into middle age, yet in all her life the worst thing she has ever done is being with her parents in a therapy session! This comment reflects the extreme amounts of conflict avoidance in the system.

As Dorothy is speaking, her husband has been sitting to the side, outside of the circle that includes Dorothy, her parents, and me. Here is another pattern that has been in many ways the tragedy in Dorothy's life: Just as he is not now rolling up his sleeves and participating in this family session to address his wife's life-threatening problems, he has stayed on the sidelines as Dorothy was immersed in her profoundly dysfunctional relationship with her parents. I now ask him to move his chair into the circle. This move foreshadows the therapeutic goal of getting him to be more a part of the family. He needs to be available to pull his wife out of the enmeshment with her parents.

[Dorothy has been talking about something that happened many years ago.]

Dr. Fishman: See, I thought you were going to be talking about Sunday mornings. [Everybody laughs.]

I am seeking to deal with a problem in the present. We can do nothing with the events of 25 years ago, but I can support Dorothy to challenge issues that are maintaining the anorexia. To the extent that she can address the key interactional patterns, especially the extreme conflict avoidance, she will be released from the anorexia. I use conflict as the lever to move the system. As it is successfully introduced and issues resolve, the other psychosomatic parameters are also changed, because they form a unit, each part of the same process.

Mother:	I wish it was that simple.
Mother/Father:	[talking over each other] We figured leave them alone . . . we don't . . . you know when they are ready they will tell us when to come over. . . . [laughing]
Father:	I'm not going to give them a guilt complex, but I miss my grandchildren, but it's all right. . . . [Mother and Father laugh.]

The anger is heavy in the room. This is the retribution that Dorothy has incurred by drawing boundaries, apparently for one of the first times in her life. The father is on the counterattack. The artillery in these systems is not overt conflict—they are too conflict-avoidant for that—it is guilt and passive-aggressiveness. Those are the materiel used in waging war. When challenged about this statement, the father can step aside and say, "I was just kidding."

Dr. Fishman:	Do you really miss your grandchildren a lot?

I am attempting to exacerbate the situation so that conflict will emerge.

Father:	Oh, I see them, they miss me more than I miss them.

This is bringing up the big guns, powerful guilt. I assume that this is the kind of guilt induction that gets Dorothy to capitulate.

Dr. Fishman:	You missed the kids last weekend, didn't you?

Again, I stir things up, so that conflict emerges.

Mother:	I think that Dorothy just said that. . . .
Dorothy:	I didn't say it.

Dorothy's mother enters to diffuse the conflict between her husband and Dorothy. She is about to demonstrate the extreme enmeshment in the system by stating what her daughter meant. Dorothy activates by further conflict avoiding. She denies having said that, and in so doing, she effectively pulls the air out of the father's sails; and as for her mother's defense, the very problem has evaporated.

One can imagine at home how unsatisfactory the problem solving in this system is. Look at the Sundays: Week after week, month after month, indeed, generation after generation, the couples are held hostage, waiting for the older generation to arrive.

Mother:	Yeah, you said come at 12:30 instead of 2:00.
Dorothy:	I'll tell you why because I know that he [pointing to her husband] gets aggravated. I know that it bothers him. So as a result I'm like that because I don't want you to know that he's annoyed. So I try to make peace, and I don't do it very well.

Dorothy, clearly a woman of peace, has now disowned even being upset by the visits. She says that she gets upset only because her husband gets upset. That, of course, indicates her triangulation. Indeed, she is very light on her feet and very hard to challenge back—she's always ducking the blows. She provides no resistance, so issues cannot be addressed and perhaps resolved.

Dorothy:	And I think it's also I had always done that. You had spent every Sunday at my grandmother's house for my whole life and I just felt that it was part of a pattern.
Dr. Fishman:	So you went to your mother's house?
Mother:	Everyone would just pile in.
Dorothy:	Every Sunday of my entire life was spent there.
Mother:	Yes!

These are the everyday-appearing but profoundly powerful patterns. Every week Dorothy and her family are trapped at home, waiting for her parents. The rigid pattern in fact replicates the rigid pattern of the previous generation. The grandparents, for their part, are equally trapped, not wanting to upset their labile, deathly frail anorectic daughter—who might at any moment be rushed to the emergency room!

Mother:	When you cut your finger it's a big thing, believe me! [laughing]

The previous Sunday, the parents unexpectedly came over very early, and Dorothy cut her finger when her parents arrived. I see the mother as chastising her daughter, suggesting that her visit is more important than the cut finger and that Dorothy shouldn't be upset about the finger. Furthermore, with her laughter, she is trivializing her daughter's injury. Communication like this is serving to increase the ambient guilt that paralyzes Dorothy. If she complains about her finger, she doesn't love her mother; if she doesn't say anything, she is disrespecting her own feelings.

| Herb: | It doesn't bother me. It really doesn't. When you go back over things, Dorothy used to get uptight and all excited, when the kids were little, Grandpa would come in and wake 'em up to look at 'em. Little things like that. Then the kids started screaming and they were up all night. . . . The only thing I object to is that she would get all excited, and that would make me aggravated because I had to live with her. |

Talk about conflict avoidance! Grandpa would want to see the kids, so he would wake them, and they would be up all night. Herb would be upset, but he would not blame the man who woke them. If he were to do that, he would have had to address conflict. Indeed, he denies that he is personally piqued—he is only responsive because his wife gets upset. The system will not allow that!

Of course, to the extent that conflict is not expressed in the system, the system does not change. But a system must change to accommodate the changing developmental needs of its members.

| Dorothy: | I was getting upset about things that were imaginary, things that maybe I didn't need to get upset about. Maybe I was exaggerating. |

This is a consistent theme in the work with this family. Dorothy was consistently "gaslighted": She would feel rightfully indignant, and members of the family would tell her, "No, it's all in your head."

Dr. Fishman:	What's a conflict that you avoided this week?
Dorothy:	I'm trying to remember. . . .
Dorothy:	We didn't have one this week.
Dr. Fishman:	I know, what's one that you avoided? I'm sure you didn't have one.
Dorothy:	I can't. . . .
Dr. Fishman:	How about today?
Dorothy:	No. . . .
Dr. Fishman:	How about this year?
Dorothy:	I don't have conflicts. . . .
Dr. Fishman:	One characteristic, it seems to me, of your family is that everybody is a conflict avoider.
Dorothy:	Ignore it and it will go away.

Dr. Fishman: Mm hmm. Everyone seems to thrive on [avoiding] it—well, almost everyone. [Looks at Dorothy.]

Dorothy: Well, what happens when you avoid conflict all the time?

Dr. Fishman: Things don't change. And to the extent that things don't change, you are focused on not eating, on the anorexia.

Dorothy: Then how do I feel conflict when I don't feel it anymore?

She is inured from feeling angry. In this system, conflict is atavistic; they have evolved beyond this—no conflict, no change, only manners! Not feeling conflict is her response to living in a system where it is considered hubris to feel indignation. She has therefore learned to guard herself by not feeling anything.

Mother: If we are talking about conflict now. . . .

Dorothy: In anything. . . .

Mother: In anything . . . for years I've been aware, not to upset you in any way, to try to avoid offering any advice unless you said, "Mother, what do you think of this?" I was conscious of the fact that I better wait till she asks, I don't want to upset her.

This is the circularity. Dorothy does not confront her parents, and they do not confront her. They live in terror that she will get even sicker with her anorexia. They dance around each other—and nothing changes.

Dr. Fishman: What about that, are there any areas of your relationship that you think need to change? Are there things that Dorothy does that bother you? Even things that have been in cold storage for all these years.

Mother: Sure. Well . . . I would like her. . . .

Dorothy: To eat. [laughs]

Mother: No, we've talked about it, and I've accepted it.

Dorothy: I think that may be the basis of the whole thing, you know. . . .

Mother: I would like to be closer to her, I would like to feel free and relaxed and say, "Hey, Dorothy, why don't we—" whatever, like free. I would like to be able to not have to think, "Will it upset her? Will I look at her wrong?" I'm conscious of everything I must say to her. I would like that to change. How, I don't know. . . it's just I don't want to upset her [weakly, while looking to Father].

[Father begins to say something, but Dr. Fishman intervenes.]

Dr. Fishman: No, let them talk about it. Go ahead and upset her . . . if you have to.

Mother: Oh, I wouldn't . . . I don't even know how I want her to be towards . . . how we . . . how I should be towards her or she towards me.

Dr. Fishman: Well, what you're describing here is 22 years of blackmail.

Father: May I add something? From my perspective I don't think it's important as far as how we [indicating Mother and him] feel, whether or not I annoy Herby on a Sunday morning because I come up. The primary purpose is how do we get Dorothy back in good physical health. Now please don't misunderstand me, if it means it's better for her Mother and I to stay the hell away and get lost, then that's the best thing to do. Regardless of whether it upset us in any way would be immaterial, I think, insofar as if it accomplished the best. . . .

Father is attempting to diffuse the conflict. That is the pattern that has kept the conflicts from being resolved. As I listen to this, I also sense the generosity. It would be a great loss to not visit their daughter and her family.

Dr. Fishman: So your father-in-law's the peacemaker, Herb?

This is another challenge to the system—I know he is a hell-raiser!

Father: I'd be subtler about it.

Dorothy: No, he raises hell, he is not a peacemaker.

Dr. Fishman: No, between you and your mother? He's the peacemaker?

Mother: No, I always quiet him down about her.

Dorothy: No, definitely not.

[Everybody is talking over one another.]

Father: You have to realize when you love somebody. . . .

Dorothy: When he gets mad, he really gets mad.

Mother: And I have to quiet him. . . .

From a phenomenological standpoint, I think another reason for the conflict avoidance in this system is that everyone is afraid of Father.

Patterns with the Children

The first session with Dorothy and Herb's adolescent children revealed patterns of extreme enmeshment and overprotectiveness. Greg, age 16, and Jenny, age 12, had taken on the role of looking after their mother, to avoid the repetition of a terrifying experience when she went into shock after taking a large dose of laxatives.

Dr. Fishman:	You're there to keep an eye on your mom.
Jenny:	To keep her company.
Dorothy:	I didn't know that.
Jenny:	You know I always ask you, "Do you want me to keep you company?"
Dorothy:	I always tell you, "No, go. I don't want any company."
Dr. Fishman:	But you know she doesn't really mean it.
Dorothy:	But I do mean it. . . . I keep telling you, Jenny, I'd always rather see you with your friends.
Jenny:	Well, I don't always want to be with my friends. Sometimes I just feel like staying home.
Dorothy:	As long as you feel like staying home just to stay home because you feel like it, not so. . . .
Jenny:	I didn't feel like going anywhere. I felt like staying home.

The children's staying home is in many ways the ultimate conflict avoidance. The conflict that they are terrified may emerge is their mother being rushed to the hospital. Of course, their social isolation is detrimental to their development. Furthermore, the kids are being protective of Dorothy by not acknowledging the real reason why they are staying home. We see here how these patterns pervade the system transgenerationally—Dorothy and her husband, her parents, and the children.

Dr. Fishman:	Really, she needs you there to take care of her, doesn't she?

My customary role in this therapy is to be gently confirming yet challenging. I'm really talking to Dorothy here and challenging her that she's allowing her children to live as her caretakers. On some level that could be construed as child abuse to the extent that it is impeding their development.

Jenny:	Yeah.
Dorothy:	No, I don't.

Greg:	I always feel guilty about the time she got real sick and I was out—the first time.
Jenny:	I was there.
Greg:	You were there and I wasn't.
Dorothy:	You feel guilty about that?
Greg:	Yes, because Jenny was there and I wasn't, and you got real sick.
Jenny:	I didn't know what to do.
Dr. Fishman:	So one of the two of you is always there.
Jenny:	Uh-huh.
Greg:	Chances are if you came to our house at any time one of us would be there.
Jenny:	Or both of us.

It is shocking that neither child seems to see their father as a resource. He has taken cover and is simply not there. The valuable part of grounded theory is that it provides a roadmap for interventions. Here, it tells us that it is important to activate father so that he can be there to relieve the kids and, equally importantly, to support his wife, both in terms of her battles with her parents and in her steps toward personal development, such as getting a job. Indeed, as we worked, one of their central goals was increased intimacy between the two of them and his increased participation in the life of their nuclear family.

Herb:	Yeah, but isn't that why the kids won't leave the house?
Dr. Fishman:	No. The kids are in the house because there is somehow an inappropriate job in your home.
Herb:	[laughing] Well, they're not in any trouble.

Here father seems to be subscribing to a conflict avoidance manual: As long as the kids are in the house, they aren't getting into trouble. In his defense, I will say that that may reflect the common lay understanding of how families get through adolescence without great upheaval, but it is fairly consistent with the pattern of conflict avoidance.

Dorothy:	Would you feel better about leaving if I ate more? Not if I ate more—if I weighed 15 pounds more?
Greg:	Twenty.

Jenny:	I don't know. [pointing to her mother's arm] You're bleeding. [A scab on her arm that Dorothy had been picking at started to bleed.]
Dr. Fishman:	Look at how they watch you. He says "Twenty" and she says "You're bleeding."
Jenny:	Well, look at her arm.
Dr. Fishman:	[to Herb] Did you see that? The way she says "You're bleeding," as though her mother were not competent enough to know that her own body is bleeding?

This is a clear demonstration of the enmeshment in the family: These adolescent children are acutely tuned into the status of their mother's body!

Patterns with the Couple

Toward the goal of grounded observation, there is an additional pattern I track when working with couples: complementary and symmetrical sequences, as described by Gregory Bateson in *Steps to an Ecology of Mind* (1972). *Complementary* sequences occur when one behavior is responded to with a reciprocal behavior—in this case, a challenge and a response in which the other person becomes ill. In *symmetrical* sequences, one behavior is mirrored in the response, as in a tennis match.

The beauty of these sequences is they are readily observable. The clinician doesn't have to rely on subjective responses ("Are you feeling less angry?"). Such grounded observation was invaluable in providing markers for conducting and, indeed, for ending therapy.

Herb:	But isn't part of life forgiving and forgetting, and going on?
Dorothy:	Yes, but I can't. I told you that meant a lot to me. I told you, "You kick me out once too often, and that was it." And you did. I told you, "You will never do that to me again, ever." Never, never again. Now you forget all these things. But I don't forget them. Because they were very, very painful, really painful. It is only now that I can even talk about it. You wonder why I think there is something wrong with me; I think you have given me every reason to think that there is something wrong with me. My whole way was not the way a lovely woman and a mother should behave.
Dr. Fishman:	What about from now on? What do you want?

Herb:	What I said before—come out of this thing and whatever your personality is. . . .
Dorothy:	I don't think you could handle me. Honest to goodness, I don't think you could.

Dorothy is suggesting that if she were herself and that if she didn't capitulate every time there was a conflict but instead challenged her husband back, he would not be able to handle it.

Herb:	If I can't, I can't.
Dorothy:	But are you going to make me feel like some sort of an inferior creep, like a streetwalker? Are you going to make me feel common? I don't want to be common, because I'm not, *really*. [Dorothy affects an upper-class accent.]
Herb:	I never said you were.
Dorothy:	I don't believe you. I don't believe you.
Dr. Fishman:	See, Dorothy thinks you are weak. She thinks you are very weak. The only way she can support you as a husband is by being weaker. And I don't think you are weak. I think you can take having a strong wife. You will be more alive than you have ever been.

My intervention here is that on some level Dorothy has been so conflict avoiding of her husband because on many levels she thinks he is weak. She thinks as she said earlier, he couldn't handle having a strong woman, so I challenge him about his weakness. It is essential that I bolster him a bit in order for Dorothy to be able to challenge him.

Herb:	I think I can too.
Dr. Fishman:	You better tell her that. I think you will be 10 times more alive than you were a year ago, when you have a strong wife.
Herb:	Dorothy, I want you to come out of this and be a strong personality—or whatever it takes.
Dorothy:	If you are willing to take the chance.
Herb:	I'll take the chance. Is it a deal?
Dr. Fishman:	Shake on it.

Her husband challenges Dorothy by saying, come on and be strong. There is an underlying suggestion in his voice, as I read it, that she is blowing smoke and that she's really weak and cannot stand up and be strong. The question is, if he gets stronger, will she then capitulate? That has been the pattern—he is strong, she is weak. But a systemic change in which Herb then became the weak one would be no better. The goal is for both of them to be strong, and both to be complementary, one strong and one being taken care of, a reciprocal relationship. According to Gregory Bateson (personal communication, 1979)—and I agree, based on my clinical experience—that is the flexibility that a functional system needs.

Dorothy:	Hey, I can't take the humiliation again, you know that.
Herb:	There will be no humiliation.
Dorothy:	You know I can't face that.
Herb:	There will be no humiliation. Shake.
Dorothy:	[shaking his hand] I will have to think whether it is worth it.
Dr. Fishman:	It is worth it. The fact is you don't really have a choice. Because if you don't do it, you'll die—either physically or emotionally.

[I get up, put on my jacket, and walk out of the room.]

Dorothy challenges him back, saying she can't tolerate the humiliation. The session ends when finally a symmetrical pattern emerges. Again, we don't want an isomorphic transformation where there is still no true change, where it's just that the other person is down. The functional system now allows for flexibility; they can be symmetrical in challenging each other and complementary in taking care of each other. At this point, the therapy had reached its goal. Both patterns were emerging.

A New Structure

The goals of the therapy were to change the destructive patterns of conflict avoidance, enmeshment, overprotectiveness, and rigidity. A new structure had to be created within the family, one in which appropriate boundaries were established between generations so that all members could meet their developmental needs. The relationship between Dorothy and her parents needed to become less intrusive on the parents' part, less needy on Dorothy's part, and more open to challenge on everyone's part. The children had to be freed from their self-imposed responsibility for their mother so that they could resume a normal adolescent distancing. At the same time, the distance between Dorothy and Herb had to be reduced so that he could have what they both sought, increased intimacy, with Dorothy taking responsibility for her own health.

During 8 months of therapy, these goals were addressed successfully. The overly enmeshed relationships with Dorothy's parents and with the children were loosened. That brought pressure to bear on the dyad, on changing the structure in which Dorothy had to be symptomatic to get her husband's attention. Toward the end of therapy, Dorothy had one more crisis: After a fight with her father, she took a massive dose of laxatives (a few boxes) and went into a coma. When she awoke in the hospital, Herb was finally able to challenge her, telling her in essence that he was sick of her behavior and she had to stop it. The implied ultimatum was "shape up, or I'm going to leave."

The psychosomatic family that had entered my office 8 months before was transformed, and the triangulation and other interactional patterns that had numerous times almost led to Dorothy's death no longer had a hold on her. The big question now would be whether these changes would hold. What would happen as new stresses began to work on this changed structure?

Follow-ups of cases are normally limited to a matter of months or at most a year, but this case was followed for a full 20 years. Both 1 year later, and 2 years and 3 months after cessation of therapy, it was clear that the changes had been maintained. The anorexia and laxative use had disappeared, and Dorothy and her family were leading happier lives. Even Dorothy's parents were happier. Dorothy still had to resist their tendency toward intrusiveness, but now she could do it without either alienating them or becoming symptomatic. The children were leading normal teenage lives and doing well. Dorothy and Herb were functioning as equals, in a symmetrical rather than a reciprocal relationship.

The initial follow-ups thus were promising. The treatment had addressed the patterns of the psychosomatic family, and the system had been transformed by the process interventions. There was still a question in my mind, however: Had the changes held over the long term? Twenty years after the conclusion of therapy, I called the family. I spoke with Herb. He told me that things had gone well for many years. He said, "The anorexia that we had addressed had never recurred." The couple was in business together, and Dorothy had had no psychiatric symptoms whatsoever over the years.

Then, a year ago, their son, Greg, died of an apparent overdose of drugs; he had had a drug problem and had been in a detoxification program. After Greg's death, Dorothy and Herb took a cruise. On the cruise Dorothy began drinking heavily. When she returned home, she couldn't stop drinking and had to go into treatment. The husband said, "You know, the problem we saw you for—the laxatives—never returned. We were successful for that."

I invited the couple to come in for a follow-up interview. Herb said that it was not a good time and asked me to call back in a few months.

When I did, I was greeted with more bad news. Dorothy had been diagnosed with colon cancer. He said that when things stabilized, he would get back to me, and I have not heard from them.

As I look at this transcript from the vantage point of time, I am struck by the power of the model of therapy for addressing the day-to-day interactional patterns. Sometimes I think of it as therapy of the banal, of the everyday. Addressing these patterns led to amelioration of a problem that had been life threatening. This was treatment over 8 months, weekly at the beginning, sometimes bi-weekly after that. No psychiatric hospitalization, no medications, no long-term care from the therapist (who, frankly, was still relatively new in the field), or any additional treatment over the years, until very recently and then for a different problem.

I have thought many times about Greg's death. Did I miss something during the course of the therapy? Did I not do enough work with the youngsters to address any developmental lacunae that might have resulted from the effects of their mother's illness on the family? I frankly don't know what I would have addressed, even if he could have been convinced to come to treatment. Greg was in 11th grade when I treated the family and already had one foot out the door, although during his first 2 years of college he did live at home.

But there is an important question regarding the nature of success. I don't believe that success in a course of therapy guarantees a problem-free life. At best, it simply sustains the person's capability to withstand extreme hardship and difficulties without totally collapsing. I am frankly impressed that, when Greg killed himself, Dorothy was in good enough shape not to collapse back to anorexia. The amazing thing is that she didn't totally decompensate.

The sense of omnipotence can be an occupational hazard in medicine and should be avoided. Once when I presented this case and the follow-up to a psychodynamic and psychoanalytic audience, the criticism was offered that Dorothy must have still been very pathologic if Greg killed himself. I think that is stretching it, going to extremes in family theory and implying intergenerational effects that are not warranted. As they say in Alcoholics Anonymous, "Shit happens." A course of psychotherapy, even effective therapy, is not a vaccine to immunize people from the "slings and arrows of outrageous fortune." A lot of life goes on that has its own impact.

In the final analysis, our impact is humble, compared with the big world out there. We are kidding ourselves if we think otherwise. I make no pretence that at the end of this work people will from then on be symptom-free and strong in every aspect of life.

CHAPTER 4

The Intensive Structural Therapy Model

You can observe a lot just by watching.
—Yogi Berra

The initial specific psychotherapeutic conceptualization of my treatment of eating disorders (ED) was based on the research done at the Philadelphia Child Guidance Clinic. The original study was done with anorectic adolescents, but at the Institute for the Family in Princeton, New Jersey, we found that this model, with certain modifications, could be applied effectively with adult anorectics and with bulimics and compulsive overeaters as well.

THEORETICAL TENETS OF THE MODEL

The treatment model of intensive structural therapy (IST) is based on four theoretical tenets.

1. *The problem is being maintained by the patient's contemporary social context.* In many of the cases in this book involving adolescents and young adults, the nuclear family is the principal focus, but the context includes all individuals and institutions that affect the patient's system. Indeed, families today tend to be embedded in larger social systems than they were a generation ago. Work with the larger system is often essential to increase support for today's overburdened families. Older ED patients usually have more complex social systems, and there are usually more people who are influential in the patient's context and must be included in the treatment. The model uses extended family, friends, co-workers, colleagues, and other therapists in the therapy. In some cases, part of the contextual problem is the *absence* of essential re-

sources. The therapist must then create a new context. The term we use is the *recontextualization of the family*—that is, the incorporation of a new context into the patient's system.

I cannot emphasize strongly enough how imperative it is to do everything one can to bring in the people influential in the system. This entire therapeutic conceptualization is based on the acknowledgment of the essential ineffectuality of the therapist as a change agent, especially when compared with the people the patient loves. People do not change for us when they are suffering tenacious problems like anorexia and bulimia; they change for the people for whom they care.

2. *Certain isomorphic (structurally equal) patterns pervade the context.* For example, the same pattern may be seen between the patient and the nuclear family, between the patient and co-workers or supervisors, and between the patient and friends. The key patterns of the psychosomatic model, as described in the last chapter, are enmeshment, overprotectiveness, rigidity, and conflict avoidance, which may take the form of conflict diffusion and/or triangulation. These patterns may be seen isomorphically replicated with people out of the nuclear family. An example would be seeing the pattern of triangulation among the parents and their child, and among the youngster and her two closest friends at school. It is these interactional patterns that are revealed in the grounded observations in the therapy session. They become the process focus of the therapy.

3. *It is essential to search for the homeostatic maintainer.* The concept of the homeostatic maintainer (HM) has proved a powerful therapeutic tool in the IST model (see Fishman, 1988, 1993). A homeostatic maintainer, as noted in the last chapter, is an individual or a social pattern that is functioning to maintain a given problem. When the forces for developmental change in the family reach an uncomfortably stressful level, someone or something responds to return the family system to its stable but dysfunctional status.

Homeostatic maintenance can also be a process problem for an individual with a paucity of social supports. In the case of Marie, discussed in chapter 9, the patient's isolation obliged her to avoid conflict; she was so desperately lonely that she was terrified of alienating anyone. Furthermore, without social supports she lacked the self-confidence to address conflictual situations.

Used together, the concepts of the HM and isomorphic patterns help the clinician recognize what is maintaining the problem. Furthermore, applying the idea of isomorphic patterns avoids the theoretically untenable position of identifying a single person as maintaining the homeostasis yet does not deny the observation of systemic contributions of varied levels of influence. Of course, the influence may rotate—for example, at one time it may be the husband who is more the obstacle to change, and at another time the wife—but at any given point one person may be identified as being more powerful in maintaining the homeostasis. Indeed, it is therapeutically useless to identify every member of the system as maintaining the status quo; that perhaps is philosophically correct, but it does not help the therapist to pinpoint interventions.

4. *Therapeutic crisis induction can be invaluable in transforming systems.* The Chinese ideogram for "crisis" combines those characters for "danger" and "opportunity." Crisis induction forces the system to address essential issues. The process can lead to reorganization of the system.

   This idea is not unique to IST with the family. For example, the change expert John P. Kotter (2002) describes eight steps to change, beginning with "establish urgency." This is the same systemic phenomenon as creating a crisis. Without it, creating change is much more difficult, be it in a multinational corporation or a psychosomatic family.

   In work with psychosomatic families, which are characterized by rigidity and extreme conflict avoidance, the therapeutic emergence of crisis is often the essential step in transforming the system. Crises are not necessarily wrenching experiences. What is essential is that they force discontinuous change. In a case described later in this chapter, I challenged the patient, whose bulimia had robbed her of her former good looks (extremely important to her) and left her negligent of her grooming, to go to the hairdresser, stressing "now," "today," and "as soon as you leave here." The key is *urgency*; the change must happen now, preferably in the therapy session, but if that is not practicable, then immediately afterward.

THE FIVE-STEP MODEL OF TREATMENT

The treatment model of IST has been formalized into a five-step model that is spelled out in detail in *Intensive Structural Therapy: Treatment Families in Their Social Context* (Fishman, 1993). Here I only summarize the main points and bring out how they are applied in the treatment (i.e., how they guide the treatment) of patients with eating disorders.

Step 1: Gathering the Members of the System

The importance of bringing together the influential members of the patient's context has been described above. In the case of the young anorectics and bulimics described in later chapters, this context is generally the family: parents, siblings, and often grandparents and other relatives. In the initial contact with the patient or professional setting up the first meeting, the therapist tries to identify everyone who should be asked to attend; as therapy gets under way, other likely candidates for inclusion may be revealed. Motivating the members of the system to attend the session is a crucial task of the therapist, one that is accomplished by emphasizing the seriousness of the situation. In the case of clinical cases of ED, the gravity of the health hazard can and should be stressed.

The participation of the members of the system can be important in two ways. First, the interactions among them expose the dysfunctional patterns at work and the homeostatic mechanism that is maintaining them; it is likely that one or more of the members are functioning as the homeostatic maintainer. Just as importantly, members of the context can frequently be recruited as cotherapists in moving the system towards needed change.

Step 2: Generating Goals and Planning Treatment

With the relevant members of the system brought together in the therapy room, the business of the first session is assessment. Again, a model of assessment is presented in *Intensive Structural Therapy* and will not be detailed here. In brief, it includes assessment of current developmental pressures, assessment of structure in the system, assessment of the history of the system and individuals, and assessment of process. Of these, the last is the most crucial to the ongoing therapy, focusing on two of the key tenets described earlier in the chapter: the psychosomatic transactional patterns that are resulting in the symptoms and the homeostatic maintainer (HM) supporting the dysfunctional structure.

Ascertaining the HM is a powerful way to assess a system. The identity of the HM can best be determined by perturbing the system; the person who activates at that point to bring the system back to the status quo is the HM. This operational paradigm in the treatment of ED is clearly demonstrated in the lunch session, discussed in chapter 5. In the case of Bonnie, described in that chapter, at moments when the parents were acting together, the child ate. When the father, whom I saw as the HM, did not cooperate with the mother, Bonnie refused to eat. Bonnie's father was encouraged to support the mother, and in broader terms the parents learned to work together in raising their children.

As therapy proceeds, if the focus on the identified HM does not yield change, the therapist searches for other forces in the system that are maintaining homeostasis. When direct observation is not possible, the experienced clinician can get a good idea of the HM through inquiry.

Step 3: Addressing the Dysfunctional Patterns

As the dysfunctional transactional patterns and the homeostatic maintaining mechanisms begin to come into focus, the work of transforming the system can begin. The HM concept continues to be used to plan treatment and intervene decisively. The therapist challenges the family to change by destabilizing the system, and not permitting it to return to its former homeostasis. This procedure induces a crisis that forces the family to address their old patterns of interaction.

The therapeutic lunch session with anorexic adolescents, described in detail in the next chapter, is the clearest example in this therapy of creating a crisis to transform the problem. Very early in treatment, usually at our second session, I have the family bring lunch. If you have a model that says it is the family dynamics, specifically the split between the parents, that is keeping the child from eating, the most logical thing to do is to invite them to have a meal together with you. The interactional patterns that are maintaining the anorexic behavior are clearly revealed, specifically the way in which the presence of the symptom diffuses the parental conflict. The therapist then challenges the family to do whatever it takes to keep their child from dying. That means the parents must work together to feed their child. Aesthetic it's not; powerful it is. I have probably done 150 of these sessions, with a success rate of 85% in getting the child to eat. It is just the beginning of therapy, however; it is contextualizing the problem. The family is brought to change their view of the problem from one that exists in the child to one that exists in the family.

Step 4: Establishing and Maintaining a New Organization

As the old dysfunctional patterns of interaction are challenged, the family members are led to enact new patterns, within the therapy session and at home. Instead of avoiding conflict and allowing it to be triangulated to include the symptomatic patient, they learn to address their conflicts directly. When necessary the therapist works with subsystems within the larger system to stabilize the behavior in a new organization.

In the cases of the young anorexics and bulimics described in this book, the changes within the family are often enough to replace the dysfunctional patterns that were supporting the system. The new patterns are often established in the behavioral paradigm that is set up to take the place of the parental stratagems that have not worked to get their child to eat. As described in chapters 5, 6, and 7, the child is prescribed complete bed rest until certain measurable goals are met, and the parents must work together to enforce the protocol.

With older patients, the context of family and friends is sometimes not influential enough to be the force for change. In such cases, it is often helpful to bring in a new context. Women with eating disorders are often isolated by their extreme conflict avoidance, unable to assert themselves in circumstances that call for indignation and confrontation, and their stress is manifested as an ED. With such women, it is important to give them a sense of greater control over their own lives and at the same time over their ED. Two contexts that have proved powerful adjuncts to therapy in this regard are feminist groups and martial arts training. In the case of Marie, mentioned above and discussed later in the book, a woman with binge eating disorder (BED) gained the self-confidence she needed to confront someone who was harassing her, and her improved self-esteem was key to dealing with her eating problem.

Step 5: Ending Therapy

In most cases of eating disorders, the amelioration of the symptoms is clear: The anorectic patient has gained a satisfactory amount of weight, the bulimic has stopped inducing vomiting, the binge eater has controlled the overeating. In the IST model, the change has come about with a reorganization of the system, in which new interactional patterns have replaced the dysfunctional ones that were producing the system. At this point, the therapy can safely be ended, with the door left open for further consultation if the family should feel the need for it. Regular follow-ups also serve to reassure the family that help is available if further intervention or support is needed. It is important, however, for the family to know that they, not the therapist, own the change, to avoid enmeshment or excessive involvement between the family and the therapist.

In the case of the family presented in chapter 7, the strength of the family commitment to the change was manifested when the family, located in a distant community, got less follow-up support from me than they would have liked. Unable to get new instructions from me regarding the behavioral paradigm, they worked out their own rules and maintained— and probably strengthened—the new organization of the system.

Of course, not all therapy leads to the amelioration of symptoms and a transformed context. When no progress toward true change is being made, the therapist should set a date for ending therapy. Sometimes declaring the therapy to be a failure can provoke a crisis that can be exploited therapeutically. In any case, the therapist should leave the door open for further work, if the family should wish it. The clinician should, of course, offer to refer the family to another clinician.

To illustrate the clinical model of IST, I include the following excerpts from a consultation I did at a university family therapy graduate program some years ago. This was a demonstration interview observed by about 100 students via a video monitor. In the 2-hour session, I was attempting first and foremost to help this troubled family. Secondarily, I was trying to demonstrate the model of therapy as it is used in cases that follow the process parameters of the psychosomatic family paradigm.

SARAH: "I'M A BAD MOTHER"

Sarah presented a state of extreme urgency. She was a severely symptomatic bulimic, and was not allowed to have her daughter live with her. The system, namely her parents and sister, had created a reality in which she was not a good mother, and as a result she was not being allowed to raise her 6-year-old daughter. With disheveled hair, she presented as hopeless and flat. The excerpts of transcript demonstrate how grounded theory allowed me to create what appeared to the observers as well as to myself a dramatic change at the time and, according to the follow-up, a profound and perhaps lasting change in the system. They illustrate how I use the concept of the homeostatic maintainer in a case where it is not a single individual but a shifting system of homeostatic maintainers. They also demonstrate the technique of creating a therapeutic crisis. This was a crisis with a small "c"—there was no great affect being created, no great drama, but nevertheless it was a therapeutic crisis.

Sarah had been seeing a family therapist at the university mental health center for 6 weeks. She had first come with her husband, Phil, describing her problem as bulimia. The problem had begun about 6 years ago, while she was pregnant with her daughter. The vomiting was a "tension relieving" event when it first began and was not severely problematic until about a year ago. Then vomiting became more frequent, and surgery was performed to correct some problems with her gastrointestinal system. She regularly used marijuana, in part to ease the pain she was experiencing. A few months later Sarah was committed to a psychiatric hospital with a diagnosis for depression; and after a brief stay, she entered an inpatient hospital program for eating disorders, where she stayed for 6 weeks. After 2 months of reported success, the problematic behavior began again. By decision of her husband, her daughter went to live with the maternal grandmother.

The case as it was presented to me was considered untreatable. As I looked at the system, it struck me that an existential injustice was being perpetrated on this woman. She was being denied, by her family, the opportunity of raising her daughter. The reasoning was not that her bulimia was incapacitating but rather that she was a bad housekeeper—her daughter had come home from school with head lice. There appeared to be a fixed alliance in the family against her. Her husband, whom I never met, apparently was concerned, but clearly he was no help in getting their child back home.

I sought to organize a system that addressed her existential injustice, her enormously distorted self-image, and her sense of powerlessness, helplessness, and depression. The corollary, of course, was an extremely rigid system that had not yielded in her therapy for the previous 6 weeks. The most important task at the beginning of the session was to contextualize the problem: to understand the dysfunctional structures in the organization and then, of course, to intervene.

In the room were Sarah, her parents, her sister, the family therapist, and myself. With light, disheveled, dishwater blond hair, Sarah would gingerly sit at the end of her chair, jumping up frequently to pace, while holding her abdomen. She would mutter to herself how much her stomach hurt.

Dr. Fishman:	You feel—what does "sick" mean now? I mean, how are you sick?
Sarah:	My heart feels like it's beating real hard and my chest hurts and I hurt right here. I feel nauseated. I feel hungry, but I can't eat.
[pause]	
Dr. Fishman:	Uh-huh. And this happens all the time?
Sarah:	Uh-huh.
Dr. Fishman:	And then you throw up?
Sarah:	Uh-huh. I can't. . . .
Father:	Makes herself throw up.

The grounded observation tells me that she gets anxious (her heart starts beating hard) and becomes psychosomatic (is nauseated, is hungry, has a bit of anorexia so she can't eat, and then throws up). I see the sequence of the tension and then the somatization. The next very powerful statement, however, is from her father: "She makes herself throw up." This is a very different perspective from Sarah's. Sarah implies that it is an autonomic process; her father says that it is conscious. This suggests a split between Sarah and her father. As the clinician, I make a mental note that the father may well be an anti-homeostatic maintainer—perhaps an ally to challenge the seemingly pervasive belief that she is medically ill. This perspective has not led to change.

One way of looking at the people in the contemporary context is that there are those who are homeostatic maintainers and those who are anti-homeostatic maintainers, people in the system who can challenge the homeostasis. The father's statement that she makes herself throw up suggests that he sees her as having free will, that this is not an illness over which she has no power but rather is conscious behavior. To the extent that the behavior is conscious, the family can get angry with her and distance, and she can get angry with the family in return. This anger and ensuing conflict would help to transform the system. When she is treated as ill, she can't be angry, because she is beholden to these people who are caring for her (and her daughter) in her compromised state. I am thinking at this point that the father may indeed be my cotherapist in my attempts to change the system.

Dr. Fishman: So where—what is it that's making you—that's creating so much stress in your life? I mean, clearly you've had all kinds of tests, and the doctors are saying that there's nothing organic, so there must be a stress that's in your life. [pause] [Looking at Sarah, pacing and clutching her gut.] I believe there's a wastebasket in the room if you need it.

Sarah: Oh, I don't know.

Dr. Fishman: Let's put on our detective hats and find out what is the stress, all right?

Of course I look to go beyond the diagnosis and find the sources of stress in their context. The introduction of the wastebasket allows me to create stress in the session and drive our therapy to crisis without having the emergence of the symptom disrupt the session. Symptoms such as Sarah's could paralyze the process if everyone were afraid that she would become symptomatic in the session. I needed to be clear at this point that we would not let the process be derailed by this threat.

If we assume that the stress she is experiencing is a result of her immediate context, then this session becomes an amphitheater in which to observe the family's response to my challenge of framing the problem as family stress.

Mother: She spent about 6 weeks in the hospital here, in the eating disorder. . . .

Mother challenges back, going directly to the medicalization of her daughter, implying that she was ill. I note that the mother's perspective is contradictory to my own, which is an implicitly normalizing process. It implies that their system may be involved in Sarah's symptomatology. At this point in the session, I am suspicious that the mother may indeed be a homeostatic maintainer.

Dr. Fishman: [to Sarah] What do you think? What do you think needs to change such that you will be happier?

I go generic—beyond the symptom, to the context that is creating the stress. I want to try to figure out, especially, what are the relationships that are obliging Sarah to induce vomiting. It is a disadvantage that her husband is not there, and it is also interesting: Here is a session that has been promoted as an opportunity to meet with an expert, and her husband is out of town on business. It may indeed be that he had business responsibilities that couldn't be avoided, but it could also be that he is a homeostatic maintainer and doesn't want to do what the expert suggests would be necessary to get Sarah out of this mess—and, hopefully, get their daughter back.

There is silence when I ask Sarah what needs to be changed. She is not accustomed to putting on different glasses and trying to see what inter-personal pressures and tensions she is experiencing. Of course, one would expect that, knowing the characteristics of the psychosomatic family, espe-cially the profound conflict avoidance, as well as rigidity, enmeshment, and overprotectiveness. For her to challenge her family would be to go against these sentinel patterns. That is, she would have to address conflict, she would have to stop being so protective of her family, she would have to be willing to be flexible rather than rigid, and she would have to counter the triangulation. My working hypothesis is that her behavior and her prob-lems keep the system stable, and that the conflict between the adults, espe-cially her parents, is not addressed because the family's focus every waking hour is on Sarah. (The conflict in her own marriage is also to be consid-ered, which of course, due to her spouse's absence, is more difficult to ex-plore.)

Dr. Fishman: Are your parents going to raise your child?
Sarah: Looks like it.

I am raising the intensity in the session by challenging her regarding her parents' raising her child. This is the beginning of my crisis induction. I am siding with Sarah against her parents and using universal concerns: her ability as a person, her right as a mother to raise her own child. The inten-sity begins low and heightens as the session goes on.

Dr. Fishman: What does your husband say about the fact that your daughter is not with you? Is he living with you?
Sarah: Yes.

We know very well that Sarah is living with her husband, but by asking if he is living with her I challenge the fact that he is not there in the session. It has been touted to them as an opportunity to meet with a highly skilled therapist with expertise on a problem that has profoundly incapacitated his wife and meant that their daughter cannot live with them. So why isn't he here?

Dr. Fishman:	Have you worked?
Sarah:	Yes.
Dr. Fishman:	How far did you go in school?
Sarah:	I had 2 years in college.
Dr. Fishman:	No kidding. How did you do in college?
Sarah:	Well, I passed.
[pause]	
Dr. Fishman:	Why did you drop out?
Sarah:	Got married.
Dr. Fishman:	You mean you couldn't go to college married?
Sarah:	I didn't really want to go.

I am searching for areas of strength, trying to see what talents she has and what supportive contexts might be available to her outside of the family. I am looking for areas of competence in an otherwise dismal life; she sits at home with very little to do except be symptomatic. In IST the search is always for different contexts that maintain and support the well-functioning self.

Therapist:	Sarah was not sick [in a previous session] as she appears today, but she was still pretty sick. She's had variations on this in the times I've seen her.

This is a dramatic session. At various points Sarah is walking around the room, moaning, holding her abdomen, dramatizing to all the world how sick and miserable she is.

Dr. Fishman:	Uh-huh. [pause] So, Sarah, what do you think I—what also should we know?
[long pause]	
Sarah:	I just hurt. I think I need the doctor.
[long pause]	

Dr. Fishman: How long have you been like this?

Sarah: About 2 or 3 days.

Sister: She told me today she hasn't eaten in days. And she ate popsicles at my house and then got sick right after she ate them. She said that was the only thing that tasted good.

Therapist: [to sister] When she had the popsicles did she go in the bathroom and gag herself? You mean, she got sick at your home?

Sister: Uh-huh.

Dr. Fishman: So you made yourself throw up? Is that what you do pretty much—force yourself to throw up?

Sarah: Yes, but I'm kind of nauseous anyway. . . .

Dr. Fishman: But then you make yourself do it?

Sarah: Yes.

Dr. Fishman: Did it make you more comfortable that we had a wastebasket here?

Sarah: I don't know. I'm all dehydrated. I just feel so bad. I'm real tingly, my arms.

Sarah: And I can't. [whimper] I just can't.

[pause]

Dr. Fishman: So I guess it is hopeless.

I add intensity by going to the extreme. This calcified system needs intensity, humor, and, perhaps, irony or it won't budge.

Sarah: It is.

Dr. Fishman: Because I'm not—you know, I have some expertise, and it's probably hopeless.

[pause]

Sister: There has to be something that can draw them out of it, though, isn't there? (Sister seems to believe there are repressed feelings that need to be drawn out, derepressed.)

Sister looks like she is potentially going to be my ally in changing the system. She has read some pop-psychology: Now she sees me as an expert who can draw the secret out that will free her sister from these symptoms. She may indeed be helpful in moving things along.

Dr. Fishman: Not if they don't want to.

I am adding to the intensity by talking about how hopeless it is. This is my leitmotif in working toward creating a crisis. In a very stable, very rigid system, crisis is the only means of creating change.

    In this case, it is more difficult than usual to stir things up because of where we are. We are in a Southern state—Louisiana—where Southern gentility and intrinsic sweetness make conflict all the more rare.

Dr. Fishman: Your sister just said that, when she feels a little nauseated, she throws up and doesn't eat. It's just a habit. This is how she chooses to live, I think.

I reframe the problem. If it is behavioral, the family can distance from her. More importantly, it is under her conscious control, so she can change the problem. Later on, the sister said that she too saw it as a habit, again allowing us to reframe and restructure.

Sarah: I'm like this all the time. I can't. . . .

Dr. Fishman: I understand that, but why can't you? If your daughter—I would imagine your daughter needs you.

I am increasing the crisis by making her guilty, as I think about it, in terms of how her daughter might need her. In my next statement, I again take it to the extreme. There is an absurdity: It appears that the reason her family won't allow her to have her daughter is because she is not a good house-keeper.

Sarah: She does.

Dr. Fishman: And I don't understand why. If you throw up, you throw up, but I don't know—you don't beat your daughter or anything like that?

Sarah: No.

The second refrain begins: that she is not "mad," she is "bad." Someone who is *mad* is taken care of. When someone is *bad*, there can be distance; people can distance themselves, and conflict can emerge.

Dr. Fishman: All I'm saying—listen, I really don't know. All I'm saying is that at some point you have to help to normalize her life. I mean, the worst—Sarah said it at the beginning, she said, "Listen, I won't be happy until I'm normal, and because I'm not normal, I can't do what will make me happy." She's implying that she wants her daughter back.

The intensity grows. I am joining with Sarah to have her challenge her parents to get her daughter back, and challenging her to normalize her life.

Dr. Fishman: Well, why doesn't she live there? Why is Amanda not living with you [to Sarah] and living with you [to parents]?
Father: Because Sarah's sick.

Father activates immediately, cutting me off. Father is stating that the system is organized so that Sarah will stay the patient and they will keep the child.

Dr. Fishman: Wait a minute, I'm asking Sarah.
Sarah: Because I don't take care of her.
Dr. Fishman: You kind of neglect her?
Sarah: Yeah.
[pause]
Dr. Fishman: Like what? What do you do or what don't you do?
Sarah: I don't take care of the house or keep house or anything I'm supposed to do.
[pause]
Dr. Fishman: And that means you can't raise her? I don't—I mean, what were you like as a mother? As her mother what were you like?

The system is organized that Sarah cannot have her daughter because she is a sloppy housekeeper. I challenge that.

Sarah: [walking] First, once when she was living with me [sits] . . . Oh. . . .
Mother: Do you want the trashcan yet?

The mother may realize at this point just how ridiculous is their justification for taking the child—thus she sees the present system threatened. The classic definition of the homeostatic maintainer is someone who activates when the system is perturbed and beginning to change. The HM activates to return the system to the status quo. The mother asks her daughter if she needs the "trash can yet," her attempt to return the system to the status quo, with Sarah as the sick, incompetent woman who cannot raise her own daughter.

Sarah: I'm just panic-stricken. I don't know.

Dr. Fishman: So, what are we to—how are we to interpret that?

Father: She'd certainly rather be at home.

Here the father becomes an ally again. Then Sarah becomes the homeostatic force, saying she can't be a good mother because she is lazy. I perceive this as meaning that she is so beaten down by the system that she doesn't have the energy to challenge the status quo; there are too many alliances against her.

What we are seeing here is a shifting homeostatic maintainer, different people taking that role. At one point it's mother, at one point it's father, at another point it's sister, and even, at another point, it's Sarah. Homeostatic maintenance is a process; the goal is to observe when it's emerging and counteract it.

Increasingly, the father becomes my cotherapist in the session. In the process, he moves from lukewarm support to become a person who stands for change. The important thing, however, is not only that there is an alliance, but that we're seeing shifting intensity. In response to the situation Sarah has manifested, there is increasing intensity toward creating change.

What's important to me as I look at this segment is that, while I am working to restructure the system, the active ingredient, I believe, is that I am working on the emotional level. Clearly, the therapy is working with the components of the family as an emotional system. This segment demonstrates working with increasing intensity with the family system. By working at this edge, I am able to address the implicit emotion that had been avoided. Indeed, this avoidance of the emotion of the conflict has been the process parameter that has both kept the system rigidified and led to the emergence of the symptom.

Sarah: And I just—I can't be a good wife or a good mother.

[pause]

Dr. Fishman: Why is that?

Sarah: I'm just too lazy. . . .

Mother: You are lazy to the extent that, if you don't want to do something, you don't make yourself do it. But if you want to do something, there's nothing lazy about you. [to Dr. Fishman:] She's done excellent on her jobs. She always did well on her jobs. Very highly paid for jobs in this town.

Mother becomes supportive in challenging the way her daughter is living, even the reality that she is incorrigibly lazy. Her words imply that the daughter is spoiled; she does only what she wants. Let's put that in the homeostatic category.

> *Dr. Fishman:* Okay. You see, this is the essential point about our meeting, with the situation defined in two words when Sarah said earlier, is she lazy or is she crazy? If she's crazy, then the two of you should raise her child. If she's lazy, then the two of you need to make it very clear that throwing up or not, pot or not, she's a grown woman.

There is a reframing and a challenge to the parents regarding how we should handle their daughter. We have a behavioral conceptualization—which paradigm is it? Is she lazy, in which case she has to be accountable (and which also means that she is pretty normal)? Or is she crazy, in which case she has to be taken care of?

> *Father:* That's true.
>
> *Dr. Fishman:* She's pushing 35. She's not a little kid.
>
> *Father:* Nope.
>
> *Sarah:* I can't grow up for some reason. That's what's wrong.
>
> *Dr. Fishman:* Well, let me tell you something. I hear what you're saying, but your family can help you to grow up by making it very clear that "we love you very much, Sarah, and you raise your daughter."
>
> [We have been looking at an attractive photo of Sarah taken some time before.]
>
> *Sister:* Actually, to tell you the truth, she got fixed up for this photo. Normally that's not how she. . . .
>
> *Dr. Fishman:* Normally she's pretty ugly?
>
> *Sister:* No, that's not what I. . . .

The sister starts challenging Sarah when I compliment Sarah on the photo. I, of course, challenge the sister on that.

> *Father:* She needs to assume the responsibility.
>
> *Sister:* She's gone for 7 years with this. You don't have any idea all the filth Amanda was living in.

Sister talks about just how hopeless the home situation is. At this point she seems to be Sarah's antagonist, allied with the forces that want to keep Sarah's daughter from her.

Dr. Fishman: You can't have your child, your family won't let you have your child, because you're not good—you don't clean regularly.

Sarah: Because my house is a health hazard.

Father: We didn't. . . .

Dr. Fishman: Has it been condemned by the health department?

Sarah: No.

She is not allowed to have her child because the house is messy, but of course there is no documentation from the health department on that. It appears to be simply the family's condemnation of the home as unsuitable for children.

Mother: We took the child when she had surgery because we needed to take the child. The child has not been able to go home for any length of time since.

This is the system organized around Sarah being a problem. She is slovenly, she is too miserably unhappy to clean her house, and for the last 6 years she has been systematically stuck. Sarah has been trapped—as has the family, for that matter.

Mother: We are talking about a child going for a little while with head lice. You get lice from filth.

Sister: More than once, you know.

Here is more grounded observation. After Sarah was hospitalized, her parents kept her child from then on. Apparently the continued justification for the child's being with grandma is that Sarah had head lice. This is gaslighting. That is, by some political agenda, this woman's apparatus for ascertaining reality has been challenged. The fact that her little girl had head lice hardly suggests that she is a bad mother. (This, of course, is a bad rap; because head lice are ubiquitous in elementary schools; they can be found in even the tidiest of households.) The sister then allies with her mother. Again, we see the usefulness of being able to read these microtransactions and then extrapolate from them to a structural map.

Sarah: I'm not fit to be a mother.

Dr. Fishman: That you're not fit, do you believe that?

Sarah: [whimpers]

Father: Lazy, I believe you're lazy.

Good news! Father may indeed be my ally. He vacillates a bit, saying that he doesn't know whether she can change, which implies that she is sick. Then he is back on my side—her side, actually—saying that she can change if she wants to herself. She has free will and can overcome her circumstances.

Sarah:	I do, too. And I don't know if it's something that I can change or not.
Father:	You could change it if you want to. You have to want to think that much of your husband and daughter maybe. And other people.
Sarah:	I've got to stop hurting.

The challenge is that Sarah believes that she has to stop hurting in order to change her life and get her daughter back. The irony is she won't stop hurting until she takes these steps. She has somehow been convinced that it is the other way around, but she will not have a cessation of her aching heart unless the system changes and she gets her daughter back and the family comes together. This, of course, is beyond psychiatric theory; it is decency; it is common sense.

Father:	Well, get up and—I've been places before where I hurt plenty, and I went ahead and had to live. I didn't sleep till noon and get up and watch my soap operas and then go back to bed.
Dr. Fishman:	He's making a lot of sense.

Father, again, is a support for change.

Sister:	That I don't think it's fair to Amanda?
Dr. Fishman:	You made your sister—you suggested that your sister was kind of a basket case for all seasons.
Sister:	No, I don't think she is a basket case. I think she just isn't taking care of her daughter.

The sister has been on a long discourse on Sarah's problems and how hopeless Sarah is, and I challenge her.

Father:	There's no way we would want her [Amanda] if Sarah wanted her. I mean, we wouldn't want to keep her at all if Sarah wanted to keep her.

Father, again, is the anti-homeostatic maintainer here. I create an enactment between Father and Mother regarding giving their grandchild back.

[pause]

Dr. Fishman: Talk with your wife about that, how you want to—see, I wish your husband were here.

Mother: Are you giving us advice? Or are you trying to—I don't know, really. . . .

Dr. Fishman: I am trying to help you be clear with your daughter.

Mother: I'm not getting anywhere with this.

In a sense, this is Mother opting for the status quo and psychologically withdrawing from the process. From my perspective, it is not that we are going nowhere; it is that we are going somewhere—and Mother is not happy with where we are going. She may, at this point, be sensing that I may not be a reliable clinician; I may actually be changing the system. Indeed, the system is changing, and she may lose the child. I suspected that Mother wanted her granddaughter right at home with her.

Sister: I don't understand if we're supposed to use Amanda as a human guinea pig and throw her back in and just see what happens, see if Sarah will snap out of being lazy.

Sister is siding with Mother, suggesting that I am a quack and experimenting on their family member.

Dr. Fishman: Sir, why don't you talk with your wife about this.

Father: We'll talk about it.

Father: [to Sarah] Do you think you'll ever be able to take care of her?

Sarah: I can't—I don't know. I know I can't right now.

Father's challenge to his daughter points to how Sarah is triangulated between her parents. To the extent that she insists that her daughter come home with her, she would be going against her mother's desires.

Of course, Sarah confuses her mother. When she says she can't take care of her daughter, what is her mother to think? It is a joy to the therapist to support Sarah and help her to get into contexts that enhance her self-confidence so that she will confidently want her daughter back.

Dr. Fishman: I believe Sarah is right now sensitive, because you [address-ing Sarah] are not working. And when you were working, were you feeling pretty good about yourself?

Sarah: I felt better than I do now.

Dr. Fishman: Were you looking as pretty as you look in this picture? That's a beautiful picture.

Sarah: Well, I'm not that young, but I looked better than I do now.

Father: You look young, though, Sarah.

Dr. Fishman: You don't look that elderly. I don't think she looks. . . .

I am searching for contexts that support her view of herself as competent, like going to her job, and even having the very attractive picture taken. From such vantage points she will have the confidence to challenge the system. I was thinking to myself, however, that this was a serious life-and-death struggle going on, and that realities had been created to rob Sarah and Phil of their child.

Father: But how about when she went with us to that funeral? I mean she was very pretty that day.

The complexity and the many levels of human communication: Father brings up the day when she looked outstandingly good; unfortunately, that was when she was going to a funeral. It is hard to handle the feelings that that brings up. Is it inappropriate that the one time she looks beautiful is at a funeral? Or is there a hidden message to Sarah that there is, as I am sure they have been told, a life-threatening aspect of her problem?

Dr. Fishman: Let me tell you what I'm concerned about. You see, you seem to think that the doctors have the answers [Sarah nods], that you're going to go to one doctor who's going to give you a magic pill. [Sarah nods] How many—how long have you been trying that?

This is the frog in the water analogy—the idea that, because frogs are cold blooded, you can keep them in a beaker of water over a Bunsen burner and they never recognize the grade of difference so they never jump out. Going to doctor after doctor has given them the hope that has kept them in the beaker. What I am trying to do is jog the beaker so the system will change. Also, I need to set myself apart from the other doctors, all of whom have failed.

Sarah:　　　Too long.

Dr. Fishman:　At some point I think you need to realize that. . . .

Sarah:　　　Oh, what can I do? [begins to cry]

I am now joining with Sarah around the fact that all of the doctors have failed her. If she wants to do it, she had better do it now.

Dr. Fishman:　You don't want to know. You really don't want to know.

Sarah:　　　I do. I want to get better.

There is a breakthrough here. Sarah is joining with me, saying she wants to get better.

Dr. Fishman:　Are you serious?

Sarah:　　　There has got to be a way to get better.

Dr. Fishman:　There is a way, but it's not an easy one.

Sarah:　　　Okay.

Dr. Fishman:　I'm not sure your family will let you, because your family looks at a lot of your negatives. [Sister crosses arms.] The fact is, there were some times here in this session already that you were sharp as a whip. You were talking about the pictures and your sister and your sister being pretty and things like that a lot of times. I think you need to get—as of today, normalize your life. Forget that the doctors don't have many answers at all. To normalize your life, get your daughter back and get a job. Get a job so that you have a—the thing about working, you probably don't need the money. But the thing about working is that you've got people around you who let you know that you're okay, and you have a sense you're making a contribution.

This is the creation of a crisis. A crisis can be as mild as "you are going to a beauty salon," but what it represents is a discontinuous change. This is what I am pushing for here. Invariably when I push this way people talk about failed attempts; I need to push beyond that.

Sarah:　　　Well. . . .

[Sarah sits down and straightens up.]

Dr. Fishman:　Now you're going to argue with me.

Sarah:　　　I had started. When I got out of the hospital I enrolled in a nursing school.

Dr. Fishman: Did you really? That's nice.

Sarah: That's something I thought I wanted to do in the fall. . . .

Dr. Fishman: Well, I don't know if you should do that right now, because you can't do it, it's in the fall. I think tomorrow you need to see if you can get a job so that you will have people around you that will tell you you're okay. I don't know that your family will let you. They love you very much, but they focus in on your weaknesses, and, you know, the fact that you fixed yourself up for the picture—Come on, I don't want to . . . [Sister, Mother, and Father laugh.] You've got to forget about doctors. If you have appendicitis, fine, but when you go to doctors year in and year out, then it becomes a lifestyle.

Sarah: And I'm trying to kill myself going on like this.

Dr. Fishman: That's true, yes.

Sarah has joined with me in realizing her situation. She realizes that she is getting worse and ultimately may indeed kill herself.

Sarah: I don't. . . . And I'm depressed. I don't want to go on like this, but I don't see how I can. . . .

Dr. Fishman: I'm making a suggestion that you have to do something even worse than kill yourself, and that's change. Change your life concretely. None of this doctor stuff. Pardon the expression. Hope there are no doctors here. . . .

Again, here is more push for discontinuous change. What I am searching for is a context that will confirm Sarah as competent. This is also my attempt to put myself in a different frame of reference from all the other professionals that have failed her. We know that the hospital and all the other doctors have not done the trick.

In disqualifying the other therapists, I am actually heightening the intensity by creating a boundary: The medical route can no longer be an escape route, where she can be protected from taking the responsibility for making changes. I put this new boundary between the work we're doing and the medical work that has been done so that she can no longer maintain her status quo position.

I'm also interested in differentiating myself from all of the other professionals, who have given the family hope that things will change without their rolling up their sleeves and changing the context. What's gone before has been false hope. True hope is that Sarah will activate to take back her life. I am challenging her, telling her it is easier to die than to change, but I am also developing a practical plan to foster her autonomy. I'm working to set up a situation where people—especially Sarah—perceive that she cannot avoid conflict and that she has to defend her boundaries, and I am working to enable her to do just that. My dismissive crack about doctors is aimed at getting her ready to get rid of all the doctors and other helpers that were keeping her stuck. Her dependence on doctors was very strong; indeed, it has maintained the homeostasis. Ironically, the major flaw in the interview was that the doctors were not present so that when she later became somewhat symptomatic she would slip back into the medical system and back to the previous homeostasis.

Sarah: I don't see how I can feel like this, though, and look for a job.

Dr. Fishman: What you do is you make yourself—you pretend that you are feeling better, and you tell yourself "I feel better." You look in the mirror and you look as pretty as you can. I would go to the hairdresser, today. After this session, go to the hairdresser. Go with your sister.

To normalize, she needs to do something functional and positive. Pushing Sarah to go to the hairdresser creates a gentle crisis. It seems almost laughable that in a highly touted consultation with a so-called expert from out of town, the major intervention is to get the young woman to go to the beauty shop. The fact is, for Sarah to go to a beauty shop—a normal, positive activity—is as drastic a change as it would be for a person who has been bedridden to get out of bed. And I push for immediate change. I have always found in these sessions that pushing for immediate change, even as minor as going to a beauty salon, and focusing on a different, more functional part can be the beginning of a significant transformation for the system.

Father: Today.

Father, my cotherapist, pushes her to do it immediately.

Dr. Fishman: Go to the hairdresser, and what you do is, you recognize that 'even if I don't feel well, I'll take aspirin. If I have a pain I'll take an aspirin or a Tylenol,' you're probably allergic to aspirin. 'And I'm going to normalize my life. I'm going to take my daughter back, because I'm her mother and I love that daughter and the daughter's asking for me.' I mean, if you showed me that school report, that's absurd. She went up—she went down in, what was it?

Sarah: Citizenship.

[Dr. Fishman has left the room.]

Father:	That's what he is telling you. All you need to do is get back and get your daughter home and get up in the mornings and do the things . . . you need to do.
Mother:	Just to quit thinking that you're sick.
Father:	That's right.
Mother:	Just ignore it.
Father:	You're not sick.
Mother:	That's what he's saying. If you think you're sick, just say I'm not sick and go on.
Father:	You've been to too many doctors. There's something you don't want to do, so you're being sick to keep from doing it.
Sarah:	I can't believe I'd make myself hurt this way.

Mom has become supportive. Perhaps she sees how her daughter has brightened up. Now that she sees her daughter's change, she pushes for her to change. I think that in the past the mother may not have wanted to see her daughter fail, but the fact that she had Sarah's daughter may have confounded her motivation.

[Dr. Fishman reenters.]

Dr. Fishman:	Well, what did you say?
Sister:	I thought you were listening.
Mother:	Let's go somewhere and rest. I'm tired.
Dr. Fishman:	Why don't you talk about that?
Father:	About her being tired?
Dr. Fishman:	Do you see I'm serious?
Father:	Yes.
Dr. Fishman:	I'm serious, because it's going to be a tremendous loss when she gets very competent. You're going to miss that child.
Mother:	Okay, now. . . .
Dr. Fishman:	Oh, now you're going to argue with me.
Mother:	Yeah, I am. You've got some kind of wrong idea.
Dr. Fishman:	I have many. . . .
Mother:	Oh. . . .
Dr. Fishman:	Just ask my wife.

Mother:	That child was 6 years old last January. All right. . . .
Dr. Fishman:	All right. . . .
Mother:	. . . so she was 6. . . .
Dr. Fishman:	Let's—I won't argue with you. You're going to prove me wrong. I already agree that you're right.
Sarah:	She really is right about that. You are wrong about that.

I am implying that Mother has a conflict of interest and was holding onto the child for her own benefit. I am pleased to be proven wrong!

Dr. Fishman:	Well, good. I'm glad to have you in my life. I want to shake your hand. Will you do me a favor?
Sarah:	Uh-huh.
Dr. Fishman:	I'm going to give you my card. I want you to send me a picture of when you're all dolled up. . . .
Sarah:	Yeah.
Dr. Fishman:	And when you have a job.
Sarah:	Okay.
Dr. Fishman:	Will you do that? [Sarah nods.] We unfortunately have to stop now, but before. . . .
Sarah:	Okay.
Father:	And you recommend she goes to the beauty shop this afternoon?
Dr. Fishman:	Oh, absolutely. Do you have a beauty shop in mind?
Father:	Your mother can go with you.

Father, once again, the anti-homeostatic maintainer, supports his daughter's making a change.

Dr. Fishman:	See how helpful your family is? You go to your beauty shop.
Sister:	People of our generation don't have a beauty shop.
Mother:	That went out several years ago.
Sister:	You just go to whichever one.
Dr. Fishman:	Wait a minute. . . .
Sister:	You don't go to weekly beauty shops.
Sarah:	I could have Carol.

Dr. Fishman: Weekly. Do you think she went last week and this is. . . .

Sister: No, you know what I'm talking about. Where you have your own beautician.

There is a bit of a skirmish between the sister and Sarah regarding the beauty shop. I suspect I am being a little old-fashioned in suggesting a beauty shop, and the sister challenges me for how out of date I am, but Sarah is supporting me. Both Sister and Mother think that she shouldn't go now. This again I come to see as reflecting the coalition that is keeping her stuck and creating the reality that she is not competent enough to have her daughter live with her.

Dr. Fishman: Okay. [stands] We need to stop. [shakes Father's hand] In many ways you have the answers and your wife has the other half of the answers, 'cause you [shakes Mother's hand] read me completely, you don't need more.

Sister: Look at her.

Dr. Fishman: [shakes her hand] And you're a tough lady. Okay?

Mother: Okay, Sarah.

[Dr. Fishman shakes Sarah's hand.]

Father: Okay, Sarah.

They did find a beauty parlor, and Sarah went. Father's support was very helpful.

As I reflect on this consultation and as I consider the immediate follow-up of this case, I realize there was a major structural flaw in the consultation. It was done in an academic graduate program in family therapy, and no one from the medical establishment was included. So when Sarah had the inevitable next crisis, the infrastructure they had been accustomed to being involved with at these points—that is, the psychiatric establishment—was brought in. Had we been able to include our medical colleagues, the consultation, which was, I believe, a long-term success (given what happened later), would have been more immediately successful. As we will see in the chapters ahead, one of the major requirements for effective care for these severe problems is to have coordinated treatment between professionals.

Several months after the consultation, Sarah and her husband had a session with the family therapist, during which they viewed the tape of our consultation. Immediately afterward, Sarah was hospitalized for 3 weeks. Although she was admitted for "dehydration," she spent most of her time on the psychiatric unit.

The videotape of the session may have created the ultimate crisis that precipitated the transformation of the psychosomatic family. Once home from the hospital, Sarah made some major changes ("all because," she reported to the family therapist, "I met a patient in the hospital that helped me through it"). Boundaries were finally created, and Sarah saw her parents only once or twice a month and her sister not at all. Her daughter came to live with her and was doing all right in school, with some tutoring. At last report, 2 or 3 years after treatment, Sarah and Phil had worked out their marital difficulties and Sarah was working part-time as a bookkeeper. She no longer vomited, and from a hypnotist at the medical school she had learned a technique for controlling the pain and no longer used marijuana. They continued to live in a small town in Louisiana, but then they moved, and recent efforts to locate them for a long-term follow-up were not successful, as their family name is a common one.

CONSULTATION SUMMARY

Although this was a single 2-hour consultation, it incorporated all of the essential elements of IST.

1. We convened the system. We attempted to bring in the key individuals in Sarah's life. This was a consultation, and the people who set up the session were not able to recruit her husband and her psychiatrist.
2. Nevertheless, we were able to assess the homeostatic process: the participation of her family of origin in Sarah's continuing symptomatology and unhappiness. The family was organized to frame her as "crazy" and thus keep her from her daughter.
3. We clearly dealt with the homeostatic maintainers in the session. A gentle crisis was created to transform the system. One indication that we transformed the homeostatic processes to some extent was Sarah's dramatic change by the end of the consultation. She was forceful and motivated, insisting that she go to the beauty salon after the session. (The rumor around campus that afternoon was that a "miracle" had happened in the session.)
4. More importantly, it appears that viewing the tape of the session several months later gave Sarah the motivation to change her life significantly by creating a boundary between her nuclear family and her extended family. This separation apparently was required to normalize her family life, eschew her "crazy" role, and get her daughter back.
5. Because this was a one-session therapy, the end of treatment was predetermined. Short as it was, it apparently did begin a process of transformation for this system, and especially for Sarah and her daughter.

A FINAL NOTE

My work with eating disorders sufferers and with families in general is based on a firm faith in the perfectibility of people. This optimism is not merely a philosophical or even a religious position. A new and impressive area of psychology is focusing on survivorship. An increasing body of literature is documenting how people are able to overcome their past traumatic experiences and not simply exist but prevail, leading full lives in every way (Heilemann et al., 2002; Hyman & Williams, 2001; Rabkin et al., 2000; Sigal & Weinfeld, 2001). The belief in perfectibility leads in turn to the concept that the self is multifaceted; to the extent that a person's context is transformed, different and more functional facets of personality can emerge. The therapist can therefore confidently expect profound change in people. Such expectations are invaluable. Cognitive dissonance theory states that humans hate dissonance; that is, we hate to be wrong. If we as therapists firmly believe that someone is incurable, we are at great risk of creating that reality for the patient. Conversely, if we expect change and even amelioration, there is a far better chance that we will get it from the people we work with. The effectiveness of this position will be seen many times in the chapters ahead.

CHAPTER 5

Treating the Young Anorexic: The Technique of the Lunch Session

Over 30 years ago, diabetologist Richard K. Bernstein (Bernstein, 2003) postulated that close control of blood sugar levels for diabetics would lead to fewer complications for the patients. It was not until recently that researchers have demonstrated unequivocally that Dr. Bernstein was correct (Gill, 1996, p. 1264). In many ways, the treatment of anorexia for adolescents presented in this chapter is similar. Salvador Minuchin, Bernice Rosman, and Ronald Liebman developed the technique of the lunch session at the Philadelphia Child Guidance Clinic in the early 1970s. This technique, extremely powerful in my experience, has been eclipsed by history. To my knowledge, there are only a few groups that regularly use it.

BONNIE: LOSING THREE POUNDS A WEEK

Bonnie was 15 years old when I first saw her in 1979. She had been anorectic for about 6 months. She had characteristic stigmata of anorexia: She had severe food restriction, she was losing weight at the rate of three pounds a week, her menstrual periods had stopped, and she had an obsession with exercise. The family pediatrician had sent her to a therapist who worked individually with Bonnie, without success. Through a circuitous path the family was referred to me at the Philadelphia Child Guidance Clinic.

The family consisted of both parents, who lived at home, a younger sister, and two older siblings, who were away at college. The parents had been married about 20 years. The mother, a manager of a large clothing store, was more successful vocationally than the father. He was a moderately successful traveling salesman whose business kept him away from the family for extended periods of time. His absence created stress on the family in many ways; indeed, it created what family therapists refer to as an "accordion family": It got larger and smaller with the comings and goings of the father.

The Therapeutic Lunch Session

For the first session, the family had been instructed to bring lunch for Bonnie. The therapeutic lunch session is a technique introduced by Salvador Minuchin for initiating the anorectic's family in treatment (Rosman, Minuchin, & Liebman, 1975). According to Minuchin and his colleagues,

> Eating lunch with the family provides exceptional opportunities for the therapist to observe family members' transactions around eating as well as to make on-the-spot interventions to change the patterns of these transactions. This session also serves broader diagnostic purposes, since structural and dysfunctional characteristics of the family are more readily apparent in this context. (pp. 846–847)

In my own experience, the lunch session provides an opportunity to see problematic family patterns exhibited, and also the intense enactment provides a fulcrum over which change is forced. To the extent that the parents are successful in getting the child to eat, not only does the child get much-needed sustenance, but also the parents' transactional patterns change as they work together to accomplish this end.

The videotape of this session reveals the subtleties of this therapeutic technique. In the therapy room, Bonnie is seated in the pathognomonic position of the petulant adolescent: slouching with legs stretched out in front of her and arms crossed. To her right is her younger sister, Nancy, and to the left her father. Also in the room are her mother and her grandmother (the mother's mother). Because it is the contemporary system that is maintaining the problem, it is essential to include in the therapy those people who are involved in the homeostatic pattern that must be changed to resolve the problem—in this case, the father and mother, and to some extent the grandmother.

The parents have been told that they must get their daughter to eat the lunch that they have brought for her. In turn, first the mother and then the father try and are unsuccessful. The following segment is from the father's attempt to convince his daughter to eat.

Father: You weren't fat at all, honey. No, you weren't.
Bonnie: I always had fat legs.

Father:	We used to go to McDonald's, let's go here, you used to ask me, right.
Bonnie:	Yes, when I was fat.
Father:	Oh, now wait, now wait, I took you more than I used to take the other kids. It's the God's honest truth too, right?
Bonnie:	Well, you're not going to do that any more 'cause you don't need that kind of food,' cause you don't need to eat junk food like McDonald's and custard.
Father:	But you always ask for it, right?
Bonnie:	I used to.
Father:	Then why don't you eat the sandwich for me?
Bonnie:	Because I don't want it.
Father:	Why don't you want it?
Bonnie:	I'm not hungry and you're not supposed to eat if you're not hungry.
Father:	Who told you this?
Bonnie:	'Cause it's just better if you don't eat when you're not hungry.
Father:	You need this for strength.
Bonnie:	I have enough strength.
Father:	I don't think you do.
Bonnie:	Yes, I do if I can jump rope.
Father:	You're always tired, you tell me.
Bonnie:	I'm tired because I don't get enough sleep. I have to wake up at 6:00 in the morning.
Father:	You don't have any energy. You're burning 'em all up on you.
Bonnie:	No it's not, because I wake up too early.
Father:	No, it isn't.
Bonnie:	Yes, it is, I've always been tired.
Father:	No, you haven't, it just started in the last couple of months.
Bonnie:	Unh-uh, I used to come home from school and I used to go to sleep.
Dr. Fishman:	She's defeated both of you.

Paul Watzlawick and his colleagues at the Mental Research Institute have identified what they call *first order change* and *second order change* (Watzlawick, Weakland, & Fisch, 1974, pp. 10–11), using the analogy of driving a car: First order change is acceleration, and second order change is changing gears. What the father is doing in this passage is first order change—more of the cajoling, reasoning, and threatening approach that the family has been using for months to no effect. What is needed is second order change: The structure must change. I intervene at this point to induce a change in the structure (Watzlawick, Weakland, & Fisch, 1974).

Dr. Fishman:	She's got to eat this right now.
Mother:	Well, then all we can do is stuff it in her mouth.
Dr. Fishman:	You have to do whatever you have to do, whatever is necessary, but she has to eat.
Bonnie:	What, do you think 103 pounds is too skinny?
Dr. Fishman:	I think that 103 pounds isn't too skinny, but not eating is. In other words, your weight is continuing to decrease.
Father:	Right.
Dr. Fishman:	If you want to weigh 103 pounds and maintain it, that's fine, but she's got to eat.
Bonnie:	And then I'll gain again.
Dr. Fishman:	[To parents] We just went through that. What she eats is her business. That she maintains this weight is your responsibility. In other words, you can't let your daughter die.
Bonnie:	I'm not going to die.
Father:	Who said you're gonna die? If you keep this up. . . .
Bonnie:	I'm not, I'll start eating regular again.
Father:	What do mean, you're gonna start eating. Why don't you start eating now then?
Bonnie:	Because I don't want it now.
Father:	What do you mean you don't want it now? You just got done telling Mom that you were going to go get something to eat. What's wrong with this? This is a sandwich; it's got calories in it.
Bonnie:	I don't like that kind of sandwich.
Dr. Fishman:	[To mother] Change seats with Nancy, and do whatever you have to do, work together.
	[Mother moves into Nancy's seat.]
Mother:	[Clapping] You're going to get the sandwich stuffed in your mouth. Come on, Bonnie. [Laughs]
Father:	Try it.
Mother:	Don't let me do this.

Bonnie:	No, Mom.
Mother:	Don't let me stuff the sandwich in your mouth, 'cause that's what I'm gonna do.
Father:	Why don't you put it in your hand.
Bonnie:	Mom, I don't want it.
Mother:	I have to do it. I'm not going to let you die.
Father:	Now come on, Bonnie, just bite it and just take your time.

With the change in seating, the mother has taken a forceful new approach in response to the therapist's directive that they must make their daughter eat. Here, however, the father is not supporting his wife. The speed at which she eats is not important—what is essential is that the starving girl gets sufficient sustenance. As the session continues, the importance of this support or lack of it can be seen in numerous "microtransactions." The girl refuses to eat whenever there is a split, however subtle, between her parents; when the split subsides, also however subtly, she eats.

Bonnie:	I don't want it.
Mother:	Now are we going to have to do this every mealtime.

Mother of course is pointing to the beauty of this intervention—it can easily be replicated at home.

Bonnie:	You're not going to be able to do it, Mom, because I'll be in school.
Mother:	Well, I'll come to school and I'll stuff it in your mouth.
Bonnie:	Mom, I don't want it. No.
Mother:	I don't care what you don't want, you have to eat.
Father:	Stop it.
Bonnie:	I'll spit it out.
Father:	Don't you dare do that. You know you want to eat.
Mother:	Come on. Bonnie, you want to do this, do that, and any other thing, you can't do that.
Father:	[Holding Bonnie's hands] You used to fight, now you can't even fight. [Grabs daughter's wrist. Parents feel her wrists and hipbone.] Look at you. Go on, look at you. Oh, my god.
Mother:	Come on, Bonnie, you have to eat.
Bonnie:	I'll eat it.

Mother: All right, then eat it.

[Bonnie takes a bite.]

Father: Take your time.

Father's "take your time" is not supporting Mother—Bonnie has been starving and finally she is eating! His statement, if attended to, only retards this essential process.

Bonnie: I'm only eating half of it.

The girl responds to the split—by manifesting anorectic behavior—refusing in part to eat. "I'm only eating half."

Mother: You're eating the whole thing, or I will stuff the rest back in your mouth.

Father: Give me my coffee, please.

Bonnie: I don't want it.

Father: You want something to drink, want some coffee, black coffee?

Mother: The coffee has very little. . . .

Again a rift has emerged between the father and the mother. By urging his daughter to have coffee, the father is not supporting his wife. Instead, he seems to be creating a diversion to avoid facing the issue of their starving daughter. These diversions continue to occur as the mother insists that their daughter eat. Indeed, the father urging their daughter to drink black coffee is not exactly supporting the mother's attempt to have Bonnie get essential nutrients. I see it as undermining the attempt.

Bonnie: It's not going to work.

Mother: Yes, it is.

Bonnie: No, it's not.

Father: Who told you that?

Mother: Yes, it is. We'll just stuff food in your guts—what I've been wanting to do for so long. Just sit on you and stuff food in your mouth.

It is often the case in these sessions, the parents feel liberated to do something that is intuitively correct—if their daughter is behaving like a 2-

year-old, she should be treated accordingly. The corollary—the youngster being obliged to eat—often results in the child feeling similarly liberated. Indeed, she is out from the middle of their parents.

Father:	Tastes good, huh?
Bonnie:	Unh-uh.
Father:	I think it does.
Bonnie:	I don't.
Father:	I'm fat, ain't I.
Bonnie:	No.
Father:	[Laughing] You always told me I was fat. I'm always eating. That's how you survive. You burn all the calories up, you've got to eat again, you know.
Bonnie:	And then I just gain it. I'm not eating.
Father:	No, you won't.
Mother:	You won't gain.
Bonnie:	I will.
Bonnie:	It's gonna make me sick.
Mother:	Well, then, you'll get sick. The garbage can is here. We'll go out and buy another sandwich and start all over again.
Bonnie:	No. I don't want it.
Mother:	You have to eat it.
Bonnie:	Mom, no.
Father:	Eat it, now come on, don't fight, just take it and eat it.
Mother:	You have to eat it.
Bonnie:	No.
Mother:	Come on, you ate the one half, now you have to eat the other half.
Father:	Come on, Bonnie.
Bonnie:	I don't want it, Mom.
Mother:	I don't care if you don't want it, you have to eat it.
Bonnie:	I don't want it.
Mother:	Well, you have to eat it.
Bonnie:	I don't need it.
Father:	Ssh! Stop your shouting.

The father's attention to the shouting is again not supporting the mother: This session is in a therapy room in a clinic, hardly a public place. Starving for food is the issue, not whether Bonnie is making noise. I see this as unsupportive to the mother's efforts.

Mother:	You do need it.
Bonnie:	No, I don't.
Mother:	Yes, you do.
Father:	Want pizza? This is going to be pizza time. [Laughs]

The father has returned to first order change, trying to convince his daughter to eat, as he has for 6 months. What this girl needs is not more advice but a transformation in the system in which she is embedded. Anorexia has little to do with food per se—it is structural change that is needed.

Mother:	Two more bites, and we start on the orange.
Bonnie:	I'm not eating dinner then.
Mother:	Then we'll have to do the same thing for dinner.
Dr. Fishman:	It's very serious. [I say this because both parents are smiling.]
Mother:	I know it's serious. [To her husband] You don't think it is serious, you think the whole thing is funny.
Father:	Open your mouth.
Bonnie:	I don't want it.
Mother:	Well, you have to eat it. I don't care if you don't want it.
Bonnie:	Always pushing me.
Father:	Nobody's pushing you. What do you mean?
Bonnie:	I don't want it. I don't need it.
Mother:	You do need it.
Bonnie:	No, I don't.
Mother:	Yes, you do.
Bonnie:	No, I don't.
Mother:	Yes, you do.
Father:	Open your mouth, that a girl. [Father puts his hand on daughter's arms so that Mother and Father, on either side of Bonnie, are gently holding her. Their daughter is eating.]

Since anorexia was first described, parents and other family members have tried, often helplessly, to get anorexics to eat. With anorexia, however, we are not talking about a conscious behavior. Anorexics cannot will themselves to eat; they are in the grip of a compulsion. For that compulsion to lift, the system needs to transform.

Every psychotherapy has a theory of change. Intensive structural therapy (IST) postulates that to the extent that the system is coherent—that is, that all the social forces in the micro and macro systems surrounding the patient agree and are working together—the symptomatic behavior is ameliorated. When there is incoherence—when there is dissonance among the people who are influential in the patient's life—stress is generated and symptoms emerge, as Holmes and Rahe (1967) were among the first researchers to demonstrate. These symptoms can be behavioral, psychiatric, or physical.

The process is clearly seen in the microtransactions excerpted from Bonnie's lunch session. When Bonnie is triangulated between her dissonant parents, her symptom emerges—a refusal to eat. Yet there is another, equally profound phenomenon that occurs when this happens. When the parents' conflict is diffused, stress in the family system is decreased. While the patient feels better, the system itself is a less stressful place to be. It is "self" interest in a broader sense; the system is more stable. There is a better chance that the parents will stay together if their conflict does not emerge.

In the IST model, therefore, the therapist strives to create a therapeutic crisis in the therapy room. Through this crisis, new structures emerge, and the therapist can monitor and work to transform the family system, observing the forces that are maintaining the dysfunctional homeostasis as the system struggles to regain equilibrium. Further, creating a crisis allows the therapist to see interactional patterns changing before his or her eyes, confirming that an intervention is successful (or, conversely, revealing that a change of course is indicated).

The crisis induced in Bonnie's lunch session is the imperative that the parents make their daughter eat, that her condition is life-threatening, and that the ultimate responsibility and the ultimate tragedy of her anorexia fall on her parents. In the treatment of the families of anorexics, I often draw a boundary, saying that *what* she eats is her business, *that* she eats (and receives adequate caloric content) is her parents' responsibility. Setting this boundary about what she eats is a way of creating distance. (Logistically, this distinction allows the parents to focus on the essential issues that their child eats and their working together. The focus on the specific foods serves to derail the process.) The structure of these systems includes tremendous enmeshment. To the extent that distance from the parents is created, the child is less available for triangulation by the system.

Following the lunch session, the change that occurred in the therapy room was maintained. The parents continued to work together around their daughter's eating. After Bonnie stabilized in terms of the symptoms, I attempted to work with the parents. Their relationship seemed to improve somewhat, but the father was not interested in returning to therapy, and I didn't push it. Over the years, the couple appeared to accept the limits of their marriage, and stopped struggling. The important point was that they no longer involved Bonnie or any of their other children in their dynamic.

In retrospect, I think my therapeutic failure was that I did not join adequately with the father. The concept of therapeutic joining is the process through which the clinician and the family establish a partnership toward a common goal (Minuchin & Fishman, 1981, p. 29). There was a functional common goal with a built-in urgency when the girl was anorexic, but when the new therapeutic goal was transforming the marital system, I failed to get the father to buy in. From a theoretical vantage point, this is a system phenomenon; practically, I believe the clinician should take the responsibility for engaging the relevant family members to embrace the therapeutic agenda. It is far too convenient to simply blame family members as being resistant!

Five Years Later

Five years after her therapy sessions ended, Bonnie called and asked for an appointment. On the telephone she told me that she was having problems with a boyfriend. Also, although she had been away at college, she found herself back at home, feeling trapped by her family. Her grandmother had died, and her family had somehow conveyed a mandate that she return home, where she had fallen into her old position as the helper. Now, however, she was helping overtly, not unknowingly by being symptomatic.

When Bonnie walked into my office, I was struck by her changed appearance. She was physically robust, radiating health and obviously with no anorexia. The contrast with the physically frail youngster I had seen years before was striking.

Dr. Fishman: What happened after therapy? Capsule what happened with yourself, with your family, what was altered following the therapy. Some of the stuff you told me about over the phone.

Bonnie: Well, I went on to school.

Dr. Fishman: Which school? And tell me the history of the anorexia also.

Bonnie: Well, after . . . God, you know, I can't even remember that part of my life. God, a junior in high school. Well, I started to gain weight. I started to munch out after . . . I'd say after August I started to eat a lot. And then, um, with my junior year it's like I went back to the same weight before I became anorexic. And then I went on to school, and I had gotten up to 140 pounds. The reason that I had gotten that fat, I think, was because I had broken up with that boy I was telling you about before.

It is important to note that the anorexia was gone shortly after the intervention of the lunch session. For a short while, after she was found tricking her parents when they were weighing her, we instituted a bed rest protocol of complete bed rest unless she gained an agreed upon amount of weight.

Dr. Fishman: The boy who wanted to change you? [This was a boy she was dating while in high school.]

I have a sense that her difficulties with boys at this point of her life are isomorphic with her difficulties with her father. To the extent that she saw her father as rejecting the family, she felt tentative with other men, expecting them to reject her. As she differentiated from the family, she was better able to relate to men, and the rejection from her father was less influential.

Bonnie: Yeah. And then I just started . . . I eat when I get depressed, you know that? I eat when I get angry. I was fine as soon as I found a friendly outlet [food]. It never asked me any questions, it never questioned me. I could just stuff it in and it won't touch me. And then, um, then I had to come home. And that's when this all started out again. But now. . . .

Dr. Fishman: When you say "this," what do you mean?

Bonnie: That I . . . that I shouldn't even have to be here again. You know what I mean? I should have been over this. There is no reason for me to come back.

Dr. Fishman: When you say "this," though, what are you really talking about? You're talking about. . . .

Bonnie: The session, right here. What we're doing now. I shouldn't have to come back here. That section of my life should have been over. But it's not. Not the part about the anorexia, I'm not anorexic. I mean I have no . . . that's not the problem. I mean the problems in general with my family. I should have gotten rid of them and I shouldn't have had to come back here after 5 years. They are conjuring it all up again.

Dr. Fishman: What are some of the problems? When I said "capsule," I know we've spoken about it.

Bonnie: My family is expecting too much from me. They are not accepting me for who I am. And my FATHER getting out of my life—my entire family's life. I don't know, I think that they still treat me as a child.

The follow-up is instructive, I believe. As I review her narrative, it is clear to me that my therapy was unsuccessful in one important way. I addressed the problem of transforming the system *only* to the extent that the parents were together around the girl. I was not successful, however, in addressing the isomorph of the father's distance from the family. The manifestation of that, in this contemporary context, is that her father is not participating as a member of this family system, certainly not as much as Bonnie would like. His distance and unavailability were still a major problem.

I have always felt, with this family and with many others, that the lunch session is a tremendously powerful intervention. With Bonnie's family I see it as having transformed even their tenaciously problematic structure. But the follow-up also conveyed a chastening message: We can be faced with outcomes that, while good, are yet imperfect, leaving problematic structures (defined as problematic by the client whom we are serving).

I had no other direct contact with the family until I called to ask them to participate in the follow-up that follows. My indirect contact was from the other anorexic youngsters that the mother referred to me over the years.

Twenty-One-Year Follow-Up

I called Bonnie's home and asked her mother if they would be willing to come in for a follow-up visit, just so I could see how things had gone. Bonnie, now married and the mother of a small child, lived in North Carolina, but during her next visit home she and her mother came in together. Excerpts from that interview follow.

Dr. Fishman: Thank you very much for joining me here. You are contributing, hopefully, to helping lots of other families. So, first of all, to do a follow-up . . . I saw you in '78. How old were you, 16?

Bonnie: 16.

Dr. Fishman: So, I guess it was about '79, rather. Okay, what do you remember of that period in your life?

Bonnie:	To be honest with you, I don't have a lot of memories of that. I think I just remember the bad parts. Well, I remember the first meeting, when we were all there in that room.
Dr. Fishman:	What do you remember about it?
Bonnie:	That someone made me a bagged lunch, and I wasn't allowed to leave the room until I ate the lunch. It was just an [orange] and a half a sandwich.
Dr. Fishman:	Right.
Bonnie:	I remember driving there a lot, but I don't really remember the sessions. I remember the time Daddy found food underneath my shirt, and I had to stay in bed till I ate it. I mean, I remember the recovery better than the sessions.
Dr. Fishman:	What do you remember about the recovery?
Bonnie:	Eating a lot. I got really heavy after the recovery. [To Mother] Remember that?
Mother:	I think you put on weight.
Bonnie:	Yeah, but I put on a lot of weight. I couldn't shop in regular stores. [To Mother] You guys had to take me to Lane Bryant for a pair of pants, remember that? I mean, I gained a lot of weight. I was eating a lot, eating everything, more than normal, overcompensating.
Dr. Fishman:	Was that okay with you at that time, to eat a lot?
Bonnie:	Yeah, I never really thought about it. I just ate and ate and ate until I thought I would burst. I always thought I should get hypnotized, because I really don't . . . oh, and I remember a wedding. . . .
Bonnie:	It's not just our meetings. I don't remember anything. I mean, I remember jumping rope like five thousand times, and I remember you giving me a lunch and me throwing it in the garbage, but those are like 5-minute memories. The biggest memory I have is the first time, and when Dad found those rocks. [At one point, during the behavioral paradigm phase of the treatment, her father discovered her trying to fool the system by putting rocks in her clothes.] I'll never forget that. I also remember you calling Dr. Fishman, and him saying that I couldn't leave the house until I weighed at least a hundred pounds. I remember that whole sequence. I don't remember going back to school.

Since Bonnie's weight was not dangerously low and she began eating immediately after the session, I did not prescribe the bed rest paradigm. It was only after the family reported that she had been putting rocks in her clothes when being weighed that we instituted the protocol.

Dr. Fishman: So how are you doing now? Is this all past history?

Bonnie: Yeah. I don't think about that stuff at all. I had a little problem when I was living in Spain. I used to take these pills to flush out my body. That was just for a little while.

Dr. Fishman: What was going on in your life in Spain? Were you upset?

Bonnie: I think I just didn't like it. It was before I started studying art. I was just working as a waitress.

Dr. Fishman: That was a short period of time?

Bonnie: Yeah. It was really short. Then I really knew. I mean, I was on this medication, and I couldn't eat for 2 days, and it was really obvious to me that it was doing a lot of damage to my stomach, or whatever. No, I never . . . I don't even diet.

Dr. Fishman: You just live.

Bonnie: I mean, sometimes I'll eat, like, a whole bag of potato chips, or a bag of chips and a peanut butter sandwich, and I'll feel really bad, but I just never. . . .

Dr. Fishman: That's pretty human.

Bonnie: It took me a long time to lose weight after I had my daughter, but I don't think I gained an abnormal amount of weight. I lost all of it.

Dr. Fishman: Which is unusual sometimes.

Mother: Yes, very.

Bonnie: Yeah. I think I lost more, actually. I think I weigh even less now than before I was pregnant.

Dr. Fishman: Okay.

Dr. Fishman: [To Bonnie] How long have you been married?

Bonnie: Let me see . . . 6 years, but we have been together for 11. We got married right before we came here from Spain.

Dr. Fishman: Okay. How about your extended family?

Mother: My mother's dead. My father was already dead. So, there's the two of them, and then there's only my sister. . . .

Bonnie: On your side.

Mother: Right, on my side. My husband has no brothers or sisters.

Dr. Fishman: Now, we had seen each other shortly after your [to Bonnie] grandmother died, right?

Bonnie:	Yeah, I came by myself, I think. Why did I come to see you?
Dr. Fishman:	I'm not exactly sure. I think you were unhappy about things in the family.
Bonnie:	Yeah, that was really hard for me, Grandma's death.
Dr. Fishman:	Were you close to her?
Bonnie:	Yeah.
Mother:	They all were, because she lived with us when they were young. They both did—my mother and father. She became their babysitter.
Dr. Fishman:	[To Bonnie] How is your dad doing?
Mother:	He's all right. He's recovering. He's had several bouts of cancer, but is recovering. He's in remission.
Bonnie:	He's a lot calmer. It's not like. . . .
Mother:	He's not as aggressive towards the children. He's still aggressive, but not towards them, because they're not around.
Dr. Fishman:	Did you see any other therapists over the years since our work together?
Bonnie:	Oh, I did. I saw this guy when I was living in Boston. He was horrible. I only went to him a couple of times.
Dr. Fishman:	How do you define a bad therapist?
Bonnie:	I don't know. He was just . . . maybe he wasn't bad. Maybe I just didn't like him. I must have been in my early 20s.
Dr. Fishman:	You didn't feel he helped you in any way?
Bonnie:	No, I didn't go to him long enough. I don't remember. I just remember not liking him.
Dr. Fishman:	Nothing else? You saw no one else?
Bonnie:	No, and I didn't go to him regularly. Before I had my daughter I was accepted into this program at this Jungian institute to go back to therapy in Washington, but I never went. I got pregnant. It wasn't a good time. Plus, it was pretty far away from my house.
Dr. Fishman:	Why were you interested in going to that?
Bonnie:	I yell a lot. I thought maybe it would be good to not yell so much.
Dr. Fishman:	Maybe you are just an emotional person.
Bonnie:	I know, but I don't know if it's so good to be so emotional around a kid.
Dr. Fishman:	How is your daughter?

Bonnie:	She's a really strong-willed kid. She has a lot of energy.
Dr. Fishman:	Your mother is smiling. Is it like the commercial?
Mother:	A little bit. [There was a popular TV commercial at the time in which a young woman is complaining to her mother about her headstrong 2-year-old; the punch line was that the mother was the same when she was that age.]
Bonnie:	She's like me, I think. She definitely has a mind of her own, and she is not easily persuaded, unless it entails a threat, and then she'll do it.
Dr. Fishman:	She's how Bonnie was at that age?
Mother:	I think so, a little bit, maybe not as strong-willed, but yes, Bonnie was strong-willed.

I see Bonnie's history of assertiveness as a plus—indeed, likely one reason that she is no longer suffering from an eating disorder. In my experience, as I have said in earlier chapters, the *sine qua non* of manifesting an eating disorder is conflict avoidance.

Dr. Fishman:	Well, when you think back on the work that we did—and be frank about this, I know it's a long time ago—is there anything you would have liked to see done differently?
Mother:	I don't think on your part there was anything I would have liked to see done differently. I would have liked my husband's participation to be fuller.
Dr. Fishman:	More so?
Mother:	Yeah. He never came. . . .
Bonnie:	He came the first time, and the last time, right? Didn't we have a closing session?
Dr. Fishman:	In my little office. . . .
Mother:	Bonnie didn't remember, but I remember. I remember the office, with the plants outside the window, but I don't remember him being there.
Bonnie:	Well, it must have been really good, because I hear it's really hard to get over, and it didn't take me long to get over it. I know a lot of girls with eating disorders that it's taken years. I don't know if it's just bulimia more than anorexia. . . .
Mother:	I think the technique that you used got positive results. I got involved with the schools, giving information on anorexia, when Bonnie was going through this. I went to two schools to talk to

the nurses to tell them what my experience was with this . . . that I really didn't realize, even living with her, until it got very serious. I had several mothers call me, and one of them had information on a clinic, and it seemed so drastic. They would lock them into their rooms, and they had a prescribed amount of food to eat, and if they didn't eat the food they were locked into their rooms, and they took away privileges, and they couldn't leave grounds, and I thought, "My goodness, how drastic." We went through what I thought was a very successful series of events without going through not only taking a child from his or her environment, but also putting that child behind locked doors and taking away privileges.

Bonnie: They were really skinny.

Mother: Bonnie, so were you.

Bonnie: Yeah?

Mother: Yeah.

Bonnie: See, I don't remember. Do most of your patients get well?

Dr. Fishman: At that time in history, Salvador Minuchin had just developed the model we used. He's a very brilliant guy, and the results are terrific.

Bonnie: American guy?

Dr. Fishman: He's Argentinean originally, actually. It's very effective. I didn't develop the model, but it's very effective.

Mother: Well, like I was saying, there were several mothers who were having horrible problems, and the procedures they were going through were horrible.

Dr. Fishman: There is tremendous chronicity. I think you said earlier that within a month, you no longer had an eating disorder?

Mother: That's why I don't think that in my mind, even today, that there's anything I would change.

Bonnie: I wouldn't even consider starving myself. I don't think I could go a day without eating. It just seems so inconceivable to me. Maybe I would do something else, though. I think that if you have obsessive behaviors, you just have them, always. It's just controlling them. I smoke a lot. It's very hard for me to quit, and that's an obsession.

Dr. Fishman: Yeah, it's very hard to stop smoking. Have you tried the patch and all that?

Bonnie: No, I haven't.

I was careful not to get involved with her smoking. She did not ask for this meeting, I did.

Dr. Fishman: Well, do you have any questions for me?

Bonnie: Is it genetic?

Dr. Fishman: No, it's not genetic as far as I am concerned. But there are people doing research in this area.

Bonnie: [To Mother] You weren't really aware of the technique?

Mother: No, I just knew we needed help, and that we weren't finding it. Afterwards, when I was talking to these other women, I heard their stories.

Bonnie: I've thought about going to someone, because I have all these gaps in my memory, but it wasn't a happy time. Maybe it wouldn't help.

Dr. Fishman: No, it wasn't a happy time. Now, you have a husband, a baby, and a career. What else do you need?

DISCUSSION

Family therapists treating a young anorectic like Bonnie routinely question family members regarding the parents' perceptions of their family and their children, various members' roles and the relationships among them, and how their relationships have changed since the problem began, when the patient stopped eating. Questions like these are interesting; indeed, any interested, thoughtful person would naturally ask them. I never ask them when I am doing the intervention of the lunch session, because if I get too involved in these issues, I get too close to the family. Therapists like people and naturally want to be close to them, but the success of the lunch session depends on maintaining a well-defined professional distance. The distancing is necessary as a countervailing force to the enmeshment in these families. I personally dislike doing this intervention. It is upsetting and unaesthetic, and I would never do it if it weren't so effective. Like many other medical interventions, it can be painfully stressful, even though the momentary pain is offset by the long-term benefit (and short-term benefit, for that matter—the young person usually begins eating almost immediately) to the patient. It is a little like homeopathic therapy—introducing a bit of poison to cure the patient. In a sense, it is vaccinating the patient against the conflict that is triangulating her, that her symptoms are diffusing.

Although it is important to maintain a professional distance from the family, the lunch session intervention cannot succeed unless the clinician joins with the family. The procedure requires the creation of a crisis, and the therapist cannot move the family in that direction if the family and therapist have not joined. One case in which it failed was that of a European family with whom I could not get any therapeutic traction. At one point, I thought the cultural difference was just too great; for example, for the lunch session they brought an elegant meal, served on fine china. But I think that was just a ruse. They were refusing to see the purpose of the session by deflecting the focus to themselves: their fine taste, high standard of living, and so on. It is not just that Europeans eat lunch off fine china while Americans eat lunch out of a brown bag. The bottom line is they could not or would not address the conflict.

The lunch session is not an aesthetic intervention, but after doing at least 150 of them over the years, I can say it is a very effective procedure as well as a safe procedure. I have never seen a casualty from it, never seen a suicide or a schizophrenic break or a homicide. The vast majority—about 85%—have showed immediate improvement with cessation of the anorexia in short order: days, weeks, and at most, a few months. In the cases I have been able to contact, the long-term follow-up shows the amelioration of the anorexia has been maintained. Minuchin, Rosman, and Baker (1978), with a sample of 52 cases, demonstrated that over 86% of the anorexics they treated showed good functioning medically and psychosocially 1 to 7 years later.

It is important to emphasize that the lunch session intervention is done only in very close collaboration with the physical health provider—the general practitioner, family practitioner, pediatrician, or internist. These are the people who determine the status quo and decide when the patient needs to be hospitalized. It is also used in conjunction with a behavioral paradigm that calls for complete bed rest for children who need to gain weight. The bed rest is administered by the parents, in a structural continuity of the work that has been done in the therapy room in getting the parents together. It is really the second part of the intervention. And it is usually essential to stabilize the changed structure.

We now have an elaborate therapeutic culture across the treatment world that is organized to avoid the salutary conflict that is invaluable to these families. Here, the culture of conflict avoidance is completely counterproductive. What *changes* these families is conflict; indeed, conflict is the active interpersonal behavior that transforms the system. In my own experience, when I have taken the family's lead and ignored the conflict, the system has not changed and the anorexic young person has not done well. When the conflict has *not* been addressed, families have suffered.

I was never completely successful with this family. The fact is that I failed to get the father and mother to address their own marital issues. We began therapy with the father peripheral to the family, and we ended therapy with that father peripheral to the family. The girl had by then been extricated from the parental dyad, and she was no longer triangulated. She was freed from her symptom of anorexia, but the system had not transformed, and she was now distanced from her family. This distance allowed her to avoid being recruited back into the triangulation position. One question in my mind was whether any of the other children had been recruited in her place, but fortunately they had not. In another family, after the first of two daughters recovered from her anorexia, the second became symptomatic, and her mother resisted the intervention of the lunch session because it made her distant from her child.

In Bonnie's family the parents seemed to have come to a middle-aged kind of acceptance of each other. They know that they will never be perfect spouses to each other, but they no longer harbor the intense anger toward each other that required the system to triangulate.

There is an important lesson here. It appears that structural change does not have to be permanent in order to be useful in cases such as this one with adolescent anorexics. Apparently the structure can change just enough to accomplish the task of containing the problem and getting the youngster over the hump. The claims of the necessity for complete systems transformation by early work in structural therapy are not borne out by these long-term follow-ups. Structural modifications can be short lived, leaving fundamental conflicts in the family unchanged. In many cases, once symptoms have been relieved in the identified patient, conflicts may reactivate, but the system does not respond with patterns that are harmful to members such as triangulation. Or conversely, the members have advanced developmentally so as not to be as vulnerable to triangulation. Bonnie is a middle-aged woman with a family of her own—the conflict between her parents has vastly less effect on her now than when she was a 16-year-old living at home. Indeed, as her mother says in the follow-up, Bonnie's father is still aggressive, but not with the children. Perhaps because they are not around.

There is another important facet of this follow-up. The fact the anorexia emerged only once in this family suggests to me that the emergence of symptoms may require dysfunction at multiple levels. After the anorexia was ameliorated, the structure reverted to its problematic organization, but the family had moved on developmentally. Bonnie was away at college, and the older children were increasingly autonomous, so other factors within the family that might have contributed to the problem had changed.

CHAPTER 6

Treating the Young Anorexic: The Behavioral Paradigm

This chapter is about two essential problems in the treatment of eating disorders: how the therapist further transforms the family after the lunch session and how to work with very complex, multipatient families. As effective as the lunch session is in getting the young anorectic to eat, the effect usually does not represent a permanent change. Just as with surgical patients, recovery is highly dependent on the aftercare. The lunch session intervention is therefore generally followed by a behavioral protocol: A schedule is drawn up that sets specific weight goals to be met by specific dates. If the patient does not bring her weight up to a particular goal by the specified date, she is prescribed total bed rest, is allowed to get up only to go to the bathroom, or, in extreme cases, is obliged to use a bedpan.

The parents thus become central to the patient's continuing care. On a day-to-day basis they must monitor her weight and, when necessary, enforce bed rest. This focal role of the parents sets the intensive structural therapy (IST) model apart from most other programs that treat anorexics. In many programs, the professionals provide the treatment, and the family's participation is secondary, in occasional or regular family therapy meetings. Where the focus of treatment is on medication, hospitalization, or outpatient group therapy, there is not a high priority on parent empowerment. In the IST model, by contrast, the parents are trained in how to handle their child's difficulty.

Just as in the lunch session, the parents must work together in maintaining the change in their child. To the extent that they resolve their own conflicts (which they must do implicitly in this process), the youngster is liberated from the triangulated position and the anorexia recedes and disappears. The process of restructuring can be a very painful one, however. To be successful, all members of the family must sign on to the new structure, as the following case makes clear.

It is important to note that, while the behavioral paradigm aids in the alleviation of the anorexia, the needs of the entire family system must be addressed. The following complex clinical case demonstrates some of the intricacies of transforming a family long after the eating disorder has remitted.

THE DAWSON FAMILY: TWIN ANOREXICS

One Sunday morning 10 years ago, I received a distressed call from a mother who said that the second of her twin daughters had just been diagnosed with anorexia nervosa. The symptoms of the first twin, Catherine, had finally yielded after a 3-month stay in a psychiatric hospital, but as she started to gain weight, her sister, Julie, began to lose weight. Julie was presently in the same hospital and losing three pounds a week. The family was furious at the psychiatrist and felt quite hopeless about whether anything could be done with their daughter.

The mother, Helen, had multiple problems when the family was referred. She was drinking heavily, was chronically depressed, and had symptoms of posttraumatic stress disorder (PTSD). The previous year, she had become severely depressed and gone into therapy. In that context, she became aware that she had been sexually abused as a child. That year was a difficult one for Helen. Her husband was working abroad, leaving her with three young daughters, thousands of miles from the community where she had grown up and where most of her support lived. The anorexia, first of Catherine and now of Julie, exacerbated her problems.

Managing the Paradigm: Segments from the Therapy

The following segments have been edited to demonstrate the thrust of our treatment. They are representative of many similar sessions. (There was one unique session, however, necessitated by Helen's mounting—and murderous—anger with her father, where Helen and her sister confronted their parents on their sexual abuse. This was a powerful, extremely emotional session in which both parents denied the accusations. After that session, there was more distance between the parents and their daughters, but Helen was less angry with her father.)

At the time of the first segment, the family treatment was still in the early stages: We were still dealing with the symptoms of anorexia. It was 1 month after the opening lunch session, and the parents were struggling to get their daughter to eat, using the behavioral paradigm. What this meant according to the model was that the parents were still conflicted. To the extent that their child did not eat, the split between the parents was still triangulating the young person.

The family had just returned from vacation.

Father:	They were pretty good when we came back, too. Julie surprised us. We didn't know what to expect. She only weighed 74 and a half at my parents' house, though the scale might have been different, she was crying, worried about it.
Dr. Fishman:	But now she's at her weight?
Father:	Now she's at her weight (80 pounds). What I told her in Portland was, "I hope you understand, if you're not at your weight [by Monday], I have to do something. . . . The vegetarianism doesn't work, Julie." And she said, "Does that mean just until I make the 80 pounds?" I said, "I know you watch everything I say very carefully. All I can tell you is that you need to make the 80 pounds. Otherwise, you're off the vegetarianism. I said, "I don't want to hear it. Make sure you do it, because you know what to do." So, she stuffed herself the night we got back, Saturday night. I don't know if you [to Mother] noticed that. She was up until about 1:00 in the morning eating bagels and cheese and Ensure (a highly caloric dietary supplement), all the Ensure in the house, which was about 18 cans for the week. She had it all figured out. She told me before we left that she had to gain a pound just about every day. And I said, "No, it's about a half pound every day. It might be 3/4 or a pound one day. If you figure it out, that puts you at 79 and a half, exactly." She says, "Well, that's still not 80." I said, "You make 79 and a half, and make a half pound a day later, no one's gonna get that upset, as long as you make 80 pounds." And she was exactly 79 and a half pounds on Sunday morning. Monday she didn't gain. Tuesday, she made her 80 pounds. And she was more talkative. [To Mother] I don't know if you noticed. She would get her book, and her binder. . . .

The father's statement shows the power of the intervention. Julie had been anorexic for 8 months at the time of this session. Her commitment—actually, her drive—to consume calories is almost unbelievable considering her condition. This behavior is the norm in my experience with this intervention once the system is stabilized, meaning once the parents are working together and the professionals are allied. If the parents do their part by working together and are unwavering in their adherence to the paradigm, the child eats.

The father's next words, however, shattered the illusion of togetherness.

Father: And I know you guys probably won't agree, but I think Helen's just gotta lighten up now. . . . Now, the foul language thing I agree with, but I think that now she realizes that she's not gonna win this thing. I think now we gotta lighten up a little bit. Like this thing, coming here, it's getting . . . like, you're the one who told us, you're the one who showed us how to do it . . . like, in the car, on the way here, Helen's fighting with Julie, Helen says Julie's crying. . . .

This reveals a pervasive pattern. The mother has been strong and clear. In fact, her intervention is demonstrably effective: Her chronically anorexic daughter has responded by accommodating—she ate. The father's response to this success is to attack his wife. The pivotal dynamic is emerging at this point: The father's attacking mother is a manifestation of his alliance with Julie.

As we will see in the follow-up, it appears that the key to the stabilization of the system—and what kept Helen from madness, and perhaps murder—may well have been the effectiveness of the therapy in creating a solid partnership between the parents. The husband's commitment and unwavering support of his wife were crucial. The segments that follow represent therapy directed to this structural goal.

In the next session, the mother and father came in without their daughter. They wanted to discuss the process of the therapy.

Father: What was she doing?
Mother: You didn't listen to me. [A challenge to her husband.]

Her husband had been supporting their daughter against her. It was a flagrant insult to mother—belittling her when she expressed concern over the girl's weight.

Father: Okay, go ahead, what was she doing?
Mother: When we got back from the trip, you took over all of the weighing of Julie, and I was left out of it. I didn't know what she weighed at all. I hadn't seen any proof at all. I got it verbally from her. Which, sad to say, is worth about zip in my book.
Father: Well, is that my fault, that you didn't look in the book on Tuesday to see what she weighed? I was at work. You were with her on Tuesday morning, why didn't you weigh her on Tuesday morning?

Mother: You exclude . . . [stops, sighs with frustration].

Helen is a shy, quiet person. She has an almost palpable oppressiveness when she fumes, but this communication seems easy for her husband to ignore. It is the therapist's job to help her to address her concerns. Her smoke signals, as it were, have not in the past budged her husband, not to mention the system.

Father: You were with her on Tuesday morning. How can you blame me for what happened on Tuesday morning? I mean, you were there Tuesday morning. I wasn't even there Tuesday morning.

Mother: [mumbling] I don't know. . . .

Father: Yes, I was there Sunday morning. And I was there Monday, and I weighed her, and she was crying because she stayed the same. But I don't know what the problem was. I mean, you were there Tuesday morning. Didn't you see her?

Mother: Never mind. I don't want to talk about it.

Father: Why were you so upset that she wasn't weighed on Wednesday?

Mother: I got dumped on, didn't I?

Father: I mean, you were very upset with me. And I mean, that's probably part of how you were brought up. Not that it's bad, but you were more rigid, more rigid than me sometimes. And it's probably my fault, sometimes. Sometimes I'm probably not rigid enough.

His use of "rigid" is a criticism of his wife. "Firm" would have been a more neutral word to use.

Father: But you are so rigid. Nutrition is Monday, Wednesday, Friday, and that's all you've got in your mind. It's gotta be Monday, Wednesday, Friday.

Dr. Fishman: But, Helen, do you feel that somewhere you were not included?

I intervene, attempting to get Helen to advocate for herself.

Father: Yeah, that's what she tells me, that she's not included. That "I was seduced again, by Julie." That Julie's getting her way.

"Seduced" is an interesting use of words. This is not a term that is often used by fathers when referring to their daughters. It speaks to the closeness the two of them have. (In previous discussions possibility of incest between the father and the girls was vigorously denied by all parties.)

Mother:	Yeah, and I think that's exactly what Julie tried to do, by trying to get out of coming to therapy. And you [to Father] gave her an ear that was, like, wide open, and you listened. And you didn't cut it off. You didn't say, "No, Julie. Mom and I will talk about that and I'll get back to you." And you let it go on and on and on. You made her feel like she's gonna get her way.
Father:	You're taking Julie's word instead of mine.
Mother:	All I'm saying is that. . . .
Father:	I'll make it clear to her. . . .
Mother:	Well, you obviously didn't make it clear to her, because then why did I get an hour tirade tonight?
Father:	Well, I'll try to do a better job, make it clear to her. . . .
Mother:	It's not just that you have to make it clear to her, okay? If you want, I'll give it all to you—all the problems, all the solutions— you can have it.
Father:	You and I both talked to her about coming here.
Dr. Fishman:	Helen, Stewart says that he will make it clearer. I'm not sure you're getting exactly what he's saying. Helen's saying it's gotta be both of you, all the time, with these things. Otherwise [Julie] drives a stake between you, and she gets too powerful.

This is my customary refrain. We were beginning the work of the middle stages of therapy—the stabilization of the new structures. The initial crisis induction—the lunch session at the onset of treatment—had transformed the system, and the child's triangulation was diminished. It would be naïve, however, to assume that the transformation would automatically become permanent. The therapist must work with the family members to help them maintain the new, more functional structures. This work requires repetition. These are family patterns that have prevailed for many years, and changing them takes practice. The behavior paradigm in the present situation was similar to the lunch session; the parents had to practice working together consistently to make it succeed.

Father:	Okay.

Dr. Fishman: [To Father] You ever play chess? You know what happens when the pawn gets to the other side? It gets as powerful as the queen.

Father: Okay.

Dr. Fishman: Go ahead, Helen.

Mother: I just think you should make it, "Your mother and I think this" or "Your mother and I feel this," but always make it, "Your mother and I," not just "Your mother said this" or "I'm saying that."

Father: [After a pause] I think you're wrong. I think he's wrong. I don't give a damn what either one of you think, okay? I've been wrong in the past, but now I think you're both wrong. And I think that this last time, you were there with me when I talked to her. Now, just because I happen to be in the bedroom, or happen to be somewhere with her, I can't say, "No, wait! Julie, stop! Don't talk anymore! I gotta go get your mother." Just like last night. It seemed like an innocent thing. I'm goin' to bed, she's goin' to bed. . . .

Dr. Fishman: So, what do you think about that?

Father: I can't think of anything else. I made a conscious effort. . . .

Dr. Fishman: [to Mother] What do you think about it?

Mother: Gosh, I don't know. . . .

Dr. Fishman: Come on. Use your voice!

[No reply]

Dr. Fishman: [Standing up to leave the room] I'll be back in a minute. [To Mother] Use your voice!

I do not remember why I left the room at this point. I sometimes leave when I feel that my presence is impeding the process of the enactment between the people in the room, that I'm stymieing them.

Father: If I've done something wrong, I'm sorry, okay?

[Mother is silent.]

[Dr. Fishman reenters room.]

Dr. Fishman: [To Mother] So you think the rules need to be changed?

[Mother is stonily silent.]

Dr. Fishman: See, Helen, it's moments like this that make you depressed. It's moments like this that are the reason you are so depressed.

[Pause]

Mother's silence is an expression of the conflict avoidance that is a classic interactional pattern in psychosomatic families. Lacking the confidence and resolve to direct her fury at her husband, she directs it at herself and becomes depressed.

Dr. Fishman: You disagree with that, you agree with that?

Mother: I agree with that.

Dr. Fishman: Now the way I understand it, Julie got his ear last night, and it changed something on which both of you had agreed. Now he didn't talk to you [Mother] about it ahead of time, he informed you that it had been changed.

Father: No, I didn't even know what days . . . because I couldn't remember. All I knew was every other day.

Dr. Fishman: I understand that, but nevertheless. . . .

Father: Nevertheless what?

Dr. Fishman: Nevertheless, it's still not exactly checking with Helen. Now [to Father], why do I have to do your work?

Father: Why do I have to check with Helen?

My jaw drops. Where has he been?

Dr. Fishman: [To Mother] Why do I have to do your work? To the extent that I do your work, I'm not helping.

Mother: [After a pause, softly, to Father] Do you want to be in this together, or do you want to do it by yourself, that's the question.

Father: I want to do it together.

Mother: Then you need to include me.

Father: Do you think you always include me?

Mother: No, I think that sometimes I don't include you because you're not there. I think that there have been times that I have told the kids that they need to talk to you about it. "I'll talk to you later, give you an answer later."

Father: I don't do that?

Mother: No, not usually. And then you come to me, and tell me that you told one or the other of them this or that, and it's all news to me.

Father: Like what?

Mother: I don't have any specific examples. It's just. . . .

Father:	[sighs] Okay.
Mother:	[After a pause] Julie looks for ways to overrule me, and she has for a long time, because she knows she's got your ear, and that you'll listen to her. And she uses that. And you don't see it.
Father:	And she knows she can get you fired up like that.
Dr. Fishman:	And to the extent that she does that, that's how powerful she is. She's so powerful because she has your ear. And to the extent that she has your ear, she can provoke her mom.

[Father nods.]

Mother:	On the way here tonight, Julie was trying to make a point, and she kept saying, "You don't even know how your own husband feels. Dad said this and this and this, and you don't even know how Dad feels." It's like she's got this [Mother intertwines her fingers to illustrate] real special thing with you . . . and you with her.

[Everyone sits in silence for about one minute.]

The silence that followed was palpable. Both parents seemed to be absorbed in their recognition of the extent to which Julie was triangulating them. I let it sink in for a full minute before intervening.

Dr. Fishman:	So what's gonna change?
Father:	I'm going to have to talk more to Helen, I guess.
Dr. Fishman:	[After a pause] Why don't you talk about that right here? [Pause] Talk about it now.
Father:	We're gonna talk more.
Dr. Fishman:	Listen, you know Missouri, the "Show Me" state? Show me how you're gonna talk more, right now.
Father:	I just said that I would do it. She doesn't feel that I do it. . . .
Dr. Fishman:	Helen, what do you think?
Mother:	I don't have much else to say at this point. I mean, he says he's gonna talk to me more. . . .
Dr. Fishman:	Are you sure?
Mother:	No. I mean, how can I be sure?
Dr. Fishman:	Well, why don't you break out some of your concerns? I don't want you to be riding home saying, or Julie saying, "I don't want to be coming here. This is a drag. We're at our target weights. What are we doing here?" How's that gonna be handled?

Mother:	I dunno. How is that going to be handled?
Father:	I guess on the way back we'll tell her.
Mother:	Well, what are you going to tell her?
Father:	What?
Mother:	What are you going to tell her? What are you going to tell Julie when she brings that up, and you know she will?
Father:	About what?
Mother:	About coming here?
Father:	Well, we'll discuss it. We'll tell her together after our discussion.
Dr. Fishman:	Is that satisfactory?
Mother:	Yeah, satisfactory. Yes. If he comes through with what he says.
Dr. Fishman:	Well, congratulations. [Shakes Father and Mother's hands] This is a breakthrough. [To Father] You see, you may not realize it, but the kind of wife who just challenged you is the kind of wife you need, because that's the wife that will be with you through the course of many years, and not in divorce court.
Father:	[Looking to Mother for confirmation] Okay.
Dr. Fishman:	Okay. Good work, guys.

Things did not go well. During the following week, Julie took an overdose—a few of the mother's antidepressants (was this an attack on the mother in taking her medication?). The family was in tumult. In retrospect, I see Julie's suicide threat as a response to the parents' newfound togetherness. She experienced a profound sense of loss as her father aligned with her mother. And perhaps it was a threat to the father: "You can't fire me, I quit!" Indeed, her statement "You don't know your own husband" suggests an almost incestuous closeness: "I can be a better wife than you!"

I believe I had made a mistake in not sufficiently including Julie in the new structure. I could have strongly encouraged the parents to vigorously attempt to get their daughter to the session—bribery can be helpful with adolescents; but instead I acquiesced to her teenage resistance toward coming to the sessions by allowing her to miss some of them. She should have been at the session just described; the essential goal would then have been for them to enlarge the system so that both parents, in their new congruent relationship, were there for Julie. Instead, she counterattacked. If we had worked to include her, perhaps she would not have felt the loss that led to her behavior.

From the perspective of the follow-up session, what Helen remembers was an alienation from her daughter in the process of our therapy. In fact, the entire family was experiencing the loss. My case notes indicate that during most of the therapy Helen was suicidal. Systemically, her daughter seemed to be realizing her mother's desire. One of the few positives of such suicide attempts occurs when the therapeutic/family system sees the attempt as a kind of reveille, a call to troops: Things need to change. The suicidal member is making a clear statement to the family on their system: "The situation is intolerable, things must change." The implicit message behind this behavior is that the system is so rigid that it is deaf to lower-decibel calls for change.

The following excerpt is from a session a few days after the suicide attempt. Julie, who was present at the beginning of the session, has left the room.

Father:	I still have . . . I still worry sometimes, about things, about Julie. I think about what's important. Sometimes I think about . . . picking her up off the floor, pants soaked through, you know, scaring the hell out of you. So. . . .
Dr. Fishman:	[to Mother] Does that haunt you as well?
Mother:	Haunt me? Um, she scared me. . . . [nodding] She scared me. I thought she was dead.
Father:	We weren't getting her to react. She wasn't making any sense. She was opening up her eyes once in a while, making sounds, trying to get Catherine to talk to her. But now she's talking about what car she's gonna drive, when we get a car trade, get her a car. Also, about getting her license, how much longer we think we'll live here.
Dr. Fishman:	Well, that's pretty normal stuff.
Father:	It wasn't prior to this. It was, "I wanna move to San Francisco. I wanna move to San Francisco." The family is from San Francisco. It was like going through hell.
Dr. Fishman:	You think the threat of a boarding school made a difference?
Mother:	No, I think we should still look into boarding schools. I think right now she's on really good behavior, but I think we should have some information at our fingertips, just in case things ever do get out of hand. I think we should look into boarding schools. Although she has been good, it's always . . . something. She was very obnoxious and antagonistic about the hospital.

I think to myself, is boarding school the only way the mother thinks she can get her husband back? Has she given up on the therapy?

Father:	Yeah. In fact, the psychiatrist [who consulted when Julie was in the hospital] called back Monday. She said she's very concerned about Julie and the family, because Julie is upset about the struggles in the family. I said, "Well, we've got that under control. We're seeing a doctor now. She's very content. We're content with her." She said, "Well, maybe it was a temporary thing." I said, "Yeah I guess it was a temporary thing." You know, maybe Julie finally realized how much we care about her. I don't know. Maybe the competition with Catherine all the time . . . thinking that we're always on Catherine's side . . . maybe she realized what we went through, that we do love her. That we're not trying to hurt her; we're trying to help her. I don't know.
Mother:	She's been nice to me, which is quite unsettling.
	[Dr. Fishman laughs.]
Father:	This way she gets home. In the hospital, she knows this. She snapped around so she got home.

The parents discuss how they are working to maintain their vigilance regarding Julie's anorexia. We also discuss their relationship and ways in which they can find time for one other. Near the end of the session, I ask to speak with Helen alone. I have learned that the best way to get a sounding on her mental status is to ask the family to leave.

Dr. Fishman:	Helen, should we talk a little bit, just the two of us?
Mother:	I don't care.
[Father leaves the room.]	
Dr. Fishman:	Well, how have you been doing with all of this?
Mother:	I'm okay.
Dr. Fishman:	I know you were feeling very guilty over the weekend. Do you still?
Mother:	Somewhat.
Dr. Fishman:	What about?
Mother:	What about? About not seeing it coming, about not taking my medication out of Julie's reach.
Dr. Fishman:	Ironically, she needed to do this. It served a purpose. And it was pretty safe, you know, taking three of your pills.
Mother:	What was her purpose?

Dr. Fishman: I think her purpose was to change things. Like she said during our session, things needed to change.

I muse to myself, they say it takes three generations to create a suicide; I wonder, is the corollary, It takes three people—two triangulating the suicidal person—to create a suicide.

Mother: You may be right.

[Mother smiles, looking very sad.]

Dr. Fishman: Why are you smiling?

Mother: I was wondering if I could be excused now.

I know by this time in working with Helen, this is her coy way of telling me she has something to say.

Dr. Fishman: Well, I'm not trying to play the parent or anything; I just need to see how you're doing.

Mother: I'm fine.

Dr. Fishman: I guess you were pretty strong through the hell of this weekend. I guess you needed to be.

Mother: I had to be.

Dr. Fishman: Hopefully, things will change, consistently, after all this. Maybe you really won't feel quite so alone, and betrayed.

[Pause]

Dr. Fishman: Do you have anything else you want to talk about?

Mother: Not really.

Dr. Fishman: You know, sometimes when people say "not really," there's something on their mind.

[Pause]

Dr. Fishman: What about all that suicide stuff we talked about?

Mother: It's an option.

Dr. Fishman: You think that's the human condition?

Mother: No. It's what it is.

Dr. Fishman: You know, there have been times when you've been hurting, when you've talked about it.

Mother: Mm-hmm.

Dr. Fishman: How about at this point?

Mother:	Not at this point, but I could change my mind in 10 minutes' time.
Dr. Fishman:	That's comforting for you, isn't it?
Mother:	I'm sorry, I don't mean to be this way, but when I pass trees, I don't just look at them. I look at them to, like, wrap my car around them. There's a good tree, here's a good tree, that one would work.

I am an old-timer in this business. When I hear words like this, I know it is usually the spouse who is implicated. There is research to support this clinical finding. A study in the *Journal of the American Medical Association* found the following factors in unremitting depression: previous depression, family history of depression, low socioeconononomic status, drug and alcohol problems, and an intact marriage (Keller et al., 1984). Not divorce, but an intact marriage. That is, it is depressing to be stuck in a system.

Dr. Fishman:	Do you think if you left Stewart, it would be better?
Mother:	I don't know. I've thought about it.
Dr. Fishman:	Do you think a lot about it lately?
Mother:	Somewhat.
Dr. Fishman:	Why don't you?
Mother:	Why don't I? I don't know. I'd have to be braver, I guess.
Dr. Fishman:	Yeah . . . but you're talking capital punishment, you know. You feel so guilty and so angry, that you want to . . . you're talking the death penalty. There's got to be something in between. Has anyone in your family ever gotten divorced?
Mother:	My brother.
Dr. Fishman:	Was that very terrible?
Mother:	Was my brother's divorce, to him, very terrible?
Dr. Fishman:	Uh-huh.
Mother:	Yes, and he's still having problems with it.
Dr. Fishman:	Is that one of the reasons that you're so reluctant?
Mother:	No, because I don't know what I would do, on my own.
Dr. Fishman:	Do in what way?
Mother:	Do. Work. Exist. Whatever.
Dr. Fishman:	But you're a smart, energetic person. Would you want the kids?
Mother:	No.
Dr. Fishman:	No?

Mother:	No. I would not. Is that a bad thing to say?
Dr. Fishman:	That's an honest thing to say.
Mother:	Oh.
Dr. Fishman:	Would you have them visit?
Mother:	I guess if I lived within a reasonable distance.
Dr. Fishman:	So, where would you go, if you left?
Mother:	Maybe back to California.
Dr. Fishman:	What's for you there?
Mother:	I don't know. Not much anymore, but I liked it.
Dr. Fishman:	[After a pause] Why are you silent?
Mother:	I just don't really want to spend the whole rest of the session talking about why I'm not leaving Stewart.
Dr. Fishman:	You don't think it's relevant?
Mother:	No, I think it's very relevant.

There is a constant tension in the therapy with psychosomatic families when pushing toward addressing conflict. At any moment the systems try to slip downhill, as it were, back to not facing the issues.

Dr. Fishman:	Then let's. Why is it that you're so mad at him?
Mother:	I'm not mad at him.
Dr. Fishman:	You're not?
Mother:	No.
Dr. Fishman:	Then why do you want to leave your marriage, assuming you want to leave?
Mother:	Sometimes I just get tired of it.
Dr. Fishman:	Well, then, let us go back one step. Why are you tired of it?
Mother:	I'm still feeling like I'm the only one there, sometimes, even though Stewart is trying hard to correct that.
Dr. Fishman:	What I don't understand is that in some ways, you're very radical in your thinking, and in other ways, you're very conservative. So. . . .
Mother:	So?
Dr. Fishman:	So why don't you say, "Enough of this BS. Let's work it out that I feel less trapped." Why don't you say, "leave your job," or "let's move" or something?
Mother:	I mentioned that.

Dr. Fishman: And?

Mother: I didn't get much of a reaction, and I was serious about it.

Dr. Fishman: You know, a lot of people live there.

Mother: I was serious about it. I said, "Let's put the house on the market now. This is ridiculous, this commute."

Dr. Fishman: Should we bring Stewart back now? Maybe you could talk to him.

Mother: No, can we talk about something else now?

Dr. Fishman: Like?

Mother: I don't know.

Dr. Fishman: I want to understand what you're afraid of. Will it make you suffer?

Mother: No, it won't make me suffer.

Dr. Fishman: I think in marriage, people can have very subtle ways of making each other suffer.

[A pause, Mother smiles.]

Dr. Fishman: Why are you smiling?

Mother: I don't think he's gonna like to hear this.

This is more conflict avoidance.

Dr. Fishman: [Sarcastic] Oh, I'm sorry, he'd rather see his wife and his daughter suicidal, right? These are things that families do all the time. Life is very tough in America these days. The sacrifices are fantastic. I think you need to speak up for yourself a bit more. If I make subtle criticism, I think we've known each other long enough that I can use subtle criticism. . . . Let me get him. . . . It's a lot easier on him than you think. . . .

Mother: Maybe I don't want that. Maybe I just want out.

Dr. Fishman: Maybe, but maybe there are steps in between. You can always do that. That's the ultimate, but maybe in between, you won't want that so much. There could be some moderation. You seem to criticize Julie as being too moderate. This seems extreme.

Let me comment on this moment from the position of the therapist. Helen is a difficult person to work with because she is so brittle. Months of sessions where she reported that she has had difficulty, in the (long) drive to my office not "wrapping her car around a tree" on the Jersey Turnpike.

She comports herself with a dignified aura of passiveness. When challenged, the anger is not far from the surface—the indignation not readily expressed with words. Not infrequently, she would excuse herself from a session, and go to the ladies' room and cut herself. Three times I was forced to hospitalize her in the local psychiatric unit.

At this point, clearly we needed to create a therapeutic crisis to have the system change. I was concerned that Helen empower herself to change her circumstances, which I saw as essential for her healthy path out of her despair. But the situation needed to be controlled, because she is also extremely nurturing and guilty if she felt that she had hurt someone, especially her husband.

[Father enters room.]

Mother: [To Dr. Fishman] Are you gonna start?

[Dr. Fishman shakes head.]

Mother: (To Father) I don't think living where we are living is working out all that well for us. I know that when we picked it, we went through a whole list of things . . . what would be the best place . . . I think the commute is ungodly. I think it's not fair to you, I think it's not fair to the kids, I think it's not fair to me. I think we should think about moving closer to your job. You could be one of those 8:00 to 4:00 managers. [After a pause] Do you have anything to say about that?

I am glad to see Helen go to a concrete topic. Clearly, there is a better chance of having observable change, such as addressing what time the father gets home from work with to help his wife with the kids.

Father: Well, I'm thinking about that.

Dr. Fishman: See, part of the question is, "How do you put less stress on the family?" Part of what's been going on is that the family's stressed.

Father: Mm-hmm.

Dr. Fishman: Helen's stressed, the kids are stressed, you're stressed. So, perhaps Helen's suggesting—and I don't know the distance; I've never been to your community—that ways of diminishing the stress will make all of you happier. Life is short. You only have a couple more years with these kids. I'll let you talk about it. [Leaves the room]

Father: Either that, or make a better effort to get home at 6:30 at the latest.

They try to negotiate Stewart's schedule and Helen's and the kids need for him to be home. I return to the room.

Dr. Fishman: Thoreau said, "Men's lives are frittered away with details. Simplify, simplify." [After a pause] Do you not know if you're gonna be here next year?

The father is a corporate executive who has to move every few years.

Mother: Is this the first job you've ever had that you didn't have to be. . . .
Father: There's a reason. It's a little different. People work different hours. It's a changed office atmosphere.
Dr. Fishman: My concern is, Stewart, I think you're losing Helen. As you speak, I think you're losing her. I don't think you're really connecting with her. Why don't you try?

More reveille! The goal is for something to be accomplished in the session. There is too much at stake, and Helen is too brittle! The crisis has to be created and resolved.

Father: [To Mother] Am I missing something?
Mother: I'm doing okay.

This is more conflict avoidance—she is stealing the wind from my sail.

Dr. Fishman: If you weren't, would you tell Stewart? "Just between you and me," you know—"don't tell Stewart."
Mother: I would try to, I guess.
Dr. Fishman: You guess, or you know?
Mother: No, I don't know. It's not my strongest point.
Father: Well, what I said, does that make sense, or no? Do you still think that it's better to try to move?
Mother: It makes sense. I think that if that doesn't work, then we should look for a house closer to your job.
Father: That sounds fair. Okay.
Dr. Fishman: Would you shake on it, as a sign of completed negotiation? [They shake hands and kiss.]

I see this as a too facile resolution. This is the beginning of many sessions where issues are addressed—with some having more effective execution. Helen is effectively advocating for herself and holding her ground.

These segments represent a fraction of the many hours of care this family received. As I review the chart, I see some important interventions. Helen was on medication and continues to be today. In addition, at one point, she began drinking very heavily in response to an exacerbation of her chronic depression. She began attending Alcoholic Anonymous, which she found helpful. During our work together, her depression and drinking varied. The year after she went to AA, her drinking decreased from a half bottle of Scotch per day to one bottle per week. During the period when her drinking decreased, her symptoms of PTSD became worse. I arranged for her to have a course of eye movement desensitization and reprocessing (EMDR). This is a technique that is well documented as benefiting people who have suffered severe trauma. The EMDR alleviated some of her traumatic memories, but she remained suicidal. (Shapiro & Maxfield, 2002; Wilson, Becker, & Tinker, 1997).

In my notes I find that she said at one point, "I am not going to do anything right now, but I think I will ultimately commit suicide."

A major part of the later treatment had to deal with Helen's sexual abuse when she was a child. To hear her describe it, corroborated by her sister who experienced the same abuse, for a number of years her father abused her. Her most poignant memory was her father placed a gun at the entrance to her vagina. During the therapy, I asked Helen to write a journal. Here is her first entry.

> Dear Diary? Dr. F.
> Who will know?
> I am not sure that I'm keen on this diary idea, however, trusting you as I do, (humm. That seems like a bad idea.) I will try this for a while.
> I don't know what to write. What do you want? I have written things over the last 2 years in an effort to make sense out of all of the confusion. I am not sure it was helpful.
> You have asked me several times about suicide so maybe I'll write about that. I don't think about suicide much. However, there *are* moments and sometimes the impulse is very strong. Frankly, though, I am surprised that I am still here. I have been very close and at those times it is very difficult to think straight. I try to think about the kids but sometimes it's hard to keep those thoughts. I first thought about suicide as a kid when I wanted to throw myself in front of a train . . . I think at some point I will kill myself. It seems unchangeable. I don't know why that is. It just is.
> My father tried to kill himself. Did I ever tell you that. He sat down with a shotgun between his knees and pointed it toward his head. I took the gun away from him. Sometimes, I have deeply regretted stopping him. I

feel guilty that he was allowed to continue all of those years of abuse. Why did I save him? Once, OK, I took a gun of Stewart's and tried the same maneuver to see if it would work, it would. Stewart has since sold the gun.

The therapy was plodding and slow—very much like the segment reviewed. (I was interested in maintaining stability and gradual change.) The one significant exception was the work with Helen's parents. At one point during the therapy, she announced that she had been shopping for a gun to kill her father. We invited the family to come up from the South and have a session with Helen, her sister (who was not married), and Stewart. During this powerful two-and-a-half-hour session, the daughters confronted the parents. The father denied everything, and the mother supported her husband. (The videotape of that session had no sound, so unfortunately is of no use here.)

After that session, Helen seems more reconciled to the situation. She was no longer homicidal toward her father—"just kind of numb," to quote her. Her daughter's anorexia had been resolved after the first month. The focus for the remaining year was doing IST with Helen. She was encouraged to move on vocationally. She enrolled in a program for social work. She and her daughters participated in the martial arts.

The family therapy proceeded. Following the session above, the father changed his work schedule, and was more available to the family. His participation as the homeostatic maintainer essentially ceased. He assumed the role as Helen's partner, as someone who can protect her from her demons.

Ten-Year Follow-Up

Ten years after the beginning of treatment, I invited the family to come in for a follow-up. Neither of the twins could come, but the parents agreed. I explained that I was planning to use this interview in hopes of helping other families.

Dr. Fishman: So how are you doing? I think when we met the kids were in high school. How was high school?

Mother: It was okay. It was probably better for Julie; the social aspect never clicked for Catherine. She was very studious. She worked really hard. She got into drama. She liked that.

Father: That was a big step. She really liked that.

Mother: She stayed with that. It's something she really loves.

Dr. Fishman:	How about the eating disorders? Was there any manifestation of that in these past years since we met?
Mother:	No. Both Catherine and Julie are vegetarians.
Dr. Fishman:	So are half the kids in America.
Mother:	Right. We didn't see any indications of it. I would say that we felt that we were always worried about it. If they were stressed out, every once in a while I would notice that I kept asking, "Are you eating? Are you sure you're eating?"
Father:	Now Catherine's thinking of dieting.
Dr. Fishman:	Is she overweight?
Mother:	She's not overweight, but she's the heaviest I've ever seen her.
Father:	The heaviest she's ever been.

Both twins had done well in high school after their treatment. Julie was always the more social of the two and had a much richer social life. Both had finished college, and one was a nurse, the other a teacher. The eating disorder did not reemerge for either. They both had jobs, were in long-term relationships, and had good relationships with their parents. Julie was teaching in one of the most distressed communities in the area.

Father:	She wrote a letter to me once about the whole situation. She had a friend who was the behavior interventionist there, at the school where she works, who really helped her [with the kids]. He kind of took a liking to Julie. He was the one the kids were supposed to be sent to, and he would help her with keeping their attention. Julie had wanted to do some dinosaur project and make it realistic with real bones. She asked us about it, and we told her to get some play sand. One night, about 10 or 11 on a Sunday, I went out to KFC, and bought like 10 buckets of chicken. I specified . . . I paid extra for legs and thighs only. She cleaned them all off and used the bones. She told me in a letter that it was because of me that she didn't quit. If I wanted badly enough for her to succeed that I did what I did, then she was going to keep going. She remembered that. One night she called around 11, very upset because her boyfriend thought they should split up. He thought she was too stressed, and causing problems. He just wanted to listen to music and party, and didn't understand that she needed to study. They had it out. She called, crying, talked to Helen and then me.

As I hear this story I am reminded of the tremendous commitment of the parents to their kids when they were anorexic. It is clear that the parents have stayed involved as a backdrop, a support when the girls need them. This is a modulated distance, not the enmeshment that families with anorexia tend to manifest. I think to myself, I hope our therapy helped in the creation of this functional process.

Dr. Fishman: She's still feisty?

Father: Feisty, but very mature.

Mother: She's really got a good head on her shoulders.

Father: I never told her this, but I think what goes around comes around, and I think the way she behaved with Helen, some of the kids she worked with acted that way, too. She never reacted, though. She handled it very professionally—called the parents. But that night, she was really upset. I thought maybe he hit her or something, because she asked if she could come back home. I drove out there. I sat with her, and her boyfriend finally showed up. I know he didn't know what the hell was going on. We moved her back, and she seemed so much happier.

Mother: So much less stressed—much happier. It must not have been easy to move back.

Father: She had lost weight. Not an eating disorder, but you could tell that she was stressed. When she got back, she ate more, looked healthier. Now that the kids are gone, she [Mother] doesn't want the sweets around, but when I think back, I think I keep sweets around because of this whole thing—ice cream, cookies. I always made sure we had around the food that they liked.

Mother: This has been ongoing. I know what is driving him, but he can't stop. It makes him feel better to have everything filled up. If one box of cookies is good, 10 boxes are better.

Father: Like ice cream. Instead of getting one or two kinds, I'll buy every flavor in the freezer.

Mother: So we end up with, like, 14 kinds of ice cream.

Notable in the session to me as I observe is the easy conviviality between the spouses. The tension that haunted them in our early work seems to have diminished.

Dr. Fishman: Okay, so no evidence of eating disorder? How about. . . .

Mother:	I just wanted to say that Catherine was treated for depression. She had a really bad time that first year. It went on for a while. She saw a therapist, and a psychopharmacologist. Unfortunately, nearly every med or combination she was on, she had the worst side effects.

During the therapy with the family, I was always more concerned about Catherine, the twin that I did not treat directly. She was shy and reserved. In my notes I noted that I encouraged the parents to actively intervene to help Catherine get a richer social life. The follow-up suggested that they had not been very successful.

Of course, we cannot say that Catherine's depression resulted from the traditional treatment she received for her eating disorder. There are way too many variables. Everything that happened, including our therapy, may have contributed to the depression. Or it may simply be that she is one of the huge number of kids who go off to college and are depressed. She chose therapy because her experience in her family told her that, when you are distraught, you should seek a mental health practitioner. It shows that she was not totally alienated from the profession by her family's experience.

Father:	She had a seizure. I was so pissed off.
Mother:	She had a seizure and ended up in some hospital in New York.
Father:	She's stressed out because of her schedule, then this. I haven't changed much in wanting second opinions, and I could tell there was something with this. Here she is in the hospital, and the supposed experts were telling her all this stuff, and I said no, she's coming home. We literally took her out of there. She went back to the psychologist, and they really clicked.
Mother:	The med issue never really got solved. Unfortunately, she is struggling again with depression and intends to see someone, but is fearful of the meds.
Dr. Fishman:	She stopped taking them?
Mother:	She stopped.
Dr. Fishman:	She stopped the first year?
Mother:	No, she probably took meds for the first year. Different combinations of different things.
Dr. Fishman:	No eating disorder?
Mother:	No.

Father:	I think this is her being not sure about wanting to change professions, thinking about her boyfriend, which I think is a lot on her mind, but it's nothing like the first year, right?

One very positive bit of information: This girl who was painfully shy when I saw her now has a stable, long-term relationship.

Mother:	But she does have a history of depression, and is going through it again.
Dr. Fishman:	So how are you guys doing?
Mother:	Good.
Dr. Fishman:	How about some of the stuff we dealt with years ago? Where is all that?
Mother:	It's still there. I take medicine. I see a therapist.
Dr. Fishman:	It's under control?
Mother:	Under control.

I frankly did not want to probe. They came in to do me a favor. I did not want to stir anything up. I was, of course, curious about her chronic suicidality, but I did not see it right to ask.

Dr. Fishman:	Does it affect your relationship with your parents at all?
Mother:	No. I see my parents, but not outwardly, no.
Dr. Fishman:	Not outwardly.
Mother:	I see them. I love them. I care about them. I don't know. . . .
Dr. Fishman:	Life goes on?
Mother:	Life goes on. I still feel a little bad about it. . . .

I ask myself, "bad about what"? But I don't want to press it. They came in to do me a favor and this is not the time to pursue therapy.

Dr. Fishman:	[Later in the interview] What do you remember of our time here? How do you feel about it?
Mother:	I have a really hard time thinking about the therapy we did with Catherine and Julie. It was such a bad time, and I know we were really desperate for something that would work, and the therapy that you proposed worked, but it seemed so . . . almost inhuman. It didn't seem to be out of kindness, or gentleness, and I sometimes wonder if it could have been a different way. I hated being the person who had to police the quarter

pound of weight gain per day. It made me miserable. It nearly destroyed whatever relationship I had with Julie. We nearly destroyed each other during that. I sometimes wonder if it could have been a different way. Maybe I could have been less mad. I don't know. . . . I could have been less angry with Julie. [Tearful]

The intervention of the lunch session followed by the behavioral paradigm is very difficult to do. The parents are asked to take charge of the patient's treatment, often after years of other treatments that have failed. They must be assertive and face up to conflict rather than avoiding it. They must stand their ground and not allow certain things to happen, often upsetting both the child and themselves. Indeed, they must disregard the child's feelings, going directly against accepted precepts of parenting in our culture. It is important to say that the intervention can never be done casually. As with any crisis induction, the stakes are high. The therapist is perturbing the system beyond its comfort level. But then, why shouldn't the stakes be high? This is a life-threatening disease. Although the intervention can be upsetting to families and is certainly not pleasant for clinicians, its extraordinary power in producing favorable outcomes justifies its use. I also see an indictment toward me as the therapist. If the mother felt that she had to enforce the paradigm, I missed something profound. Nice Guy Dad seems to have, by sleight of hand, disappeared from the process. Had he been part of this enforcement, the mother's relationship would not have suffered to this extent.

Dr. Fishman: I hear what you are saying, and I agree with you. I hate doing those lunch sessions. I've done a lot of them, and they have almost always been effective. There's not much psychotherapy that is that effective. There were a lot of kids coming out of hospitals, and going into hospitals, especially in those days, and a lot of pain and suffering. I had a girl who came here, and she had been on a feeding tube for 2 years. She went through this, and it worked, but you're right. It's not pleasant at all.

Mother: I guess I'm not talking just about the therapy we did here, but the whole therapy experience—all the therapy prior to it, that was dismal . . . the whole psychiatric hospital experience for the first twin who was anorexic, Julie.

Dr. Fishman: What was that about?

Mother: Catherine was taken in to the emergency room, and they said she was anorexic. We had been trying to work with Julie to gain weight, [telling her] "You can be on the swim team if you" . . . whatever. She kept not working with us. We kept telling her that she would have to go in the hospital if she didn't comply. I don't think she believed it. They called one night, and there was a room. Catherine had come home by then, and I had to forcibly drag Julie to the hospital. She was there for . . . 6 weeks. She didn't comply at all there. She didn't eat there. The director of the program there kept taking things away, making it harder and harder, thinking she would break, and she didn't. Nothing made her turn around.

This hospital seems to have had a model of punishing the kids when they don't eat. They limited family contact severely.

Father:	It was the way they talked to her, too, telling her she was a bad person—"Why are you doing this to your parents?" She hated Helen.
Mother:	She hated me for taking her there. It affected the relationship between Julie and I. At some point, they wouldn't let me visit her anymore.
Father:	They told us one time she ran away to the cornfields. She said she got out to the fields and stopped, because she had no place to go. She couldn't go home.
Mother:	I saw her in the field that day. I didn't find out until years later that it was she. It was Julie.
Father:	She went back to talk to the director—to tell him how it affected her.
Dr. Fishman:	Helen?
Father:	Julie. When I asked her about today, she said, "You got to be kidding." I could tell she didn't want to talk. Catherine was pretty good. She said she would talk. She didn't talk too much about the therapy. She said she tried to talk to you about how to be more outgoing. Catherine said you could conduct a telephone session if she couldn't make it down here. I remember we told you that you saved their lives, but Helen had to deal with it—I didn't. You never want anyone to go through that, and I think you know better than we do what works. I remember you telling us to bring some food, bring some snacks. I remember you telling us we had to do it. I don't know if there are any improvements, or different ways, but it's stuff you just want to forget about.

Mother:	I still feel so much guilt. I am glad that they've done really well, everything's fine, but it is hard to think about that time.
Father:	It's a miracle. . . .
Dr. Fishman:	Why do you feel guilt?
Mother:	For not seeing it in the first place, initially . . . not coming up with the right . . . you know . . . everything we tried. . . .
Father:	Catherine tried to tell me. She tried to tell us. I remember her showing me an encyclopedia. I remember talking to a doctor in the hospital in the community we moved from, and him telling me he didn't think it was. . . . Catherine was trying to tell me in her own way about her own problems. I was traveling back and forth to Europe. I should have just stayed, because Helen had her own issues. It's hard enough with two parents, let alone with one not doing well. My guilt . . . if I could take it all back again . . . you always think, is there something else we could have done?
Dr. Fishman:	I think everyone who has raised an adolescent has these feelings. I think it is a fairy tale that anyone could feel like he or she raised a child perfectly. They needed to go through this. It helped them to be strong individuals and to separate from the family.
Mother:	Right. They are doing better than some of my friends' kids are doing. They are wonderful.
Father:	You told me once that the one that gives my wife the hardest time ends up being the closest. The best story was when we went to California. We didn't fly out there. We drove 3,000 miles—Julie and I. We packed and did it in 3 days. She wrote me that she didn't know of many dads who would do that, and it really meant a lot to her. It was a lot of fun. It was something that you never forget. She's learned how to deal with adversity. The school she's [teaching] in is difficult, and she's had to develop her own lesson plans, and a testing system, and discuss all of that with the principal and the teachers. She went in there with basically nothing, and I think she's good at facing adversity. Catherine is the same way, with working in a hospital, in neonatal intensive care.
Father:	Did other families you saw have the same results? Did they go through the same process, and were they successful?
Dr. Fishman:	Yes. The same process, usually with success.
Father:	What about the parents? Did you find out anything about them—the divorce rate being higher or anything?

Dr. Fishman: I have rarely seen divorce. I have heard many times that the intervention is tough, but it saved the child's life. It was very effective psychotherapy, thanks to your work as well.

DISCUSSION

The family's situation 10 years from the beginning of treatment is clearly good. The symptoms are gone and all of the family members are functioning well. The anorectic twins are in fulfilling careers. The mother, although she still takes medications, is stable. She is functioning well in her marriage, is training in a new area that greatly interests her, and has an increasingly close relationship with her children.

As the follow-up with the parents makes clear, however, the therapeutic process was extremely painful for the family. Indeed, Julie may have refused to revisit the pain by attending the session. The mother found the therapy almost inhuman, not something done out of kindness or gentleness. Having to police Julie's weight gain of a quarter of a pound per day made her into a person she hated to be. It nearly destroyed her relationship with her daughter.

At the same time, the mother's testimony vindicates the theory and challenges the common belief that limit-setting is wrong and that conflict-avoidant behavior should be allowed. The parents' impulse to surrender in the name of love and tenderness had to be forestalled. In all extreme cases, the intervention brings about a deterioration in the relationship between the youngster and the adult who won't let the child die. The mother was miserable, but the system was transformed. To the extent that the children were distanced from the parents, they were no longer available to be triangulated. They also improved their connections with their peers, which their parents experienced as a loss.

The intervention requires no less of a commitment from the clinician than from the parents; a few gestures will not suffice. The clinician is replacing the hospital. This is community-based treatment, and as such it does not have the extra supports that the hospital can offer. It takes some courage to roll up one's sleeves, profoundly unstabilize the system, and challenge the family. Yet the approach is deeply respectful of the parents: The professionals are seeing them as the agents of therapeutic change. The question is whether the parents can indeed be responsible and can be trusted to change not only their daughter but themselves and ultimately their family. Sometimes parents cave in in the face of the adolescent's opposition, and the clinician's control efforts must win out over the parents' dislike of policing, of taking charge.

The parents may, in fact, fear that their new level of intensity will lead the child to complete starvation. In my experience, that has never happened. It truly takes that new level of anger and intensity to prevent the youngster's self-destructiveness. With parental tenacity, the eating disorder disappears, if not overnight then within a few months. And, as in this case, the diminution or disappearance of symptomatology appears to be permanent.

The case of Julie's family contains a lesson about how parents succeed with this procedure. In the follow-up the mother describes the misery and self-hatred she felt in the weeks of policing Julie's weight gain, but she never backed down, and in the end she brought about the needed change. I believe she succeeded because she had a partner who supported her and coordinated with her in her struggle with the child. Her husband was there for her even when she had to become a hated person she didn't want to be. This was a truly family-based effort. But, as I said earlier, her husband may not have been there enough during the most difficult days.

There are parents that cannot do this intervention, at least not with me as their therapist. Chapter 11 discusses cases where the outcomes were not as successful, cases in which I was not able to join effectively with the parents or there was a cultural component that would not allow them to address the conflict.

Families who have the most difficulty with the intervention are those with a history of chronic, severe conflictual relationships. They are so embattled that the parents cannot work together, no matter what. Families with severe psychiatric problems also find it difficult. In Julie's family, the emergence of the anorexia provided a focus for the chronically disturbed parent. According to IST systems theory, the emergence of the symptom always serves as a focal point around which the family can avoid conflict, but in families like this the need is more intense. Helen was chronically suicidal and even, at one point, potentially homicidal.

Other parents at risk of failure are those who value their child's relationship over the child's life. Of course, there is circularity here; parents who are estranged from their spouses will tend to need and often to depend on closeness with their child or children. As we have seen in this follow-up, when the intervention is successful a distance develops between parent and child. In these enmeshed families, this distance is essential to liberate the child from triangulation and to bring the parents closer together.

In general, it is easier to join with and motivate parents who have not had severe problems such as sexual abuse in their history or who do not have too much dysfunction in their present families. Similarly, parents who do not feel defeated by many previous failures in treatment tend to do better with the intervention. The parents most at risk for becoming continually depressed as the anorexia recedes are those whose child has undergone repeated episodes of unsuccessful hospitalizations. These parents are exhausted and defeated when they are asked to replace the hospital as the site of treatment for their child. The intervention can be an extraordinary burden and sacrifice for them, especially because they are already emotionally depleted from waiting around hospitals, building expectations that were never met. Parents who have not been through repeated unsuccessful hospitalizations tend to be less exhausted and do not feel so disoriented by amelioration of the anorexia. For them, the anorexia had not been the center of their lives for many years.

Like many families, Julie's family had had the experience of being tethered to the hospital for a length of time. While Catherine was in the hospital, she was on a strict behavioral paradigm; the parents were not involved, and if she did not eat she was not allowed to see her parents. Clearly, that paradigm was not adequate to transform the family, because as one twin recovered, the other assumed the baton of anorexia. None of the interventions with Catherine allowed the transformation of the system that was needed for the anorexia to be ameliorated. Given the family's experience, it is amazing that they had the will to try a new approach. Ironically, what worked to my advantage was that they were desperate.

CONCLUSION

One focus of this chapter is the behavior paradigm that stabilizes the new structures introduced by the lunch session. Another essential component of the chapter is the IST concept of recontextualizing the family. In this case, of use were the introduction of EMDR, the family session that provided a context where Helen could address her parents regarding the sexual abuse, and the addition of medications to help stabilize Helen, even to the present.

There has been a controversy over the years between Salvador Minuchin and Jay Haley. Haley posited that the transformation of the system would put the system in a new structure that would maintain itself (personal communication, 1979). Minuchin believed that the changes in systems needed to be stabilized through additional work (personal communication, 1981). As I review this chapter, I am reminded of an interview with Bette Midler I once watched on television. They asked her what it's like to make a movie. She said it's very redundant, like working in a pineapple factory. Therapy with this family was an experience of redundancy in that it took considerable repetitive work to stabilize the new structures. I was pleased by the follow-up, seeing that they seem to have had held so far.

CHAPTER 7

Treating the Young Anorexic: The Family as the Delivery System

As the previous chapter described, the lunch session is followed up with aftercare in the form of the behavioral paradigm. If the youngster does not gain weight at a satisfactory rate, total bed rest is prescribed. This protocol places the family directly in charge of the care. To me this is the beauty of the intervention. As the child is being cared for by those who are an integral part of her life—and with whom she is deeply emotionally involved, to say the least—the behavioral paradigm itself creates ongoing pressure for the transformation of the system. In the very process of enforcing the paradigm, the parents work toward a more functional structure in which the child is no longer triangulated.

There is a profound challenge for the family when they are asked to participate in this model of care. They are challenged to move from a passive role, waiting expectantly as the experts do the job, to action: "You can't sit there and let your daughter starve to death!" Clearly, if the therapy is to succeed the family must buy into this new role. Their previous experience with clinicians, hospitals, and dashed false hopes can severely impede the joining process, or it can facilitate the process. In the case described in this chapter, the parents had exhausted all other options available to them and were willing to go with the program even at a distance.

The family as the delivery system for care makes a great deal of sense. Many anorexics and their families are left with a sense of abandonment as they go from program to program, professional to professional, medication to medication. There is a lack of continuity. Centering the treatment in the family—the one permanent element in the young person's life—ensures a much greater continuity of care. It also allows for the treatment to be developed into a system that uniquely fits the family. As the family does its work of healing, however, guidance and support are crucial. The case that follows illustrates the importance both of these factors and of their absence when they were needed.

FAITH: LIVING WITH A TUBE

The treatment of the Evans family was initiated under duress. A friend and colleague who lives in a western city told me about Faith, a girl in her church, who at age 11 had been anorectic since she was 9. During those 2 years, the family had seen psychiatrists, psychologists, and other clinicians, and none had been successful in helping the girl to eat. Faith had an indwelling tube in her throat, through which she was periodically fed. The family was desperate. They had exhausted all the options in their community, and their health insurance provider now was pushing to have the girl committed to a state mental hospital where she would be the youngest patient.

I told my colleague I would try to find someone in the family's area who worked with the structural therapy model, but numerous phone calls turned up only one possible resource: a family therapist who had been trained years before in structural therapy but had no experience with eating disorders. He lived 2 hours away, but he agreed to help with maintenance therapy.

Out of desperation, I offered to treat the family if they would fly to Philadelphia for the weekend. They did so, and I worked with them for a total of 6 hours over 2 days. The session the first day included a successful lunch session intervention. On the following day the lunch session was repeated and the behavioral paradigm was introduced: The girl had to gain a specific amount of weight every day or every other day; if she did not, she would have complete bed rest. By the end of the second day, Faith was eating readily. With the consent of all family members and Faith's medical doctors, my wife, who is a family practitioner, removed the nasogastric tube.

A Weekend of Therapy

The family that came to the weekend sessions in Philadelphia included the parents and their two daughters, Faith and Donna. Roseanne, the mother, had a job in a social service agency. The father, Lionel, a graduate of a prestigious university in the East, did not work and spent his time exploring his intellectual interests, especially in the area of the environment.

The segment below comes from an early part of our first day's session. The parents were in the therapy room without Faith, asking questions about the therapy. As we speak the father is writing down everything that is said by the other participants, so I am essentially talking to the mother and father while the father acts as the scribe.

Dr. Fishman: So what's going on, what's this all about? For 2 years she hasn't eaten, she drinks?

Mother: Right. Water and herb tea.

Father: Looking back, actually I have to tell you going over this history is not real pleasant, it's been a real trying time.

Father: Yeah . . . and looking back through some of the things—within weeks or several months she had quit eating her snacks at her friend's.

Mother: We didn't know that, though.

[Mother is looking sternly at Father as he begins his soliloquy.]

Father: We didn't know that, but she would bring her lunch home from school uneaten, then I'd fix her something to eat and she'd eat it. I don't know if this is true because we didn't really have the proper feedback from the counselors, but I think the counselors were telling her she should finish her lunch or something. This is why I thought she was just stubbornly not doing it, because they were telling her to do it. So I have no idea if this is true, but all I know is she was bringing her lunch home and then she was eating a second lunch after she came home. But there were also some things that surfaced at that time about body image: She had been looking at her stomach and so forth, but at the time she was really sick, I was really sick too, and I didn't care if I ever ate again I felt so bad. And this is why I said I don't know what this is about, because I don't know if there is only one model, if there is more than one model. My mother's friend was telling me that, like, when I mentioned we had gone to the dentist she said "oh" [he laughs]. Evidently she has a son who is, I guess he is paraplegic, he's in a wheelchair . . . people who have plastic in their bodies have to take mobs of antibiotics because it unleashes all these bacteria and so forth into your system so if you have plastic parts it can cause problems, so I don't know . . . I guess . . . I don't know the answer but I guess juvenile diabetes. . . .

Mother: But what do the plastic parts and the dentist have to do with Faith?

Mother has little patience with Father's reverie, but it is clear to me as a clinician that he is completely confused about what is going on with their daughter. They have been to too many experts—all the experts in their community and even beyond their community—and have received little guidance. Their daughter continues to refuse to eat.

Father:	Well . . . [holding his hands palms up] I mean, I don't know whether it's a medical, physiological explanation similar to juvenile diabetes, where something invades the pancreas. . . .
Dr. Fishman:	Right, but she's medically healthy.
Mother:	Right.
Dr. Fishman:	And there's no physiological reason for this, right?
Mother:	I don't think so. I think the part that I started to say about the history was that the summer before this started is, in retrospect, when I think she started to have difficulty, or at least a point where I could see something was starting, and I remember it starting when she was on this trip—for about 3 or 4 weeks, is that right? [addressing Father, who nods] And she was—I was in stripping wallpaper in this room, I spent all day doing that. I remember her kinda screaming and yelling and crying, sort of, and then I remember off and on she seemed, starting more in the winter, to be more anxious. In fact at school they wanted a conference because they noticed these anxious behaviors, like pushing her hair back and things. And I thought, well, that doesn't seem like a big deal, you know. But I noticed she spent a lot of time looking at herself. She was a little bit chunky and her stomach stuck out a little bit, so she'd be looking at herself and at times she didn't want to wear clothes that were bulky. I mean there were quite a few body image things. But. . . .
Dr. Fishman:	That sounds normal, right?
Mother:	Well, it was too—I mean, it was to the abnormal point. You couldn't really—when I took her to buy some new clothes, it was a terrible experience, because she cried and fussed and felt like she looked terrible and everything. I mean, beyond the point of the way she was before or the way she is now. And they wanted to have her tested by a speech pathologist, because she wasn't finishing sentences in class. She would start saying something and she wouldn't finish. And they wanted to know if she spoke normally at home. Because she is a very bright kid and she's always talked a lot and she's finishing sentences at home fine. So I basically, I knew she wasn't having a speech problem that was stopping her from finishing

sentences, so I didn't let them pursue that. I said, well, maybe she is feeling anxious, and I pushed for a school counselor to meet with her regularly and we had to go round three or four times and finally got that going, but I don't think that was particularly helpful, and I didn't realize . . . I mean, in retrospect you see we were in real trouble already, but at the time you don't really understand that.

The parents talk for a few minutes about the various interventions that have been tried and in many ways their hopelessness. Now I begin the intervention and talk about my model of therapy.

Dr. Fishman: Well, let me tell you what I want to talk to you about. The fact is, she should eat.

Mother: Mm-hmm.

Dr. Fishman: And you're going to have dinner.

Mother: Mm-hmm.

Dr. Fishman: And if she refuses to eat, I'm going to ask you guys to feed her.

Mother: Hmm.

Dr. Fishman: Now, does that sound crazy? I'll tell you, this model I've utilized myself with patients for 25 years. It has almost always been effective. I mean, I can't guarantee it'll work this time, but I'd be surprised if it didn't.

Father: It has always been what?

Dr. Fishman: Effective.

The father cannot believe his ears that anyone would have this level of self-confidence and would be foolhardy enough to stick out his neck to this degree. Then the father rightly wonders about the flipside of this: If it's so effective, why isn't it more widely used?

Father: To what level of bodily force? [He laughs.]

Dr. Fishman: Oh, that depends on the family. The bodily force depends on the family. I mean, for example, she will have to eat and gain a certain amount of weight or keep her weight stable or she will have to have complete bed rest with a bedpan. That will be the extent of any bodily force.

Mother: Now are you talking about [doing this] at home?

Dr. Fishman: At home.

Mother:	So it's kind of behavioral privilege model like they sometimes do in the hospital, only you're doing it at home.
Dr. Fishman:	Right, because you guys can do it forever.
Mother:	[Laughs] Well. . . .

Mother is actually right that this is a behavioral paradigm. Of course, the value is that the family is providing the intervention—and they can do it forever. Then I reassure her that in my experience that is not necessary. I have never had to prescribe feeding at home following the lunch session; mandating bed rest achieves the same purpose and is much less intrusive. I have found, however, that the bed rest paradigm is more effective if the treatment has begun with a lunch session—the initial crisis transforms the system.

Dr. Fishman:	You won't have to, but you can do it forever. The tube has got to go, not necessarily while you're here, but when she gets home.

I am trying to join with them. I know that if I tell them that the tube must go this weekend, they will see me as a snake-oil salesman. All they have known over the last 2 years is defeat. Also, of course, I don't want to promise more than I can deliver. I would rather give them a surprise.

Mother:	So what . . . maybe this is not the time to ask about these things, but how are you suggesting that be done—the tube being taken out?
Dr. Fishman:	I would just pull it out. I'd check with the doctor, of course, but I'd just pull it out.
Mother:	Mm-hmm
Father:	Well, excuse me for asking, I mean this is so obvious, where are all those other professionals? I mean—I don't want this to come out wrong—suppose she . . . how do you handle the physical health if she were to not eat anything for 2 weeks?

These people think I'm crazy. If it's so simple, why didn't the other people do it? The parents are concerned about their daughter's safety, and I don't blame them.

Dr. Fishman:	If she doesn't eat, you put the tube back in. That's the downside. You're already there.
	[Both Mother and Father laugh.]
Mother:	Right, been there a long time. You're not further down than you were before, in a certain sense.

Dr. Fishman: Right, but you guys have to be together on this. The power is in the two of you being together on this. To the extent that you are not, you will fail.

A refrain I will repeat over and over again is that the parents need to be a coherent unit. At this point in the session, the father has his hands over his mouth, his body language telling me there is quite a bit he doesn't want to say.

Father: How can you . . . you've seen how buoyant she is. How are we going to keep her in bed without watching her all the time?

Father rightly challenges their ability to keep her in bed. I see this challenge to the parents as one more opportunity to strengthen their bond.

Mother: Maybe we are watching her.
Dr. Fishman: You may have to. Or bring in other people to do it—family members, friends.
Father: I mean, why is this method effective in your experience?
Dr. Fishman: Because it's a family problem, and this corrects a lot of the family problems.

I don't want to blame the family. But they know very well that there are issues, and if I deny them I lose credibility and fall into the same conflict-avoidance pattern that has kept this family stuck for at least 2 years.

Mother: So by together you mean that we are together insisting that she stay in bed? Is that what you mean?
Dr. Fishman: And tonight in terms of her eating.
Mother: That we continue to insist?
Dr. Fishman: Sometimes more than that, sometimes physically.
Mother: Mm.
Dr. Fishman: And the fact is, you can do this every meal if you have to. She has to live a normal life.
Mother: That's why we are here, I think.
Dr. Fishman: Yeah.
Mother: But we have never managed to get to that in all the other things we've done.
Dr. Fishman: Right.

Mother:	So the things you are talking about are basically forcing her to eat right now and taking the tube out and doing the bed rest with the bedpan.
Dr. Fishman:	Yeah, and you'll see to it that she eats.
Mother:	Okay. So you're saying each meal go through the same pattern?
Dr. Fishman:	I hope not. In my experience, usually that is not the case. In about 3 weeks there will be a challenge to your authority, again, but you shouldn't have to do the feeding. But first things first, let's see to it that this is effective.
Mother:	Mm-hmm.
Father:	You don't think she has to go to an inpatient hospital to remove the tube? The tube just comes in and out, but when I say remove the tube, you said she doesn't have to be in a hospital setting when she stops her nutrition from the tube. Am I making myself clear? A lot of people that don't know about the tube, they don't realize that you just pull on one end and the other end comes out.
Dr. Fishman:	Right.
Father:	Until we came to you I was under the impression that people were contemplating that she would be in some hospital-setting care when she was on her liquid nutrition with the tube and when she tried to eat, and are you saying that would be done at home?
Dr. Fishman:	Well, I talked to the pediatrician.
Mother:	Dr. Cole?
Dr. Fishman:	Dr. Cole. I said can she eat as well [with the tube in place], and he said sure.
Mother:	[To Father] Well, you're saying does she need to be in a behavioral program back in the hospital to supervise her gradually working back to eating, is that what you're asking? Not the medical part so much.

This is really the battle for joining, the battle for leadership. Father is asking should she go back in the hospital; that had been the last recommendation, prior to their coming to Philadelphia.

Dr. Fishman:	I think you've tried that, haven't you?
Mother:	Well, initially, yeah. That was the proposal—to go through that again, I think.

Father:	Where does the antidepressant medication fit into this? Is it an important part?

Again the father is trying to reconcile in his own mind the difference between what I'm suggesting and what the other doctors have talked about for the last 2 years.

Dr. Fishman:	I don't think so. Has it helped?
Mother:	Not the central part, no.
Father:	[mumbles something] [laughs]
Dr. Fishman:	Well, it doesn't matter. If you want to keep it, keep it. It's up to you.
Mother:	If you suddenly take 'em off medication like that, is there any. . . .
Dr. Fishman:	Let's talk about that later. It's not doing anything, it's immaterial.
Mother:	Yeah, okay.
Dr. Fishman:	To answer your question, I would taper it, but that's not the point. In fact, I would keep it; if it's keeping her in a good mood, keep it. But I doubt if it's doing anything.
Mother:	[Laughing] Well, we don't know if it is or not.
Dr. Fishman:	We know one thing it's not doing.
Mother:	Right. I mean, I think it was one of the original hypotheses that if she gets over being depressed by this medicine we're giving her, then she'll. . . .
Dr. Fishman:	I understand.
Mother:	Well, we are certainly here to try anything you suggest.

Although the mother is ready to follow my protocol, the father is sitting with his finger to his temple and his fist over his mouth. What ensues is 30 minutes of the mother trying to get the father to commit to the program. I'm trying to be sensitive to their attempt to trust me in their confusion, caused by the cognitive dissonance of the conflicting models. I do come highly recommended by a good friend of theirs who is in health care, but nonetheless this is very different from what they have done in the past.

Dr. Fishman:	Ask your husband.
Mother:	[To Father] Are you?
Father:	Another question is are we just supposed to wing it on our own feelings on what to do or where to stop? My only uncertainty is

I'd feel bad that through my own blundering I forced her to harden her position about not eating.

The challenge is relevant and frankly daunting: How do they do this on their own? They are 3,000 miles away from me. Father sees a frightening parallel with another incident.

Father: I mean, when we were trying to get the tube changed once, the nurse said if you don't do this we will take you in the other room and strap you to this board and force it in. It didn't really make a lot of sense to me. It turned out the reason the tube wouldn't go in is because they had too big a tube.

Dr. Fishman: I don't think you have a choice.

I have been inducted in the rules of the family system. I start to disregard the father, and to the extent that that happens I suspect he needs all the more to have the role of taking care of his sick daughter. He has no job, and the mother essentially supports the family. In a system like this, where one member is so marginalized, it is not rare for that member to need to have a child at home, sick; caring for the child provides a sense of importance and gives direction to that person's life.

Dr. Fishman: But listen, you could just have dinner and you could do this tomorrow night. The two of you can go take a walk, whatever, and think about this.

I pull back and suggest that really I don't want to sell anything to them. They have to be willing to subscribe to this paradigm, this mode, and my leadership. In my experience, if I push too hard and the parents go through with the lunch session for me, it's not nearly as effective.

Mother: [Addressing Father] Are you saying you are worried about forcing her for fear that it will do something bad?

A good reaction, from the therapist's point of view, is the mother's challenging her husband. It is their unit that has to change for this girl to be liberated from anorexia.

Father: No, I'm saying I don't know whether we should have a repertoire of things to try when we go to eat or if we should just wing it.

Dr. Fishman: Well, I can help you with that.

Mother: [Addressing Father] He's going to be here. Are you willing to attempt doing this, or do you have other concerns about it?

Father: No, I'm willing to do it, I'm just not. . . . I'd kind of like to know the best way to approach it.

Dr. Fishman: There is no best way. You just approach it.

Mother: I mean, are you feeling overwhelmed because of all the times we've tried to get her to eat before and we couldn't get her to eat?

Father: No, I mean I would rather have done this 2 years ago if somebody had told me that this would. . . .

My sense is that unless they move decisively, he will go into smaller and smaller circles.

Dr. Fishman: You see, she's too powerful. She doesn't really have a choice not to eat.

Father: A choice. . . .

Dr. Fishman: What's her choice? She's a little girl, she eats! It's not an option. She has a responsibility, like she has a responsibility for not putting her feet on the furniture. Twenty minutes for that to barely change. She's too powerful.

At the beginning of the session the girl had sat down and lounged with her feet on the furniture. Clearly it was antagonizing the parents, but it took them 20 minutes to challenge her to get her feet off. I'm using this as the same behavioral model; if her not eating is seen as sick, they will not intervene behaviorally, but if this is a behavior problem they will be liberated to do that.

Mother: Yeah.

Dr. Fishman: And this is a manifestation of her power.

Mother: [Addressing Father] I guess I don't know exactly where you are on this. You seem kind of hesitant.

I feel sorry for the father. I feel him almost losing something. It drives him crazy that his little girl is so sick, and every cell in his body wants her to be cured and to lead a normal life, but I see his resistance because perhaps it represents some loss for him.

Father: Well, I guess I just would like. . . . I don't mean to seem hesi-
                   tant, but does that mean if she doesn't eat, does that make her
                   more powerful?

[Mother shifts her body away from Father, and Father moves away from her.
They glare at each other, then avert their eyes by looking at me.]

Dr. Fishman: Well, you'll have to find out

Father: You just said. . . .

Dr. Fishman: There's only one way to find out.

Father: You just said that we should invite her to eat, and if she doesn't
                   eat we should feed her or try to feed her. Should we give her
                   any consequences if she doesn't eat?

Dr. Fishman: Yeah, you're going to force her to eat—physically. Listen, it's
                   not pretty. I mean this is medicine, it is not. . . . I would much
                   prefer to go out with you guys to one of these lovely restau-
                   rants.

Father: But I mean are there any medical things about eating when
                   you haven't had food in your mouth for 2 years?

Dr. Fishman: Her doctors said no.

I have checked with their pediatrician beforehand, so I can refer all the
medical questions to her. That is essential—this is a partnership between
the two sides of health care.

Father: She won't gag and choke?

Dr. Fishman: I hope not.

                   [Mother and Father laugh.]

Mother: He's a doctor, he can revive her.

Mother's comment suggests to me she is with the program.

Dr. Fishman: The consequence is she may be mad as hell at you.

Mother: Mm-hmm.

Dr. Fishman: But your life is going to get easier.

Mother: That'll be a plus [laughs].

Father: Should we give her a reason why she's eating, other than it's
                   her responsibility to?

Dr. Fishman: It's up to you. It's whatever you think.

[Long pause]

| *Mother:* | [Addressing Father] Did you have any other questions you wanted to ask? |

It is notable that the father never looks at his wife.

Father:	I mean, I really tried hard to do this 2 years ago when she was ill, and she had to go into the hospital. I talked to nurses, and I have a friend who is a pediatrician in Illinois, and the best thing we could get into her was Pedialyte® [a mineral supplement], and having tried to force-feed her 2 years ago. . . .
Dr. Fishman:	Did you do it alone or with your wife?
Father:	Well, mostly. I don't remember. A lot of it was alone, because it was during the day.
Dr. Fishman:	See, it will not work with just one of you. It has to be both of you.
Father:	Why's that?
Dr. Fishman:	That's how it works in my many years of experience. But let's have dinner. If you guys don't want to [do the intervention] you can go home and think about it, but let's at least have dinner. Are you okay with that or not?
Mother:	[Addressing Father] Well, I think you and I should decide what we are doing on this before the kids come in. I guess I don't really know where you are on this. You seem very hesitant.

I leave them to talk.

The lunch session that followed was a classic lunch session where the parents succeed in getting the child to eat. At first, Faith was resistant; she locked herself in the bathroom. The parents cooperated in cajoling her out of the bathroom. Then, in the usual dynamics of the lunch session, whenever they worked together, Faith took a bite. At the end of the session, on her way out of the room she picked up a cookie and spontaneously ate it, much to her parents' amazement.

The next day we had a second lunch session. There was some initial resistance, but after that Faith began to eat and the mood lifted in the room. She ate voluntarily, with her parents sitting on each side of her. When she asked, "So I have to finish it?" her mother glanced at her father and they both said, "Yes."

In the fifth hour of our working together it was agreed by all that my wife, Dr. Tana Fishman, a family practitioner, would remove the tube.

| *Dr. Fishman:* | Are you sure you are ready for this? Is the family ready for this? |
| *Mother:* | We are ready for this. We're well ready. |

Donna: Yep

Dr. Fishman: You think it's time?

Mother: It's time.

Father: [Beamingly happy] It actually comes out all the time, it's just another one not going in is the thing that we're celebrating.

Dr. Fishman: Yeah, absolutely. I mean this is it. This is "Sayonara, tube!"

Father: It is nice to get the feeling of Philadelphia and then get to leave the tube behind. . . .

Donna: And everything that goes with it.

Dr. Fishman: And everything that goes with it, that's right.

Mother: Well, we actually have to take the pump back. . . .

[Faith is snacking on crackers when Dr. Tana Fishman enters.]

Dr. Tana Fishman: Do you replace this tube every so often?

Faith: Yeah.

Dr. Tana Fishman: And do you usually infuse this yourself, or does somebody put the liquid in for you?

Faith: Um. . . .

Dr. Tana Fishman: Who puts the liquid in?

Mother: I think she means *how* are we doing it.

[Faith takes another cracker.]

Dr. Tana Fishman: Well, no, I mean *who* does it. Do you do it, or do your parents do it, or does your sister do it? Who puts the food in?

Father: Well, it goes in by a syringe, that's all you have to do. It goes in by the pump.

Dr. Tana Fishman: Okay, and you sit with the pump then? How has this been used—at night is when it's infusing?

Father: Actually, we are just getting rid of it so. . . .

Dr. Tana Fishman: I understand, I'm just trying to figure out when she last had anything infused and how was it done.

Father: Oh. Yesterday morning was the last time.

Mother: No, wait, maybe yesterday about lunchtime, because we did some in the early afternoon by syringe.

Dr. Tana Fishman: Okay, but normally she would have to stay in one location and have it run in over a period of time?

Mother: That's what we've done also.

Dr. Tana Fishman: It has been at night while she's sleeping?

Mother: Yes.

Dr. Tana Fishman: [To Faith] And who took it out for you the last time?

Faith: I don't remember—somebody at the hospital.

Dr. Tana Fishman: Are you ready to do it?

[Faith sits up. Dr. Tana Fishman prepares her equipment then quickly removes the tube.]

Dr. Tana Fishman: Are you okay? Take a deep breath now.

Father: [Patting his daughter on the head] It's over, Faith.

Dr. Tana Fishman: Are you okay? You're pretty brave, I can tell you that.

Faith: Can I have a Kleenex®?

[Tissues are found. Everybody starts clapping.]

Follow-up

The next 6 months or so were difficult and arduous for the family and for me. The distance proved daunting. The local colleague with training in structural family therapy met with the family regularly, but he knew little about eating disorders, and by all accounts their work had no therapeutic effect on the inevitable backsliding. An occupational therapist who had been seeing the youngster for years and whom the family respected continued to supply valuable emotional support to them. We also had an informal information network in place that included Lois, the colleague who had referred the family to me and who saw them in church every week. Once, when she noted that Faith was not looking well, she called me, and I called everyone together for a meeting via speakerphone. I saw them occasionally when I was visiting in the area, and I tried to be available to them by phone, but I was mortified to learn in our follow-up interview they thought that I was far less helpful than I could and frankly should have been.

Four-Year Follow-Up

Four years after our last contact I arranged to set up a family meeting via videoconference, both to find out how the family was doing and to get their retrospective views on our long-distance therapy.

Dr. Fishman: Thanks very much for meeting with me. Now, who couldn't make it? Faith couldn't make it?

Mother:	No, Faith didn't want to be here.
Dr. Fishman:	Okay. I completely respect that. That's a chapter of her life that she may not want to revisit, and I certainly understand that. Now, how long has it been since we met?
Mother:	I believe it was in '97.
Dr. Fishman:	Right—summer of '97. You got to experience the Philadelphia humidity, I think. So, what I would like to do is to follow up on where things are, the course of things since we met, what has transpired, how Faith is doing, and how everybody else is doing as well.
Mother:	Well, she's healthy. She started doing gymnastics at a gym this summer. She's been taking community classes, and she wanted to do something more demanding. So she decided to sign up for classes. On the first night, she broke a piece of bone off her elbow and had to have surgery. So that was kind of discouraging. I went to see her, and she told me to go away. You know how 14-year-olds are. So I went and made coffee, and hung around, and then she was calling me, of course. So that was kind of discouraging, because it was very hard for her to do gymnastics and to do her other activities. But that healed up, and she's hoping to start gymnastics again over Christmas break. She's doing a lot better in terms of just starting high school. Starting middle school, I think she was very frightened, and withdrawn, and all those things. I felt some concerns sometimes. Lately, I have been finding lunches she didn't eat, things like that. So, we've talked about just weighing her once a week to make sure she's not going down unnoticed.
Dr. Fishman:	As far as you know, she's pretty stable?
Mother:	She's all right, yeah. We just had this discussion this week, so I can't . . . she looks all right.
Donna:	She's filled out.
Mother:	Yeah. She's filled out a lot, and people have commented about how much better she looks—just her whole demeanor. She looks like a high school student now. She just got back from a school trip where she did very well. She's in some very difficult classes. She's in an advanced biology class that has a college textbook, and she's ahead a year of high school math. She's handling it a lot better than she has in the past.
Dr. Fishman:	Lionel, what do you think?
Father:	Yeah, I think she's doing really quite well in high school.

Dr. Fishman: Do you have any of the sorts of concerns you had years ago?

Mother: She's eating, and seems more outgoing. . . .

Donna: I think it's more of the social aspect that makes a difference. She's really participating. She just looks a lot more mature, and is a lot more involved. That's a big part of it.

Dr. Fishman: Okay, if I could ask you to give a brief review of how things have been since we met. I know we have met various times over the years, but kind of a snapshot. You guys came here for a weekend, and we did this very difficult bed-rest protocol, which was tough, but I think perhaps ultimately effective. So if you could talk a little bit about that. It's really good to have kind of a historical document.

Mother: I think it was the middle of '97.

Dr. Fishman: July of '97, I think.

Mother: It's been a long kind of process, and if I look at the begin-ning . . . in the summer of '94, she was having a lot of crying, and yelling kinds of tantrums, and being upset a lot, and I think she was depressed, but I didn't understand that that was what it was at the time. In '95 was when she stopped eating, and we went to a number of different doctors, and psychologists, and psychiatrists, and clinics, and so on, including the medical school, and that was a 2-year period when she was on a tube. It started with 2 weeks in the hospital, and then they inserted a tube because her heart rate was going down drastically, and it was getting into a really dangerous area. That was when she turned 9, and she had a tube for 2 years, and she didn't eat anything, and nobody was able to get her to part with that.

                   So we went to Philadelphia. Then I kind of thought the prob-lem was over, and we weren't prepared for her to relapse. I think part of it was the long distance. We weren't in close con-nection with you, and maybe that would have been part of the process. If we had actually been going to you, instead of going to somebody close by. I'm sure you would agree with that. I mean, I was grateful that she started to eat during that week-end. It was totally miraculous, from our point of view. So I think we didn't have a plan laid out for what we were going to do, and she started to slide backwards again during the summer. I think it took quite a while for us to figure out something that would work that would incorporate us, and start working for her, and what you were telling us, and it was really agonizing, because it's a really strict program. You're telling your child

	that she can't do this and she can't do that, and she's lying in bed, and you're concerned about that and where that's going, and she's just getting more depressed. So finally, after about a month, I think, we figured out something that would work.
Dr. Fishman:	Can you talk about that—what your own kind of resolution was?
Mother:	I'm trying to remember. I think we ended up that if she didn't gain weight she had to eat an extra serving. Isn't that the plan we had? I haven't thought about this for a while.
Father:	I don't remember exactly, but I remember we made a menu.
Mother:	It had certain types of food, and certain amounts of cereal, and with a certain amount for different fruits, or different items that she had to eat, and we added on extra things if she didn't maintain her weight at a level that was healthy. So she could escape going to bed if she agreed to add this extra serving, or whatever the specific thing was. She could do that instead. Usually she would choose to do that. That somehow seemed to . . . and I believed we still had the negative consequence still there if she wasn't eating. Does that sound like what we were doing?
Father:	Yeah. For a smart kid, it's easy to teach the math, and take a prescriptive approach. . . . The worst was when we had the visitors and went to the local amusement park and made her stay home alone because we were led to believe that this approach was something to be adhered to, and she just kind of gave up after that. Then we had to create all this other stuff. I knew she liked to negotiate, so I tried to mix that in, and that's where we got the idea to give her the choice of staying in bed or adding something.
Mother:	I think we kind of misunderstood where you were coming from, because you were saying we needed to strictly adhere to it, and I think it was a small amount of weight loss that kept her from doing something she really loved, and we stuck to it anyway, and later in our conversations with you, you were saying, "I would have let her go." That was discouraging to us, because I always thought we were behind what you had said, and at great cost emotionally to us. My best friend was there, and she felt really bad, too, because she just happened to be visiting during this week, and we go off and do what Faith likes to do the most, which is go to this amusement park, and everybody else goes except her, and we leave her because she didn't eat the sweet roll, and her weight goes up and down so easily

that sometimes you don't even know. So we were sticking strictly to it, and we did that for a long time, and it wasn't going anywhere until we added this other element where she had a positive choice to make, and that was something that we kind of came up with on our own, incorporating that so that she could kind of negotiate in a way, in that she had a choice and she could get out of bed by agreeing to whatever food group. I mean, we were kind of in control of it—it was a limited choice—but she did have some leeway, as she saw it, I think.

I think the fact is that the parents stayed the course and that they invented a way of negotiating instead of holding to the rigid protocol because they didn't want to break her soul and wreck her spirit. Given the positive results of the lunch session and the paradigm, they didn't want to just disappear and let her have her way. So they stayed in there and modified the protocol a little bit, but they kept control.

Mother: It's not like we had a community of people who were dealing with similar things—greatly to the contrary. I was talking about the miracle cure, but they didn't know me. It's like, who is this person who just walked in off the street? There are volumes written about this [anorexia], but when I went back and I tried to read about everything that we encountered here, I didn't find anything about the things you were saying. One part of the winter before we came to you, I was seeing a psychiatrist at the medical school, and taking Faith every week for a year, and she wasn't making any progress in terms of eating, and her solution, because we didn't have medical coverage for any of this. . . . Our HMO wanted to put her in a state facility for children and adolescents. I read about the state hospital program, and it was very, very similar to what they were doing with kids in detention. You were encouraged to visit once a week if you could, and this was like in '97, when she was 10. I asked about success with kids, and they had one girl who had been there a year, and she was doing a lot better. I had some concerns about the violent kids.

I empathize with the family. They are still upset that the alternative of the state hospital was the only option offered for their 11-year-old daughter.

Father: The only alternative was to go to the state hospital.

Dr. Fishman:　You deserve a lot of credit. Tell me, during the course of the years, have there been other changes in your lives? Anything else going on?

Mother:　Between everything that was going on, I lost my job of 15 years or so. I have a new one now that is fine.

Father:　Well, I would like to preface this by saying that no one is more thankful for what you did for our family, but I really felt that after we left Philadelphia we were abandoned by you three or four times, times when I specifically asked for your help, and felt that it wasn't there. It was communicated to us in Philadelphia what to do about the bed rest thing and so forth, and I assumed that that was brought up with Dr. Peters, and either it wasn't or he didn't understand. So, we went back this time when Roseanne was taking her to the doctor, to the nutritionist to try to keep her weight from going down when she was kind of backsliding, and we ended up with a nutritionist who was really so passive and weak that it wasn't any kind of a directive thing. Then Heather [an art therapist] got alarmed because the school was giving us messages that she was acting depressed, and they knew, I guess, because there are a number of kids at school that were withdrawn, and they knew what depressed kids looked like. Then, she had been on an antidepressant because they told us in the hospital that they thought she was depressed, and I had just thrown that away a couple of weeks ago, before I needed it, and then when I needed it, I couldn't get anybody to get it so we could at least start it to see whether it made a difference. I just felt that the ownership wasn't there on your part, and when I got worried about her, I remember calling you and specifically asking you if you would oversee and direct her care with Peters, because I could see that he didn't know what to do.

The father lets me have it—and rightly so. I discuss this in detail later in the chapter.

Dr. Fishman:　Well, I apologize for that. If I hear you correctly, the continuity was not there to the extent that it should have been.

As I write this years after this meeting, I am ashamed at my answer to the father's appropriate indignation. This is my professional foxhole. These words blunt the pain—and my honesty. Did I really say "continuity"? What I really should have said is, "Please forgive me."

Mother: Yeah. It seems to me that before we got to you, we had been basically what my social worker friend calls case managing, without knowing anything about it aside from what we had learned from our own experience. I think that if you're doing something long-distance, you need to overcompensate for the distance somehow. . . . I think it would have been helpful for you . . . we were focused on the immediate thing—she's starting to eat. That was basically all we were thinking about. [It would have been helpful] to talk about the longer term, to say, "Well, this might be kind of like smoking, when you take five times to quit," or that there's some backsliding, and to be prepared for it. To me it was pretty devastating to feel like we were going back to where we were. I think it would have encouraged us to realize, "Okay, she's sliding back, but we have some tools." I felt like we got that. I don't feel the way I did then. The tools were in place, but if we could have come back to you and tell you we were having trouble, that would have been helpful. Even if we don't go there—have periodic check-ins with us, at certain specified intervals, that's what I would recommend. I felt like during that summer, we were trying to make something up with you, and I did feel like you were withdrawing. I didn't feel the withdrawing as soon, but when I had that conversation one day, when I felt like you were giving up on us, and it was very hard because you were the only person we knew in the United States that I felt had a handle on what was going on. We didn't have a backup person that I felt had the insight that you did to go to, out here or anywhere, and I didn't know where we would find that person if you left. It was very hard, I realize, for you, professionally, to be dealing with us out here.

Dr. Fishman: No, that's not an excuse, because I volunteered to do that. Clearly there was a communication problem, because once I agreed to treat you, I would never abandon you. I think what I was trying to do was to get you and Lionel on the same page, so that you would be together with your message to Faith, and to the extent that would happen, in my experience, it would be very effective. In my experience, which you know well, professionals are not very good at this.

Mother: I guess I would suggest overcompensating for the distance by making sure it's really clear that there will be check-ins at certain points. I wasn't feeling like I was being overly dependent. It's hard to think, "Okay, we know what to do." We did eventually come up with something, but when you feel like all the

	people you went to didn't know what to do . . . you see what I mean? It's scary.
Dr. Fishman:	First of all, let me apologize for that. I've learned from that now, and I appreciate that. I do know that it's always frightening. What we should have done is perhaps you should have arranged to come back, or I should have come out there, something like that.
	[Pause]
Dr. Fishman:	Let me ask you this: Are there any other suggestions?
Father:	I think, and this is just from our experience, there needs to be support for the parents or the family when they're going through this, and we were very fortunate. We had Peters [who is my friend who made the referral]. She gave me the words to use to take to the doctor, but I'm running all over town again, kind of déjà vu, driving to the pharmacy to say "Refill this," 'cause I know that I'll have to go to the doctor. You hope when it goes to the doctor they won't make a mistake and approve it. So, anyway, Lois gave me the words, and I go over to the doctor about this thing, and . . . but I think somebody needs to check that the family has some sort of support.
Dr. Fishman:	Right, I agree. So, the obvious thing is this Tower of Babel kind of situation—all these different voices.
Donna:	The challenge is to figure out how you can get all these different people to communicate and work together.
Mother:	That's what needs to be done.
Dr. Fishman:	It's beyond communication, though, in many ways, because they don't agree. Those folks that Lionel went to see, I would imagine, take a very different approach to care.
Mother:	I don't think it would have a negative effect on what you were doing in this case.
Dr. Fishman:	No, but still. . . .
Mother:	I think he [their medical doctor] did a lot of things well, but when she was relapsing, I think he was saying, "Well, she's doing okay." The doctor wasn't responding to our concerns like you were, I think.
Donna:	I mean, no one could sense better than us, because we had been around the whole time, and I think there were tiny signs that weren't overt.
Mother:	I think one of the things that was really discouraging to me in trying to figure out what to do before we got to you was, my

brother went on the Internet and got a lot of information, and . . . it's very discouraging stuff. You hear all these horrible stories . . . it does permanent brain damage and wrecks your bones, and this and that . . . and when I was asking around—how long is the program, do people need additional help—it takes months and months, and it's not clear to me that people are really over it by that point. So the idea that people don't need ongoing care, or chronic, episodic care—that's in contrast to what's happening in a lot of other avenues.

Dr. Fishman: I agree. Girls and their families shouldn't suffer the way they are. Many of the reasons for suffering are the medical treatment that's being offered to them.

Donna: Is this a chronic problem?

Dr. Fishman: To the extent that it's not ameliorated properly. To the extent that treatment is not effective, it is prolonged. Whether it's directly exacerbating the problem—it may well be exacerbating the problem. It's research that I'm doing now. We will document the effectiveness of the program.

  Well, I want to thank all three of you, and give my best to Faith as well. You've been very helpful. No one should have to go through what you guys went through.

Father: From my heart, Charlie, I really want to thank you. There's no doubt in my mind that we wouldn't have had this successful outcome without you. [Tearfully] I wanted to mention the other difficulties, but what I feel most strongly is profound thanks for saving our daughter's life.

Dr. Fishman: Thank you. The work, really, all of you did, and I am glad I could have a part in this.

Mother: I wish you could see how different she looks now.

Dr. Fishman: Well, send me a photo, if you would.

DISCUSSION

The circumstances of this case had created an unusual situation: An experienced clinician had set the stage for the family to treat their youngster's anorexia essentially by themselves. The follow-up makes clear that the family rose to the occasion. They manifested an intelligent creativity, and in so doing they furthered our theoretical understanding of how the lunch session/behavioral paradigm intervention should be used, as well as the pitfalls to be avoided. Faced with the facts that the girl was slowly gaining weight but was also pressuring the parents to abandon the paradigm so that she could have a more normal social life, the parents had to be creative.

Part of their creativity was forced upon them by what they experienced as my relative unavailability. I had clearly misunderstood their needs and was not as available to them as they seem to have needed me to be. In retrospect, this may have been therapeutically valuable; they had to muster their own resources. Indeed, my unavailability may have helped to transform the system, in what Carl Whitaker used to call the "battle for initiative" (personal communication, 1981) in which the family takes the initiative to push for change. The therapeutic misunderstanding certainly moved things in that direction. On the other hand, this may be a bit too facile; I hope it is not self-justification for sloppiness.

Like so much in psychotherapy, there is a tightrope here that must be walked. To the extent that the therapist is less available than the family needs, there is a danger that treatment will suffer. On the other hand, if the therapist is overly available, the parents are less inclined to say, "We've got to work this out together," and thereby strengthen their unit. And indeed, strengthening the parental unit is the central goal of the therapeutic work with these families. Anything that facilitates that end facilitates curing the child's anorexia nervosa.

Following our weekend sessions, the family was at risk for a long period, even though the initial 6 hours of treatment were successful. The intervention had enough positive power that the girl immediately began to eat after 2 years of self-starvation. She continued to eat spontaneously for a time, but problems arose with the parents' commitment to the protocol. They were caught between my instructions to adhere strictly to the protocol and their desire to be responsive to their daughter's needs. They didn't want to break her spirit, yet they didn't want just to let her have her way, which they had done for two very painful years. They needed guidance in how to be flexible in a context of negotiation, guidance that I was not providing when it was needed. On the amusement park issue, for example, they were surprised when I said later that I would have let her go.

In time, these intelligent, loving parents realized in my absence that there needed to be flexibility, and they invented a way of negotiating. When her weight fell below the specified minimum, Faith was given a choice of bed rest or eating an extra portion of food. Instead of stopping their policing, they created choice-making possibilities for their daughter. There was, of course, the danger that if the parents became too tolerant, the structure would collapse and the structural dysfunction surrounding the girl would resurface. In this case, the father and mother acted very well together, I believe. They were able to set up a system that provided both the appropriate latitude and the appropriate structure.

Indeed, the experience of this family indicates to me that our behavioral paradigm needs to be modified so that when we empower the parents we can allow them negotiating powers without losing control. After the initial period of bed rest, when the child is no longer in danger (and the parents are very likely exhausted), a second stage may be called for, introducing more flexibility in the choice-making possibilities. Choice making is a formidable part of the theory: After the parents take charge, the patient has to choose to eat to get them off her back. In a second stage, choices can be negotiated with the patient around the paradigm. There are dangers to this flexibility, however. Treatment is impeded drastically if the negotiation goes too far one way or the other and may be paralyzed if the focus of the negotiation becomes content issues such as the correct minimum daily calories. When this happens, the treatment system is mirroring the driven obsessiveness of many anorexics, seen, for example, in their cutting their grapes into small pieces.

It is important to remember that our treatment of these adolescents must be coherent with their developmental needs. I see the negotiation model just described as an essential template for the family to use in the years to come as other issues arise, as the family makes a smooth transition from the clinical situation to normal development.

The generic notion of the parents being the center of the therapy is pivotal, regardless of the proximity of the therapist. Faith's parents arrived at a successful balance of being strict and creating positive choice, and they got results. On reflection, however, I am not advocating long-distance care to families. I am not sure it is adequate. If competent clinical care is unavailable locally, and if the protocols can be sufficiently clear, it may work. Reliable and affordable video conferencing technology would certainly help.

FRONT LINE FALLACIES

This case and the cases in the two preceding chapters elicit a number of lesson caveats against several popular biases about the treatment of anorexia.

Bias 1: The expert must be in charge. In this therapy, the parents are in charge. They are not only the treatment modality, they are the case managers. They provide the continuity and therapeutic consistency. To the extent that they serve this function, their system is transforming and their pathologies are consumed by the collective process of healing their child.

Bias 2: Conflict is bad for treatment. Conflict needs to be manifested in psychosomatic families to transform them. The lunch session is profoundly effective, and the behavioral paradigm is powerful in maintaining the intensity and forcing the parents to continue functioning as a unit.

Bias 3: Therapeutic crises should be avoided. The therapist must be willing to create a crisis. Indeed, it is the crisis that is curative; it is the emergence of conflict that transforms these overly protective systems.

Bias 4: Institutions are the ideal place for the treatment of anorectics. The corollary of putting the parents in charge of the care is that institutions are not reliably there for families over time. Often institutions tend to peripheralize families, and often it is unclear who has the ultimate authority and accountability. In the IST model, hospitalization is used only when the patient is too frail to be treated as an outpatient.

Bias 5: Medications are the key to successful treatment of anorectics. Medications are only adjunctive, as the American Psychiatric Association guidelines say (2000b). Many therapies focus only on the depression. Indeed, these young people may be depressed, but there is a broader systemic phenomenon that must be addressed.

Bias 6: Teamwork is not important, and nonprofessional support is irrelevant. It is absurd to say that the family is completely responsible for the youngster's care. A team of professionals and friends is needed to support the parents and enhance their efforts. There must be a medical doctor working with the mental health clinician. It is the pediatrician who determines whether the child needs to go into the hospital. In the case of Faith's family, the local support team was there; I was the only one who was not there to the extent that I would like to and should have been.

CHAPTER 8

Bulimia

> Conflict precedes change; all of nature is based on conflict;
> conflict is a natural part of growing.
> —Don Coghis, Mohican Nation

As was indicated in chapter 2, there are less data supporting the effectiveness of family therapy with bulimia nervosa. In my experience, however, the model fits just as well. The treatment tends to be more difficult because bulimics tend to be older, so there is not always a close family context with which to work. Nevertheless, as this difficult case demonstrates, the problem yields well to a clinical model such as intensive structural therapy (IST) that transforms the patient's social context. In this severe case, for over 2 years this 19-year-old young man had been purging to such an extent that his serum potassium had dropped to near fatal levels. A brief treatment course of less than 3 months ameliorated the problem, which was confirmed by a 6-year follow-up.

Brad was referred to me when his family changed health insurers. He was 19 years old, he had been purging for over 2 years. He had been hospitalized 15 times, and in addition he frequently was rushed to the emergency room to be given intravenous potassium. A week before our first meeting, he had been hospitalized with a potassium level that his physician said "was so low, he shouldn't have been alive."

During the 2 years of purging, Brad had been in individual therapy. He had also been on Prozac, although he manifested no suicidal ideation, thought disorder, or severe depression. Nothing was working, and he and his parents were apparently deeply pessimistic about whether he would ever get better and get back on a normal developmental track. Because of the frequent medical interventions he had been unable to keep up at school and had dropped out in the 11th grade.

The family reported that the problem had begun when the young man's maternal grandmother died suddenly of a heart attack at the age of 61. According to the mother, "the family fell apart." The mother was briefly hospitalized for depression, and in addition to his bulimic behavior, Brad began to assert his autonomy in more typical adolescent ways, such as drinking and reckless driving.

The family showed manifestations of a psychosomatic family—triangulation, conflict avoidance, and rigidity—and there was enmeshment between Brad and his mother. Of course, what parent would not attempt to be as close as possible to a child in imminent danger of dying? The family reported, however, that they had always been very close. The father, by contrast, rarely spoke, and he seemed very comfortable with his silence. I was struck by his inaction in many situations, even those concerning his dangerously ill son. What was not consistent with the psychosomatic model was Brad's behavior; he not only did not avoid conflict but also was a hell-raiser in the community. He drank heavily, did not follow the rules, and partied frequently.

My treatment assumptions were very different from those of the therapist who had treated Brad in individual therapy. The system had to be transformed to free Brad from his bulimia as soon as possible, as it was a life-threatening situation. Even though this was a chronic problem, only the induction of a crisis would transform the system. And while Brad certainly had developmental issues, it was his contemporary system that was maintaining his problems and thus had to be the target of the care. The developmental changes would follow.

FIRST SESSION

Present at the first session were Brad, both his parents, and his cousin. The interview was motivational and goal-setting as well as diagnostic—what was the context that maintained such a severe and unusual problem? The young man was eager to change his life and agreed readily that lying to me would be counterproductive, for we wouldn't know if we were making any progress. We established the following protocol, comparable to the paradigm used with younger anorectic patients: Brad would have his potassium level measured every morning. If it was within the normal range, Brad would go about his normal day. If it was dangerously low, he would have complete bed rest, enforced by his mother. Ideally, both parents should be there to enforce the protocol, but his father was a factory worker and could not afford the time away from his job. (They had little financial stability. They lived in a poor, inner-city area and the father had little flexibility regarding time away from work.) We therefore expanded the pool of help for the parents and brought in members of the extended family and friends to support the mother.

Dr. Fishman:	So things are not particularly good, huh?
Mother:	No.
Dr. Fishman:	[To Brad] How are you feeling?
Mother:	He's gotten used to his potassium being low, so it doesn't bother him; he doesn't know when it's real low like that.
Dr. Fishman:	[To Brad] Do you feel it, when your potassium is low?
Brad:	Not as much as I could before, but I can feel it. Before I could tell. Now, I can't feel it as much.
Dr. Fishman:	What are you thinking?
Brad:	I'm scared.
Dr. Fishman:	[To Father] How about you?
Father:	I'm frustrated, that's for sure. I see a lot of it [the vomit], especially when I take the trash out.
Mother:	What can you do?
Dr. Fishman:	That's the issue. What can be done to help him, to stop this?
Mother:	I made him stay home from work on Saturday, and he seemed to be okay. Sunday, Monday, and yesterday he went to work. I got a call from Dr. Nelson saying his potassium was low, that he needed to stay home. It's frustrating. It's hard. I don't know how much more of it I can handle.
Dr. Fishman:	What are your options?
Mother:	I don't have any options but to take care of him. I'm not gonna throw him out on the street. I know I have to take care of him, but I'm scared. I want him to get it back together. I can't make him stop vomiting. He has to do it, but I want him to do it.
Dr. Fishman:	Is this the kind of thing when you wake up in the morning, and you feel, okay, you're gonna get rid of this thing. . . .
Mother:	I don't wake up in the morning feeling that, because I know how the day's gonna go. He [Father] wakes up in the morning to come in the kitchen with you [Brad].

Sunday night I caught him with a big bowl of ice cream. I said, "Don't you think that's a little bit too much?" He said, "No, I'll be okay." About 10 minutes after he ate it, he went upstairs. He threw up out the window of my house—in my yard, and my neighbor's yard. I told him to use a toilet like a person would. It's disgusting. My house is stained with vomit. I caught him red-handed. We had words. I told him I was disgusted, and frustrated. I can't take this anymore. |

Dr. Fishman: Okay, let's take a break, so I can just talk to Brad.

[Parents leave room.]

Dr. Fishman: So, do you feel guilty when you eat?

Brad: Sometimes. When I don't feel good after I eat, I feel real guilty that I ate it. I know I shouldn't try to eat that much.

Dr. Fishman: Do you eat anything that you don't throw up?

Brad: Yeah. I don't want this to happen anymore, because I'll go back to the hospital. I was able to keep down everything there.

This is the classic situation with hospitalization: The symptoms remit because the individual is out of the context that maintains the symptoms. This the classic "parentectomy," where asthmatic children would be sent away from their families to the mountains. They improved—until they returned home.

Dr. Fishman: You didn't throw up anything?

Brad: I was feeling like I was gonna throw up at the hospital, when I first went in. They gave me a tray, and I ate it, and I just went to sleep, even though I felt sick.

Dr. Fishman: If we're gonna work together, you gotta let me know. Sometimes the patient will lie to me, and then I can't help.

Brad: That would be stupid. Then they get nothing out of the treatment. They would just be sitting here telling stories.

Dr. Fishman: That's a very good point.

Brad: I want to get better. I won't do that. I want to get better. I don't want to be like this no more. I can't keep going on like this. I hate throwing up, and I hate being this way. Sometimes all I think about is food. I don't want to be like that all my life.

Dr. Fishman: So you don't like this anymore?

Brad: No. I don't want to have this problem no more. I want to get on with my life.

Dr. Fishman: Are you seeing friends this week?

I am thinking let's find some strengths. Does he have a supportive social system of friends? If so, it is a valuable context to tap to help him normalize his life. It would help his transition out of home, which is developmentally appropriate for him in our culture.

Brad: Yeah, I'm seeing a couple this week.

Dr. Fishman: How about a girlfriend?

Brad: I couldn't get hold of her to make plans. I always go over to her house and spend time with her. Her mom likes me a lot. She'll do just about anything for me, her mom. One time her mom was making banana pudding, and she didn't make it because her daughter wanted it, she made it because I wanted it, and it has potassium in it.

Dr. Fishman: What does your girlfriend look like?

Brad: I have a picture [shows it to Dr. Fishman].

Dr. Fishman: Your girlfriend's really cute.

Brad: She's always been my family, too. She really cares a lot about me.

Dr. Fishman: Do you have a romantic relationship?

Brad: Yeah.

Dr. Fishman: That's good.

Brad: We talk to each other about everything. She talks to me about her problems, and I talk to her about mine. I talk to her mom about everything, too.

Dr. Fishman: Can you kiss her?

If is it is a sexual relationship, it may be a context that can help as a support in his differentiating. If is it is more of cousin situation and their families are friends, it may be less useful.

Brad: Mm-hmm.

Dr. Fishman: That's even better than talking about problems, you know. [Brad laughs.] One thing is, if you get better, when you get better, you could go to the shore with her, Ocean City or something.

His girlfriend sounds more like a cousin, a home-away-from-home type thing. This is not the kind of relationship that we would expect to help him trapeze out of his family (like trapeze artists, one way of leaving relationships is that the person does not let go of one hand without first taking hold of another). But diagnostically, it is a good sign that he has such a friend.

Brad: That would be real nice.

Dr. Fishman:	You could drive down, hold hands, not talk about your problems at all, and just talk about life.
Brad:	I'd love that.
Dr. Fishman:	You'll get your life back, you know.
Brad:	I'm tired of running in this cycle. I want it to be over with, and just have good times, a normal life.
Dr. Fishman:	Brad, your potassium is so low—
Brad:	It got real low—
Dr. Fishman:	You shouldn't be alive.
Brad:	That's what the doctor told me. He said if this happened to someone who wasn't used to it, it would kill him.
Dr. Fishman:	What's your girlfriend's name?
Brad:	Sandra.
Dr. Fishman:	What would you do to take Sandra to the beach?
Brad:	I would do anything.
Dr. Fishman:	So what's the goal? Healthy family? Healthy person? I'm not sure you can do it yourself, without your family. Are you and Sandra going out this weekend?
Brad:	Yeah.
Dr. Fishman:	You could go to the beach.
Brad:	Yeah. That would be nice. We used to go when I was little—for 2 weeks every summer. I remember going to Atlantic City when I was little.
Dr. Fishman:	What beach would you go to with Sandra?
Brad:	It doesn't matter.
Dr. Fishman:	Wildwood?
Brad:	It's maybe an hour ride. And I would. . . .
Dr. Fishman:	So let's get your parents back and talk together for a few minutes.

[Parents reenter room.]

In this conversation I am joining with Brad and trying to focus on the positive. This is the search-for-strength technique described in *Family Therapy Techniques* (Minuchin & Fishman, 1981). Focusing on the non-pathological, developmentally appropriate aspects of people is the most human and loving way to be with them. In part, patients change for their therapists. If I see Brad as functional, it is likely that he will want to prove me right. If, on the contrary, I see him as dysfunctional, the chances are he will not want to disappoint me. I also want to have as sturdy a relationship as possible with Brad, considering the intervention I am about to suggest. For the same reason, I chat briefly with Brad's cousin and parents when they come back in the room.

Dr. Fishman:	[To cousin] What are you doing this Sunday?
Mark:	Hanging with friends. Work.
	[Several family members talk at once about the job, which cousin got through mother's sister.]
Mother:	I have four brothers and four sisters.

I am glad to hear this, because additional family members means more support for the family during this period. This is especially important in terms of monitoring Brad with the protocol. Now we move on to the introduction of the behavioral protocol.

Dr. Fishman:	Here's what has to happen, I think. We need to monitor Brad's potassium, every day. I talked to Dr. Nelson. If the potassium is not at the level where it should be, he's in bed. He can have a bedpan. He's gotta stay in bed. The two of you [to parents] need to make sure he stays in bed. Okay?

[Everyone agrees to these terms.]

Dr. Fishman:	[To parents] Do you know Sandra?

I then switch back to the girlfriend. This saltatory intervention in therapy, carrying a number of different themes simultaneously and jumping from one to the other, I learned from my work with Carl Whitaker. I find it is a way of modulating the tension in the room: As the tension rises, I go to a less charged, mostly conversational topic.

Mother:	Yeah, we know Sandra.
Dr. Fishman:	Is she okay?
Mother:	Yeah, she's a good girl.
Dr. Fishman:	Are there any questions about the protocol? It is of life and death importance that is begun immediately!

Back to the tension!

A CRISIS SESSION

Things were progressing well. A few weeks later, however, the family system went into crisis. Brad had been willing to adhere to the protocol for a time, but then his purging escalated. One evening he refused to stay in his room. He became violent, and when his mother went to the police he left the house. The following session represented a turnaround in the therapy. Because I was away, my colleague was the therapist in this crisis session. Although she was a part of our eating disorders program, her orientation as a therapist was somewhat different from my own.

The therapist asked to see Brad alone at the beginning of the session. The short segment that follows gives a sense of Brad's subjective experience of his compulsion to purge.

Therapist:	You can stay, Brad. I just want to talk to you first—just the two of us, okay? Brad, is there something going on that you would just like to talk about privately?
Brad:	No.
Therapist:	Something bothering you, something changed, something happening?
Brad:	The only thing that is really bothering me is that I can't—I hate not being able to do all the things that Mark can do. [They are the same age.] But obviously getting sick isn't going to help that.
Therapist:	Well, you know that, so what's up?
Brad:	I've been getting sick. Not every day, but every once in a while. I left it in my room, in bags.
Therapist:	Yeah. When did that start, Brad?

The major question is why today, why this weekend or last week for that matter, did things unravel? Being able to unearth these interpersonal stressors allows the therapist to direct therapy toward an efficient cessation of the problem. The homeostasis has changed—from his controlling the purging, to the present situation of no control. What patterns are maintaining this new status quo?

Brad:	About a couple of weeks ago. The last time I think was on Saturday.
Therapist:	The first time was a couple of weeks ago?
Brad:	Yeah. I haven't thrown up since Saturday, but I haven't been eating that much either since then.

Therapist:	So do you think you're angry at Mark?
Brad:	I'm not angry. I'm angry at myself.
Therapist:	So when you're angry with yourself, you think that's when you throw up?
Brad:	Yeah.
Therapist:	Yeah. So you're angry with yourself for what reason?
Brad:	For *being* sick. So I get sick.

Being angry with himself for being sick is an extremely understandable reaction. It is also profoundly homeostatic. To the extent that his problem is addressed through that lens, at no point does he challenge others to modify their behavior, which may be causing the stress that's making him symptomatic.

Therapist:	Then it kind of becomes a circle, like a vicious circle? So you're angry with yourself for being sick. Can you say more about that?
Brad:	I wish I never started. I hate being like this. Every time I eat, my food just comes up in my mouth, so I have to swallow it back down.
Therapist:	But there are times when you are *making* yourself throw up?
Brad:	Not really. Sometimes I think I've eaten too much and it will just come up, but I don't really make myself throw up anymore.

When people say "not really," I assume that they are really answering in the affirmative. He does make himself sick.

Therapist:	Well, what—you said you were throwing up and saving it?
Therapist:	I would have to throw up so I wouldn't go to the bathroom so no one would notice so I would throw up in my bedroom and throw up in a bag.
Therapist:	Ah ha.
Brad:	But my food just comes up that way, a lot of times, after I eat. It'll just come up in my mouth and I'll swallow it down a lot of times.
Therapist:	Are there things that really make you so angry that you just want to—you feel violent?
Brad:	Yeah, sometimes I feel violent, but I don't know really why.
Therapist:	Are you angry with anyone else besides yourself?

Exploring his anger at himself leads nowhere. He has had this problem for 2 years, why is he suddenly so angry at himself that he resumes the bulimia? This is what we need to know: Who has created the present stress? Who has made him angry?

Brad:	Not now.
Therapist:	Hmm. I think this is something that we really need to explore, because it has the potential of being pretty dangerous. I mean, not your anger, your throwing up. I mean the way your anger is coming out. Do you know what I mean?

The therapist brings up the medical aspect, adding intensity; the symptom is dangerous. I would then have put on my prospector's helmet and sought those relationships and patterns that are causing the stress.

Brad:	Yeah, I know what you mean.
Therapist:	Right. What do you think about the danger part of it?
Brad:	It's *real* dangerous, like a heart attack could be caused.
Therapist:	Well, how do you explain that your potassiums were—you know, like last week, they were all normal?

She is going medical—going to symptoms and not addressing the cutting edge of the problem, the relationship that is obliging him to purge. The therapist's behavior is isomorphic with the conflict avoidance of the psychosomatic symptom. It is much easier to hide behind the professional cloak than to roll up your sleeves and push the system, which dealing with the conflicts they are experiencing would have done.

The therapist then invites the parents back into the room.

Therapist:	So we are having this special meeting because of concern, great concern. There is big concern on your part [indicating Mother]. Does Brad know what your concern is?
Mother:	Oh, yeah, he knows. He knows that sometimes we feel like we're wasting our time and our money, that sometimes we feel like he's going to fall back down and either die or be back in the hospital again. He's aware of our fears.
Therapist:	[Addressing the parents] What do you—either one of you, whichever one of you feels can answer this question—what do you feel has happened, what's your perception? I mean, things changed for a while. What's happening?

Mother:	Personally, I think—John's not going to agree with this, but I think it's an attention grabber, because when he sees me giving the girls time or taking time for myself, he falls.

Mother's reaction that this is an "attention grabber" is extraordinary to me, because it is the rare psychosomatic family that looks at the manifest symptoms in behavioral ways. It is true that Brad's presentation is very different from that of the usual bulimic, perhaps because he is male. Unlike the common picture of the bulimic as a shrinking violet, phobic of conflict, this boy is a hell-raiser, but not in the family. Within that context it is very easy to see Mother's perspective on Brad's purging.

As I reviewed the video of the session when I returned, the distance being manifested by the family fascinated me. In the framework of symptomatic behavior as "mad" or "bad," psychosomatic families invariably see the sick child as "mad"—as ill. That they have no control. A lot of the therapy we use is designed to reframe the behavior as bad behavior, because if it's bad, family members can distance themselves from the individual. The structural goal is to increase the distance in this enmeshed system. The mother's statement that she sees this as bad behavior suggests that I as a clinician may need to reconsider my assessment and diagnosis of this young man and his family. I ask myself, am I missing something, and may Brad and his family not respond to the protocol I have designed? Or, as was probably the case, was the mother speaking within the context of enmeshment—how people who are very close lash out? It is not true distance, because everybody knows that they do not mean what they are saying. She would never, in a thousand years, act on her accusation and ask Brad to move out.

Finally, from the perspective of the symptom serving a function in the family, Brad is improving, thus presenting less of a focus to diffuse the conflict in the system. For years, the bulimia has been the focal point. In particular, the stress, especially between the mother and her emotionally absent husband, had been diffused by Brad's symptom. Now Brad as a manipulator—an attention grabber—may function as a deflector.

Therapist:	[addressing Father] What about you, Brad?
Father:	[To the therapist] It's like you can't reach him. You can't give him the room he needs, where he should be. He actually wants to be treated like a little kid.
Therapist:	[Addressing Brad] What do you think about that, Brad?
Brad:	I don't want to . . . that's the last thing I want to be treated like.
Mother:	Then how come every time you get a little bit of space you crumble again? Every time you're not underneath my thumb, you crumble.

Brad:	I don't know.

From a family systems perspective, Brad would not be aware of the pressure on him by the system to be symptomatic. I see it as a "sixth" sense controlling members of a system.

Therapist:	Do you think that happens, what your Mom and Dad are saying?
Brad:	Yeah, I think it does happen, but I don't want to be treated like that, I hate being treated like that.
Mother:	Well, we don't want to treat you like that. Believe me, that's not what we want. We want you to be an adult and to be treated like an adult, but it's impossible when we have the fear that you're going to drop dead all of a sudden. And that *is* my fear. Friday night, Saturday night, when I tried to put him in his room and he kicked the door off, I did go to the police. They can't do nothing about the eating disorder, but if there are any more outbursts in our home, when he's destroying our home, they *can* come and remove him. That's not something I want to do neither, but I can't have my house destroyed.

The question is, is this an eating disorder? Is it a behavioral manifestation? Or is this something that began behaviorally and then became a compulsion, as sometimes happens with anorexia? It may well be that the family still has the lens of bad behavior for this boy but that in reality he has as little control of his purging as the anorexic girls in the preceding chapters have of their self-starvation. The origins were somewhat different in the sense that the anorexic girls—the overly compliant adolescent girls—were expressing themselves in a Gandhi-like passive resistance. Brad's expression came from another mindset, that of a young man raising hell, but each one led into a compulsion, within which they had no control. For both the bulimic and the anorexics, it is a monkey on their backs; they do not have conscious control. Regardless of the diagnosis, their family systems were similar—there were the psychosomatic family characteristics such as enmeshment, triangulation, rigidity, and diffusion of conflict. There was conflict, but it was tantrums and not interpersonal conflict, as such conflict continued to be avoided.

Therapist:	What about that, Brad? What happened, what made you feel so violent or so distraught to kick the door down?

Brad:	I didn't want the door shut, 'cause it stunk up there.
Mother:	Why did it stink? Your throw-up.
Father:	I mean, how many bags of throw-up?
Brad:	Ten.
Mother:	Can we ask you why you don't use the toilet?
Brad:	I don't know. 'Cause I guess I don't want to be. . . .
Mother:	You don't want to be caught.
Brad:	Yeah.
Father:	But you hide it anyways behind. . . .
Mother:	Yeah, I mean we cleaned out the basement. . . .
Therapist:	What is this about being caught? What is that for you?
Brad:	I hate throwing up. I don't know why.
Therapist:	You feel ashamed?
Brad:	Yeah.
Mother:	But I've told you before, there is nothing to be ashamed about. We know you have this problem. Your sisters know it, Mark knows it. There should be. . . .
Brad:	It makes me feel real dumb.
Mother:	I understand that, but there should be no reason for you to be embarrassed or ashamed, because everyone in the house knows you have this problem.

The mother flips: Suddenly it's not behavior, it's a problem, it's medical. There are a number of ways of looking at this. One is that the family may indeed capitulate when faced with this behavior; they do not maintain the behavioral perspective that allows them to distance and manifest consequences. I introduced a behavioral paradigm that made it impossible, or at least very difficult, for Brad to continue this behavior. Because it was behavioral and had to do with being accountable, he had no way out; he couldn't hide behind the illness defense. I must emphasize again that the real power of the paradigm is not that it is a facile chess move, trapping the young man, but a powerful lever to transform the family. Mother's statement does support my earlier speculation that her criticism of Brad—"his behavior is an attention grabber"—is a lover's criticism, stemming out of enmeshment.

By the end of the session we still don't know what the contemporary social pressures were to precipitate his increased purging, other than the speculations mentioned.

Mother:	I've thrown numerous glasses, numerous Tupperware away. You went upstairs and threw up on your floor. That's disgusting! We found 10 bags with at least two quarts of vomit in each, hidden, surrounding his bed.
Therapist:	That's sounds more like . . . more than just something just coming up. When you say it just comes up automatically, so much comes up, everything that you've eaten comes up?
Brad:	A lot of it.

Before the conclusion of the session, we do learn more about this fragile system.

Mother:	And you do know that when we put you to bed before it *did* help.
Brad:	That's not what did it, 'cause I threw up all over my bed.
Mother:	What did it then?
Brad:	When you burnt down.
Mother:	When I had a nervous breakdown?
Brad:	Yeah.
Therapist:	What's this about a nervous breakdown?
Mother:	I thought he OD'd on potassium pills. I found two empty bottles of potassium up in his bedroom, and I thought he OD'd on them. And my body shook uncontrollably for an hour. I believe I had a slight nervous breakdown then.
Therapist:	When was this?
Mother:	Maybe June. Do I have to be admitted to a hospital, a psychiatric ward with a nervous breakdown, to make you realize?
Therapist:	Can we go back to the very beginning of when this first started? I recall you saying that this started just about the time when your [addressing Mother] mother died? Can you tell me a little bit about that time and what was going on and how your mother died and what the situation was. . . .
Mother:	Brad was always very close with my mother. She had a massive heart attack.
Therapist:	So it was very sudden?
Mother:	Very sudden. . . .
Therapist:	Did she have any . . .
Mother:	She had heart problems, she had two heart attacks when I was younger, but she was on medication, she had been at the doc-

tor's, the doctor said she was okay as long as she stayed on the medication. My daughter found her dead in the living room. We all went over there; he [referring to Brad] was off with his friends. I found him, Mark told him that Mom-Mom died.

Therapist: How old was she?

Mother: Sixty-one. He reacted the way I expected him to: he punched a couple of walls. Then I asked him please . . . I lost touch a bit with reality after my Mom died.

Therapist: What do you mean when you say you lost touch with reality?

Mother: I functioned as a mother. I did what I had to do, not because I wanted to, because I had to do it. I wanted my mother back, I wanted to watch her grow old, I wanted her to see my kids have kids. Me and my sisters took turns taking care of my father and my brother [12 years old when their mother died]. He [referring to Brad] refused to go with me, so I left him home with his father, but he went on a little joy-ride. I had asked him not to drink . . . he had a little drinking problem there for a while. I don't know if it was his way of dealing with her death or hiding the fact that she died.

Therapist: Did it start about that time, when he had the drinking problem?

Father: He was drinking heavily, very heavily.

Mother: Yeah, because we were in the process of being evicted from our home because of his drinking.

Therapist: So how long had that been going on? Brad, did it *start* when your grandmother died, or were you drinking before she died?

Brad: No, before.

Mother: And my mother had actually mentioned bulimia to me before she died.

Therapist: What did she say?

Mother: She thought Brad was bulimic because I would talk to her about him vomiting. [Pause] I did lose a lot of time myself. I didn't want to go on.

Therapist: [To Father] What was your reaction to your mother-in-law's death?

Father: Shock, because it was sudden.

Therapist: How did you see your wife's relationship with her mom?

Father: It was very close.

Therapist: You talked to each other every day?

Mother:	Yeah, she lived about three blocks from me. And I crumbled bad.
Therapist:	Okay, so it affected everyone in the family? And she was a pretty important person?
Mother:	Yes, she was the role model. She was the rock that held us all together. If I couldn't get something through to Brad, I would call my mother up and she would say [to Brad] the exact same words that I would say but because my mother said it, it was gold. If my mum said it, "Okay, I'll do it." If I said it, "You're a moron, you don't know what you're talking about." So I used my mother a lot on him. It worked, it made things easier. He wouldn't go against her for nothing. And I was very proud of their relationship, I wasn't jealous of it at all. In fact, before she died he spent every weekend with her.
Mother:	Sometimes I feel like I was robbed of my grieving time for her because of this illness. But then again this illness brought me back to reality. I had to face the fact that she wasn't coming back and that I had to pull her strength out of me somehow.

This statement is an indication of the function of Brad's symptom in the system—Mom's focus on it diffuses Mom's sadness. Of course, there is a circularity to this, to the extent that she does not go through the grieving process and continues to need a distraction. To the extent that she has a distraction, she doesn't go through the grieving process. . . .

Therapist:	Well, you certainly have had to be very strong.
Mother:	I try. Some days it's wrong, especially when you think your son's dying, especially when you don't know if they are doing it on purpose, when I *know* he can stop it if he wants to. [Addressing Brad] You have, you've got it under control, and I know you can do it.
Therapist:	So, Brad, did this throwing up start before your grandmother died?
Brad:	Yeah, a little bit.
	[Parents and Brad dispute when it first began.]
Therapist:	The process had begun, but it really hadn't gotten out of control?
Mother:	No, not where it was controlling him.
Therapist:	See, the reason that I bring up the painful situation surrounding your mother's death is I think it was such a huge loss in the family for everybody that everybody reacted to it, and no one, I

think, has really had a chance to mourn the way families usually have the time to do that.

The session ended inconclusively. It was clear to me when I saw the
videotape the next day that we did not have the answer as to why the bulimia had exacerbated. I presumed that even though Brad was improving,
the system had not transformed. The structure was still the same: Father
was essentially absent from Mother. Indeed, the crisis at home in the week
following the therapy session, as the family implemented the protocol with
a resistant young man, seems to have been the crisis that transformed the
system. What transpired was the turnaround in therapy.

After this session the paradigm was enhanced. One of the adults, especially the father or Uncle Tom, had to be there with Brad at all times. The
father used his vacation time to stay home with Brad. He and his wife,
often with the support of Brad's uncle, saw to it that the protocol was followed. As the graph (Figure 1) shows, following this week, his potassium
steadily rose.

In retrospect, years later, I believe that the extent to which the parents were able to distance themselves from Brad and see the situation behaviorally helped them to adhere to the paradigm. It was the crisis
around the paradigm that resulted in Brad's cessation of the purging.
When we met that next weekend, the parents were thoughtful. They were
sobered by the realization that they had to work closely together in addressing Brad's problems. While this may not be a great insight to many
people, especially to family therapists, it was indeed profound to them.
And the power of their seeing that this new approach resulted in their
son's ceasing his purging—virtually overnight—was profound enough, I
believe, to maintain the new structure of the system. It gave them an operational roadmap that would decrease the likelihood that the purging
would resume. In my opinion, learning to function as a unit is one of the
powerful attributes of the IST model of therapy. As the follow-up to this
case shows, it was indeed the lesson that the couple derived from the
treatment.

There undeniably is intrusiveness in this intervention. One might say
that Brad's room had greater psychological significance than just as a place
where he slept; it was his "safe zone," his refuge from the family that allowed him to avoid the conflict that the vomit evinced. The fact that the intervention happened there, his being in bed in that place, had greater
significance in part because he had no place to hide. But the intrusion in all
of these interventions is indeed intended to create what the cyberneticists
would call a "runaway." The system implodes to such an extent that the
entire system seeks to redress the boundaries.

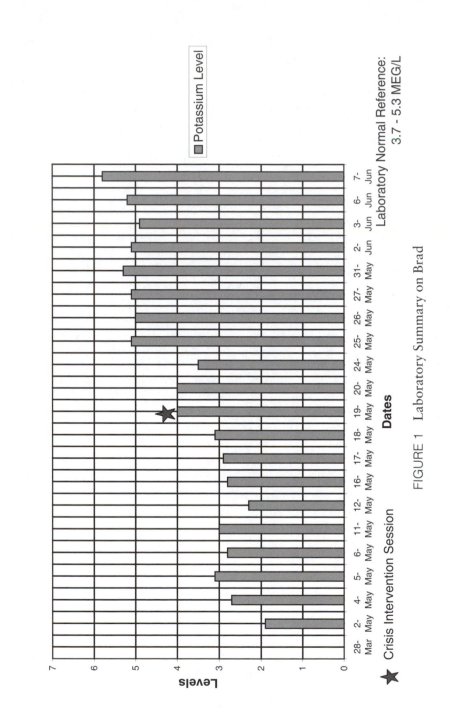

FIGURE 1   Laboratory Summary on Brad

SIX-YEAR FOLLOW-UP

With some anxiety, I called the family. We had not had contact, and frankly, after a very short duration of treatment, I had concerns. It was 6 years after our first session that I invited the family to come in for a follow-up session. Present were Brad and both his parents. Brad was no longer the gangly, frail, anorectic-looking adolescent; he had filled out into a robust, healthy young man.

Dr. Fishman: How are things?

Mother: Good, good, very good. Brad's problem never returned after our work together.

Needless to say, this was music to my ears.

Dr. Fishman: Yeah?

Mother: And nobody knows what triggered it to stop?

That worries me. I was hoping that she would see the connection between the system change and the cessation of symptoms. But this does not surprise me—it is the rare family that shares our clinical lens. This is not a model that puts much reliance on insight; families just seem to have different ways of behaving together.

Dr. Fishman: Well, we have some theories. I've got some theories.

Mother: You've got some theories—are you going to share them with us?

Dr. Fishman: Let me see if I can share them with you. Part of it is that your family changed. The family changed, I think, and when systems change, kids get better.

Mother: You mean as far as us two [pointing to Father] working as a unit?

Mother was with the program! She knew that there had been a major change at home.

Father: Yeah.

Mother: Yeah, 'cause towards the end there, he was helping out a lot more!

Father: Yeah, I didn't have to go home as much because of problems with Brad.

Mother:	Yeah, I mean, you were giving me more backing, more moral. . . .
Father:	I told different guys at work anyway, but I didn't realize a lot of this stuff was going on.

I think that's about the extent men share with their pals!

Dr. Fishman:	It was a tough period for everyone.
Mother:	Yeah.
Dr. Fishman:	It was really tough, wasn't it?
Father:	Mmm.
Mother:	Even for the girls, it was hard on them, it was real hard on them.
Father:	Yeah.
Mother:	'Cause my youngest was just in kindergarten when we started. She remembers you [looking at Brad] falling and scaring her. She felt like she was neglected.
Dr. Fishman:	Well, she made you pay, didn't she?
Mother:	Oh boy, she made me pay.

Mother means that when her daughter was in her adolescence she raised hell; she challenged all the rules, especially her mother's authority.

Mother:	Yeah, I've paid big time. She really did feel that I neglected her. I just kept trying, kept saying, if you had been the sick one, I would have been at the hospital with you. I just did what I could do and what I felt that I had to do. Yeah, she made me pay for that. And I've got another child entering adolescence.

This is a common occurrence in families where one child has been ill or problematic. The other kids receive less attention and often suffer. The corollary is the fact that the parents, in this case the mother it appears, feels guilty for neglecting the other child or children. These kids are then at risk of being treated differently: Their parents give them milder consequences for misbehavior because they feel guilty.

We also must be aware that the system may not have restructured as much as we had hoped and that the daughter took on the role of "the problematic child." This role, as I have said, serves the function of diffusing the conflict in the system—as per the psychosomatic model. On the

other hand, the adolescent's behavior appears to be tame and pretty normal—as compared to her brother's.

Dr. Fishman:	Oh yeah, but she'll be easy.
Mother:	[To Brad] Yeah, you never gave me a hard time.
Brad:	I gave him [points to Father] a hard time.
Mother:	Yeah, and then the girls don't give him a hard time; the girls give it to me.
Father:	[To Brad] But then you gave you a hard time.
Brad:	Yes, I gave me a real hard time.
Mother:	Yeah, he beat himself up, he beat himself up.
Brad:	Yeah, I wish I never did it; I lost three of the best years of my life, that's the worst of it.
Dr. Fishman:	Well, yeah, everybody says that in retrospect.
Brad:	I tried to make up for it when I got better.
Mother:	Boy, did you, I was going to say. Because he kind of went from being a kid who was in the house all of the time to party ani-mal. A few tickets here, a few this, a few that, and in the begin-ning I thought, okay, he is just alive and living, okay, it's all okay, and then the tickets got to be a little bit more than they should have been, yeah, got a bit heavy. But he's grown up, so those days he's slowed down too.
Dr. Fishman:	Right, now let me ask you this. How are your teeth, because the vomiting is very hard on teeth.
Brad:	The bottoms are rotted.
Dr. Fishman:	Wow.
Mother:	His teeth are bad.
Dr. Fishman:	You'll have to have some dental work at some point, perhaps.
Mother:	Umm, yeah, when I first thought I'd take him to the dentist, they told me there was no enamel, so there was nothing to bond anything to, so he's got to have major teeth work.
Dr. Fishman:	[To Brad] What kind of job do you have at this point?
Brad:	Roofing.
Dr. Fishman:	Roofing?
Brad:	It's a hard job, roofing.
Dr. Fishman:	I can imagine!
Brad:	Real hard job.

Dr. Fishman:	Yeah.
Brad:	The money's good.
Dr. Fishman:	Is it?
Brad:	Yeah, real good, and they pay double where he is [points to Father].
Father:	Hah.
Dr. Fishman:	And you don't have the risk?
Brad:	Yeah.
Dr. Fishman:	This is risky work.
Brad:	Yeah, it's hard work, sometimes I'm so tired, I just want to go to bed.
Dr. Fishman:	Yeah. What do you have on your tongue?
Mother:	It's a piercing.
Dr. Fishman:	It's not through your tongue is it?
Brad:	Yeah.
Dr. Fishman:	It's through your tongue?!!

I think my reaction shows my age and what circles I travel in.

Mother:	Show him.
[Brad shows tongue.]	
Dr. Fishman:	And do all your friends have this as well?
Brad:	A couple of them. I've had it for three years.
Dr. Fishman:	You know, you opened your mouth and I saw it glister, a little sparkle in there. [Pause] So what are your plans for the future?
Brad:	I don't know. I only have a plan [for] right now. I'm working right now. I want my own place. I don't want to do the roofing forever.
Dr. Fishman:	Yeah, it's a young man's job.
Brad:	Yeah, I see guys doing it at 50 and 60, but I don't want to be doing it.
Dr. Fishman:	It's tough, dangerous.
Brad:	I only want to do it now. I don't want to go back to school. . . .
Dr. Fishman:	What is your thinking?
Brad:	It's the future, and there'll be a job out there.
Dr. Fishman:	Oh yeah, you bet. You did very well in school, didn't you?
Brad:	Yeah, when I tried.

Dr. Fishman:	When you tried, on a good day, right?
Mother:	He was actually at a genius level, but he never excelled himself.
Brad:	I got good grades up until high school, and I got good grades while I was playing sports, and then when I stopped playing sports they went downhill. [Brad reflects.]
Mother:	In the beginning, you were terrible, because you didn't want anything to eat because you threw up everything.
Dr. Fishman:	Yeah, well, it was a nightmare. You've woken up now, right?
Brad:	Yeah.
Dr. Fishman:	You're awake now, right?
[All agree.]	
Mother:	Fully awake.
Dr. Fishman:	Fully awake, right, that's a good way to put it. [Later] Were there any lessons that you learned, from the illness and the therapy? I'm going to ask everybody that question.
Brad:	Don't try bulimia.
Dr. Fishman:	I'm sorry?
Brad:	Don't try bulimia.
Dr. Fishman:	Don't try bulimia, okay, and what else?
Mother:	I don't know if there were any lessons. It's just, just . . . um, motherhood.
Dr. Fishman:	Yeah, but you got to learn how to deal with it, you know, what it was all about.
Mother:	It was a lot easier having other people and knowing it wasn't just us going through it, and listening to other people's stories too, that was a lot easier, it didn't feel so isolated.

Mother is referring to the parents groups I held during my program.

Brad:	Learned a lot about nutrition.
Father:	Yeah, and then learning that the other one [anorexia], which was very similar to . . . anorexia and bulimia weren't too far off.
Dr. Fishman:	Right, absolutely.
Brad:	I learned a lot about potassium.
Brad:	I couldn't, I'd throw them up, and pills were a lot easier to keep down. But those are the different things you find out down the road. Now we've learned a real lot about nutrition, I could be a nutritionist now.

Dr. Fishman:	You could do that. [Brad nods head] It's probably safer than roofing, anyway.
Brad:	A lot.
Dr. Fishman:	Okay, that's all the questions I have. Thanks for coming in. Good to see you.
Mother:	Yeah, it was nice seeing you. When you see other people from the group, tell them we were asking about them.
Dr. Fishman:	Sure, definitely.
Mother:	I'm glad to hear everybody is doing good.
Dr. Fishman:	Those I have spoken to. And maybe in five years I'll call you back.
Mother:	And hopefully I'll have a grandkid by then.
Dr. Fishman:	[To Brad] Great to see you. You really have changed, you're grown up.
Brad:	Thank God.
Mother:	It was nice seeing you again. I'm just glad it was on a better footing this time.
Dr. Fishman:	Oh yeah, absolutely.
Mother:	I don't want anybody to have to go through that.
Dr. Fishman:	Yeah, well, you've all worked hard.
Mother:	Yeah, I guess it was a battle worth fighting.
Dr. Fishman:	Oh you bet, big time.
Brad:	I'm still here.

DISCUSSION

Brad did not present as a typical young man with an eating disorder. He lacked at least some of the characteristics of a bulimic. This young man showed no fear of being fat, no signs of dissatisfaction with self-image, and no prominent desire to attain the culture's ideal of thinness. The vomiting was not driven by fear of gaining weight. Indeed, he did not fit the *DSM-IV* criteria: He lacked the body weight distortion and the compensatory behaviors. On the other hand, Russell (1979), in his paper describing thirty bulimic patients, found that these patients are generally different from anorectics in their extroversion and impulsiveness and their tendency to sexual acting out. Brad may have been a youngster who began with a transient legitimate GI tract problem, symptoms of being unable to keep the food down, that eventually got captured at the service of larger family dynamics until he became a compulsive purger. His peers also seem to have been important in the inception of the problem; he recounted that he used to vomit to make his friends laugh. One could speculate that he was socially ill at ease if he had to resort to a parlor trick such as this.

Whatever the background of Brad's bulimic behavior, it soon developed into a stabilizing force in his psychosomatic family. His grandmother, who had been his mother's mainstay in bringing up her children, died suddenly, leaving the mother bereft. The father was not there for her, frequently away from home and distant even when at home. She became depressed and was hospitalized for a time prior to the onset of purging. Brad's becoming symptomatic stabilized the system. He threw up constantly, concealing bags of vomit for his parents to find. He combined this behavior with other misconduct such as drunk driving. His dangerously low potassium levels and close brushes with death galvanized the family's attention and defused the anger in the parental system.

Nevertheless Brad showed a warm relationship with his endlessly forgiving mother, who began to look for new ways to handle the bulimia. She became more concerned with where he vomited (it should be in the toilet, not in bags or on the floor) than with the fact of his vomiting. That is, she became more behaviorally oriented, wanting to put limits on his behavior rather than eradicate it. This drift toward setting limits was capitalized on by the crisis induction therapy paradigm that I introduced: that Brad be restricted to bed if his potassium was low.

The parents finally had some control, which, by the way, was never hateful or too aggressive. This fact may be relevant to theory. Mother was strong, yet she never rejected him; their warm, comfortable relationship was still there. The crisis induction tactic was no immediate magic bullet, however. Mother did not pull back so that Father could step in immediately. The turning point occurred when Brad refused to stay in bed. The recruitment of Father and his family to enforce the paradigm turned the corner on the problem. Brad's chart shows that shortly after that crisis, the purging ceased.

Why did the treatment work? One cannot deny that it was effective: 6 years later none of the presenting symptoms are present. Beyond that, the system has changed; the young man is more autonomous, and the parents are somewhat closer and working as a unit. The crisis induction clearly correlated with the cessation of the symptom. The structural family issues cannot easily explain the young man's remarkable transformation, however. We could even be skeptical and suggest that the system did not change very much, or very enduringly, but that what changed is that other children in the family took on the mantle of symptom bearer. Brad's younger sister in particular was giving his mother a very hard time.

The broader contextual issues were also important to Brad's recovery. In IST we attempt to transform clients' systems by helping them connect with corrective extrafamilial contexts. Work was such a context for Brad. In part, work took him away from his compulsive purging because he wanted to keep his job. Also, as he recovered, his social life improved. He became more sociable in a developmentally appropriate manner.

In summary, as I reflect on this therapy, I am impressed by the power of the model. This is not complex family therapy theory—this is basic Structural Therapy concepts–create boundaries between generations and strengthen the subsystems, especially the parental. What is new is data such as presented in this chapter. A few months' work to restructure the system and 6 years later, the problems are still gone–and all of the family members continue to do well.

CHAPTER 9

Compulsive Overeating

> Ah, but a man's reach should exceed his grasp.
> —Robert Browning, "Andrea del Sarto"

Compulsive overeating is an immensely difficult problem to treat. Generally a lifelong problem, it is health endangering and often socially paralyzing. In its treatment it presents a somewhat different challenge from anorexia and bulimia, which are socially maintained; for most morbidly obese people, there is a biological component (Pi-Sunyer, 2000). Even when there are biological factors, however, there is always the question of the degree to which stress is exacerbating the patient's vulnerability, and it is that aspect that I address in treatment.

In the case that follows, there was an especially daunting element to the patient's situation: She had no immediate family available. As we have seen in the preceding cases, the profound power of the approach is with the family. Indeed, the family—the people with whom the patient is most closely involved—represents the delivery system of the therapeutic techniques. In this case, however, the patient was not a teenager living with concerned parents but an adult living at a distance, both physically and emotionally, from her family. The technique used here was to scan her context for difficult relationships, identify key isomorphs, and support her as she addressed these patterns.

Eating disorders in later life are the most difficult to treat. The problems, by definition, are tenacious; the person has usually had the difficulties for many years. Many of these patients are limited both physically as a result of the ravages of the disease, and socially from the social withdrawal that results from the opprobrium generated by their appearance. The corollaries of the social withdrawal are cognitive and affective retreat.

BETSY: ISOLATED AND OVERWEIGHT

Betsy was 39 years old when she called me, saying that I had helped her friend with her anorexia and that she hoped I could help her with her own weight problem. She was 5'10" and weighed 350 pounds. Struggling with the demons of compulsive overeating, she had been in numerous weight-loss programs to no effect.

Betsy was divorced, after having been married for 8 years. She had no children. In the 10 years since the breakup of her marriage, she had had no relationships with men and had lived a celibate life. She was extremely isolated. She was not close to any members of her family, who all lived at some distance. Her mother had Alzheimer's disease, and her father had partnered with another woman, whom Betsy knew only slightly. She had a casual relationship with her three siblings and their spouses. She had one good friend and a number of co-workers in the social service agency where she was employed.

By her own admission, Betsy was terrified of conflict. Whenever conflict arose or even threatened to arise, she would turn into a "sniveling wimp" and eat uncontrollably.

There were a number of goals for our therapy, all of them connected. The first was to overcome Betsy's terror of conflict. According to a simple repression theory, her socially generated yet unexpressed fury led to her binge eating; to the extent that she avoided conflict, she ate compulsively. As my friend Virginia Satir would say, "The body says what the mouth won't" (personal communication, 1981).

Closely tied to her fear of conflict was Betsy's seeming inability to have an intimate relationship. For there to be true intimacy, conflict must emerge and be resolved. If the capacity to address and resolve conflict is lacking, a certain distance must be maintained. Thus, the paradox is that one can safely be intimate only if one can have an independent voice and not be lost in the relationship.

Of course, there was circularity in Betsy's conflict avoidance and her social isolation. The more she avoided the conflict of social situations, the more she ate and the more isolated she became. In turn, her isolation compounded her eating, making her less vulnerable to public opprobrium and leaving her alone at home with her refrigerator. An immediate goal of therapy was therefore to address Betsy's social isolation. Without close friends and family to support her, it would be harder for her to overcome her self-doubts and summon the nerve to overcome her tendency to avoid conflict.

Building a Therapeutic Context

One of the tools of intensive structural therapy (IST), is to recontextualize the client's system—to bring in contexts that enhance transformation. This was especially important in Betsy's case, because she had no spouse or significant partner. I started with the obvious, her extended family. I invited her father, his partner, and her siblings and their spouses to come to Philadelphia, and we had multi-hour sessions over a weekend. These meetings were pleasant, but of no direct use to the treatment. Betsy's was a distant family, polite almost to a fault; if there were conflicts, they did not emerge in these sessions. Nor would they contribute to her socialization; they were too far away, both physically and emotionally. In retrospect, the real value was in Betsy's gathering the courage to invite her "perfect" family to come to family therapy sessions. Therapy was more than a foreign concept to them, it was anathema.

In the absence of family support, other contexts were needed to recontextualize Betsy. First, she was encouraged to date. For the first time in a number of years, she began to go out with men. Dating was brought up as one of the numerous contexts that we would introduce in therapy that would be potentially conflictual. Addressing the conflict in these situations would indeed create profound changes in Betsy. She expressed considerable apprehension about doing so, but like a good soldier she cooperated.

The second new context we introduced, the martial arts, also called for her to be a good soldier. Betsy was being treated in an eating disorders program that I designed and directed, and one of the contexts we used was a martial arts program with which we worked closely. Why the martial arts? The motto of the program we worked with was "Go to the heart of danger; there you will find safety." That could be the motto of eating disorders treatment in the IST model. In offering patients a means of defending themselves, it gives them confidence in themselves, especially when they are in conflictual relationships. This can be especially important for women. Betsy's social isolation was undermining her confidence to address troublesome interpersonal conflicts, and to the extent that she did not address conflict, she would always have trouble achieving emotional intimacy.

It should be said that an intervention such as martial arts must be carefully monitored, to be sure that it is meeting the needs of the client. Our program had established a relationship with a *tae kwon do* program whose philosophy meshed with ours and focused on building clients' confidence in self-defense with a practical, nondogmatic style. I took the training myself, and a female staff member participated in some of the groups to monitor how sensitive they were to the different needs of our eating disorder clients.

For Betsy, the martial arts did indeed prove beneficial, as she reported in the first follow-up we did, a few months after the conclusion of therapy.

Dr. Fishman: How were the martial arts useful?

Betsy: When I found out I had to do martial arts, I didn't think I could do it, to begin to accomplish something like that. I was mortified and terrified, and miserable. Within 4 weeks I began to love it. . . . There are four major things that have happened. One was that I did not know that I was afraid that I couldn't take care of myself in certain situations. I thought, I'm so independent, I can sit on people. Who's going to threaten a woman of 350 pounds? I didn't know that the knowledge I could defend myself in a clinch would be so important to my own self-esteem. Second, I was sure that he [martial arts instructor] had never worked with overweight people before, and he'd make fun, but he was so understanding. He helped me. Rather than demand what a person of 85 pounds would do, he would demand I'd do the best I can do. Third, the active exercises—he paced it. The fourth thing was being able to work with other people in the program at martial arts. All of us had misgivings about our abilities. The others would offer encouragement.

Dr. Fishman: How do you think it's affected your relationships in your life outside the program?

Betsy: A couple of major ways. Like, the date I had that didn't go real well, and I realized at one point that I was grateful that I knew martial arts, and I actually said to this man, "Are you aware I've been taking martial arts?" And he said, "Why do you think you'd have to do that?" And I said, "It comes in pretty useful." And in 5 minutes he was gone. Unconsciously, it just sprang to the fore that I knew I was in a tight position, probably a dangerous position. I would have done what he wanted to do, and it was clearly not what I wanted to do, and I had a means to tell him no. The other thing is, when I tell people I do martial arts, they want to do it, too. They've noticed the difference in me; they want that, too. It's a very important program. Looking back at it now, I can't believe I dreaded it.

Addressing Conflict

The martial arts seemed to be a very useful context; in fact, it was only in the 7-year follow-up that I learned how important it had been to her over the years. Her participation in the program was a marker for change number one. The next contextual marker would be her demonstration that she could address conflict in situations that she thought important. Here, I am making a distinction between assertiveness training and taking on people who represent important relationships, people with whom she is emotionally involved or people she needs professionally. These are situations where she has a lot to lose; they are more difficult, and they lead to more profound change. By contrast, the traditional assertiveness training program is often acontextual; it is between strangers.

Here, our work floundered for a time. I could not find an important context within which to support, coach, and challenge Betsy in dealing with conflict. The group therapy in the program proved to be weak, lacking in intensity because none of the people had any enduring relationships with one another, as they would have in a family therapy context. Then one day, Betsy came into a session, bristling. She had realized that she was being sexually harassed.

For some time Betsy had been receiving sexually explicit letters and phone calls from Edward, a man she knew slightly through his family, who were friends of her family. She found the letters upsetting, but it had not occurred to her to mention them in our sessions. What triggered her realization was the testimony of Anita Hill at the confirmation hearings for Clarence Thomas's appointment to the Supreme Court. The hearings were dramatic. Hill galvanized the country with her accusations that Thomas had sexually harassed her when she worked for him in the Justice Department, and the challenging and even bullying responses of the white male senators made her testimony even more compelling. As a result, sexual harassment became an issue that appears to be permanently fixed in American sexual politics.

The following excerpt is from the session in which Betsy brought the letters up in therapy. A female co-therapist is in the room with us.

Betsy: [Holding a piece of paper] You know the Thomas hearings? I had my first out of control weekend since I started this [program]. And I was racking my brain. I went grocery shopping on Saturday night and bought some fruits and vegetables, and I spotted this bag of potato rolls and I ate them all at once. I know I don't do well with something like that—eat them all at once. I can't describe it, it's like I had to get them. I told myself a lie—you don't have to eat them all, you can eat one, you don't have to eat the whole thing. Well, within 2 days I had eaten the whole thing. They are Pennsylvania Dutch, they're really good. Anyway, it was the first time in a long time that the food has controlled me. That's what scared me. I went into the office and Joy said, "What is going on?" And I said, "I got another one of the letters, Joy." She asked, "When did you get it?" I said, " Friday morning."

Then I realized I never told you about them. That amazes me, that I haven't told you about this. This is a guy . . . I have known his mom and stepfather for about 10 years. I met him for the first time in 1982 or '83. This was one of those passing things, then he moved into the area from DC. There are more problems in that family than you could possibly imagine. Whoever isn't in prison for God knows what, and they are alcoholics and drug addicts. . . . His mother I get along with fine.

Co-therapist: Is this the man you used to be involved with?

Betsy: No, this is a man who I met, him and his wife, through friends. He told me that they need some counseling. Now I just do peer counseling through our church. His mom said, "Well, maybe you can help. They have two little kids and they are ready for divorce." Well, my first mistake was to offer to go to his apartment in Jersey. Like, a 10:00 meeting with both of them. Unbeknownst to me, she wasn't there when I got there. He said she would be there in a minute. Well, I became very uncomfortable. The topic became very sexual. He kept talking about his wife could not satisfy him—he was oversexed, she was undersexed, or something.

So I kept trying to change the subject and asking, "Where is your wife?" He would say, "She will be here any minute." And this [went on] for two and a half hours—you talk about no boundaries and stuff. Finally, he told me he had always loved me and when we first met he knew that we were soulmates, and that we would be together and all this kind of stuff—I didn't know the guy from Adam. I remember feeling frightened, that this was out of control. I would say that I have to go, and he would say his wife would be there in 10 minutes.

Finally, he said that he wanted to show me an album that he had in his bedroom. I said, "I've got to go." I think I lied, I said, "I have an appointment." I said, "Your wife isn't here. I don't know where she is, but I have to go." And I left. Before I left he handed me a letter, and he said, "Don't open it until you get home." [Holding the present letter away from her body, with a disgusted expression on her face.] It told me what he wanted to do, how he wanted to do it—it was very explicit. The language was like, I am embarrassed to even mention it.

Well, did I tell anybody about that one? I don't think I did—I was afraid to. . . . Two weeks later I got another letter. He apologized for anything that might have offended me. He was "just pouring out his heart," "needed to talk to someone," I was there. With the rest of the letter being as sexual as the first one. With every third line saying, "I hope I am not offending you." That is the one I showed to my board of trustees. I asked, "This letter I got and I have to know how to address it." So one of the board members sat down with me and we wrote a letter to him. I just didn't know what to do. And all the while, I must tell you, part of me was flattered—I hate to admit it—that someone could actually be sexually attracted to me with this body. Part of me was flattered by it. The other part of me was terrified, because he does have a violent temper. We sent the letter, and the letters stopped for a few months and then they started up again. He has called two times. Each time he has called I start talking around the lines of the sexual business. We kept all of the letters.

After changing her address, Betsy continued to get the letters.

Betsy: About that time I got a real strange phone call. The woman said she was from Macy's in New York and they were checking up on accounts and they wanted to know my PO box and wanted to know my residential address. I said send it to the post office box. When I hung up, it worried me. Was Edward trying to find my home address? I never gave them the address, but it never occurred to me—so when I got this letter on Friday I'm reading and thinking, we're on the same page. I got up to the third page and I thought, holy, holy, holy shit, this man is, you know what, this man is sexually harassing me. . . . I just got it on Friday. It doesn't say things about my honey pot or anything like that in there, but on the last page he invites me to a hotel so that we can talk. So that he can do with me what he knows that I want and what I need and that type of stuff. I almost had the sense that when he was writing these letters he was masturbating or something. . . . This has been going a year and a half, a year and nine months about.

The Intervention: Betsy Confronts Edward

Here was an opportunity for Betsy to take on the challenge of facing conflict and dealing with it directly. We arranged for her to call Edward from the therapy room in my presence and that of my co-therapist. We sat in a small circle around a speakerphone.

Dr. Fishman: In various places like divorce court they have a sign that says, "This is the first day of the rest of your life." Let's pretend this is indeed the first day of the rest of your life—that you will tolerate no more of this!

Betsy: All right.

Dr. Fishman: A person is pushing you around and you're so nice and so enthusiastic and you're such a wimp when it comes to addressing conflict.

Betsy: A sniveling wimp.

Dr. Fishman: So how are you not going to be like that? Why don't you do the opposite of what you are afraid of doing?

Betsy: The thing I do not want to do is what I term pissing him off. Up until the last couple of days, I didn't think he was pushing me around.

Clearly her fear of not "pissing him off" is the isomorphic pattern that has allowed the situation to be continued. It has led to the stress and anger that she soothes with her compulsive overeating.

Betsy: The sadness of it, it wasn't until the Hill hearing that I realized what he was doing and that it was sexual harassment. That I began to realize that maybe something was not healthy about this. I began to realize then it was not healthy, it is more than sick, and I mean . . . my own guilt about, it's my fault, but it's not, but I'm guilty about somehow responding to the fact that somebody thinks I'm sexually desirable. Even admitting it to you that there has been that part of me that has . . . it's like, how low can I get in self-respect?

Co-therapist: Women tend to blame the victim.

Betsy: Those letters—he's living in lala land. This is a fantasy on his part that has nothing to do with reality. I have in no way, shape, or form ever given him even the slightest encouragement that there was any interest on my part with him. This has always been a one-sided thing, and it's a fantasy. I don't want the letters. I want the letters to stop.

Co-therapist: What will happen if they don't? What will you do?

Betsy: I may even tell him that after this weekend of watching the hearings I realized that this is a form of sexual harassment.

Co-therapist: You're still being very nice.

Betsy: And I just want him to stop. He's going to be pissed.

Co-therapist:	Usually men who are abusive are passive and are very afraid of conflict. . . . When someone challenges their authority they often back off.
Betsy [with a nervous voice]:	What I want to do and what I will do when I get on the phone are two different things, but what I want to do is tell him that, you are not going to agree with this, but explain why I've been so nice to him and never given him any indication that these have been offensive to me. I've been real nice about it. Letters will come and even when I've written letters back to him and the Board has been very clear and concise that we cannot have anymore contact, that he needed to have a male sexual counselor—I couldn't do it anymore, that he should break contact and just get help. I don't believe in any way ever, in any of the letters, or phone contact or even in personal contacts, when I would visit his mum and he would be there, never in any way did I give him any hint that these letters frightened me. Actually, I didn't even know that they frightened me until this weekend, but I just knew after reading one I would get real uncomfortable. So what I could do, may do, is say, "Listen, Edward, you've been sending me these letters for about a year and a half. I've been reading them, feeling very uncomfortable about them, trying to let you know in the best way I know how that you shouldn't be sending them. That you need to stop and get your life in order. I can't help you, you need other help. You haven't been able to hear me. Now I need to tell you in a real clear way that you cannot send any more of these letters. You absolutely cannot. Whatever you are feeling, going through, you need help from somebody else. I cannot give it. The letters must stop, the phone calls must stop, any contact between us two, must stop.
Dr. Fishman:	Do you think that's strong enough, or will he see it as part of a game because it is such a change of face?
Betsy:	He may not think I'm serious. I can tell him that I just realized this weekend that this is very serious. Much more serious than I ever even thought before. And that if they don't stop then I will have to file for sexual harassment.
Dr. Fishman:	Not strong enough, not strong enough.
Betsy:	I'll have to go an extra hour of karate a day.

What I'm doing as she prepares to make the phone call is setting up a situation where she addresses the conflict directly. For months she has skirted around the issue. Part of her avoidance, of course, is not completely irrational; she is physically afraid of the man. But if she does not address this, she is a hostage and is in greater personal danger. The structure we are setting up, an enactment where she addresses him by telephone, is of course a safer way for her to confront him.

As we are speaking Betsy is reading his letters over and glancing at the telephone.

Dr. Fishman: You've shown it to the police and the police think it's sexual harassment.

Betsy: [Gasps and grabs her neck] That's very strong. . . .

Dr. Fishman: This is the first day of the rest of your life, and you go to these people who are pushing you around and push yourself around and you gain weight.

Betsy: Oh, boy, you're probably right, it's worse than the cops telling his mother. I could tell his mother.

In my experience incompetent people like Edward very frequently have discernable social supports such as parents who still treat them as young, irresponsible individuals. They are forgiven and not held accountable. With people who act like children I always speculate who in their lives is still treating them like a child. From a developmental perspective, this man indeed is acting like an irresponsible delinquent boy in whom the testosterone is charging unfettered.

Betsy: [Picking up the receiver] Please God let him be home. [Dials.]

Dr. Fishman: You have to tell him your phone doesn't work, you can only use the speakerphone. So we can all listen.

[Edward answers the phone after two rings.]

Betsy: Hello, Edward, this is Betsy.

Edward: Hi.

Betsy: My phone is acting up and I have got you on the speakerphone, so if it sounds like echoing and stuff, that's why. I received your letter on Friday, and, uh, Edward; we have to talk about this, Edward. You've been sending me letters now for about a year and a half, and these letters have been very, very explicit, and the Board has spoken to you and has told you that nothing that we say, nothing that we do must be misconstrued, your wife should be able to listen in on all the conversations, she should be able to read all of these letters, and anything that you say to me like that.

Edward: How come?

Betsy: How come? Well, this letter concerns me because I've come to recognize, especially this past weekend, that the reason I am so unsettled about these letters that you send is because they really seem to me to be a form of sexual harassment.

Edward: Okay, I won't write any more letters.

Betsy: Thank you. That's all I was going to ask you—not to write any more letters, please. Our contact cannot be misconstrued by your wife and I don't want you to send any more letters because I feel very uncomfortable

Edward: I won't.

Betsy: All right.

Edward: Okay?

Betsy: All right. Well, Edward. . . .

Edward: How are you doing otherwise?

Betsy: It's very busy, and I'm all right.

Edward: That's the main thing.

Betsy: You and your wife need to get your lives together. Please take care of things. If these letters don't stop then I'll have to take steps.

Edward: Okay.

Betsy: All right. Thank you, Edward.

Edward: You're welcome.

Betsy: All right.

Edward: Okay.

Betsy: All right.

Edward: [With great anxiety in his voice] You'll what?

The therapists have been writing notes to Betsy as she speaks in this coaching format. In his last utterance Edward appears to have misheard her and to think this is another threat. Betsy doesn't reply but hangs up, clicks off the speakerphone, and covers her face with her hands. She doubles up, picks up the phone and hangs it up a second time. (She has to be sure he's gone.) She smiles and looks at the female co-therapist.

Co-therapist: He wasn't even offering you any opposition.

Betsy: He caved in so quickly! I don't think I'll see any more [letters]. If I see any more, I'll be surprised. [Grasping her chest and heaving a great sigh of relief] I don't think he will. Boy, it was easier than I thought it would be, and it was very hard.

The following week, Betsy reported a phone call from Edward.

Betsy: He called me, and I said, "Leave me be," and I choked him off. I said, "You are not even hearing me. We are not going to get together, we are not going to phone, not going to get together, not going to have any contact any more. Not any. You need to take care of your family and your kids, that's what you need to do. I need to take care of myself. . . . Goodbye Edward."

Concluding Therapy

I terminated therapy with Betsy when I thought the system was stable and she was moving along. She was losing weight on a regular basis. She was swimming every day, up to as much as three miles a day. She was working on relationships, actively dating. At work she had a much better sense of her relationship to her board and the other employees. She felt very much in control. The following excerpts are from her last session.

Betsy: I might be here because I have had a very big problem with food and dealing with my life, but everybody in my family has benefited from my participation in the program, and yet everyone in the family dreaded the thought. . . . We were all so scared. Everybody kept thinking, Now she's dragging us into it, we didn't do it, what does she think we've done? What are they going to tell us we did? All this kind of stuff. And it wasn't any of that, so this is really something.

Dr. Fishman: What would you say you've learned?

Betsy: There's a lot. Food alone—when I came here 6 months ago it was a battle. I was in a war, and food was the enemy, and I couldn't even go and shop. I did not have groceries at my house without eating them all. I didn't know what to get. Now I can walk into a bakery, anywhere, put it at home. Food is no longer the enemy.

First Follow-Up: A Few Months After Termination

Betsy: I have learned that I can get mad at people, mad about things.
              I can feel angry about something and the world doesn't stop
              rotating on its axis. I've also learned that something may hap-
              pen today, tomorrow, the next day, and even though I cringe at
              the idea of trying to take care of it, I know that I can, and be-
              fore this program I didn't even acknowledge that something
              was wrong, let alone know that I could deal with it. There were
              things in my life, this Edward person—by the way, he's called
              a few times again. The first time he called was 4 months ago.
              He'd got a new job, and his boss knew me, which gave him a
              foot in the door. But I told him on the phone at that time, "Just
              because your boss knows me doesn't give you a chance to
              begin communication again." I was at the office and Joy was
              there, so she just came in and sat right there while I talked to
              him, and I was very, very clear and said, "This isn't going to
              work. You cannot call." He went into this whole thing about
              "What's the matter? I stopped the letters. I'm not writing letters
              anymore. What about our friendship, we have known each
              other so long" and saying all this other stuff. And I said, "This
              has nothing to do with friendship, this has nothing to do with
              anything. The letters were just indicative of something else
              much greater that I can't have in my life." And Joy was going
              "Yes, yes," and I just felt so good to be able to do that, and I
              hung up and I felt really good about that, to be able to handle
              that. So he won't call anymore. You know, if he calls I will hang
              up. I would never have been able to do that. God forbid that
              somebody didn't like me. So that has changed.
                  And of course my relationship with my family has been real
              good. And my relationship with myself.

Dr. Fishman: So the two of you are doing much better.

Betsy: Yeah, [laughs] all of us. I'm starting to feel a lot more than just
              one person anymore . . . I feel like I have—it's not like a split
              personality or anything, but there are parts of me that I hadn't
              even known existed that I'm discovering, and one of which will
              surprise you, maybe. I'm almost embarrassed to say it, but I'm
              a woman. I'm not like a little girl. I haven't been married for 12
              years and raising stepchildren and all of that, so there has al-
              ways been that part of me that has never felt really grown up.
              What am I going to be when I grow up, what will I do in the real
              world, how will I handle this as an adult?

One never knows the ideal point to terminate therapy. It's always quite obvious when to start therapy—the symptoms mandate it. Stopping is a greater challenge.

In a grounded therapy one looks at the interactional patterns. The major patterns that concerned me in the work with Betsy were her conflict avoidance and her isolation. We worked together in our therapy for about 5 months altogether, meeting about once a week. By the end of therapy she was not isolated; she had increasingly close friends, and, by her account, she was addressing conflictual situations in her life.

It turned out, however, that all was not well. Shortly after this last meeting, she became involved in an extremely conflictual relationship and in many ways became a captive within it, and she did not act to remedy the situation. A major focus of our therapy had been to connect her with the broader context, including a prescription that she start dating. Doing this was difficult for her, because she was embarrassed by her body and was an essentially shy person. Nevertheless, she did date and eventually entered a difficult marriage. Ironically, what she needed in her relationship with her dominating husband was just what we had been working on in our therapy, that is, to be able to stand her ground and not let him ride over her. Of course, when she finally began to stand up to him, he capitulated, as she demonstrates in the following excerpts from her later follow-up.

Follow-Up Interview

Six years after the therapy had ended, I invited Betsy to come in for a follow-up session. I had not spoken to her since the follow-up shortly after the conclusion of therapy.

The Betsy who came into the office was still an attractive woman, but she struck me as having gained weight since we ended therapy. My memory could have been wrong, but I had recently seen videotapes from that period.

Betsy: The most important thing that happened to me since our therapy is I got married. We went to a marriage enrichment seminar last week; he came to the seminar with me. It's been rocky. For 4 years it's been rocky, but he went to the seminar with me and from the point of going to the seminar with me, he's now open to marriage counseling, which he never would do before.

Dr. Fishman: Tell me about the marriage being rocky.

Betsy: It feels like Niagara Falls, like so much water over the falls in the last—is it 5 years? I think it's been 5 years since I've seen you last. . . . I needed to be able to be in a relationship, it's been so long since I've been in any kind of, well, intimate relationship, any relationship, so you know from the time I left here I continued to lose weight, kind of slow but steady. Wasn't massive amounts, but I think from the year and a half that I was with you till about 7 months to another year, all told I think I lost about 46 pounds.

Her memory is not precise. We worked together about 5 to 6 months.

Betsy: I was feeling good, and then I met Mike. We struck up a friendship. About 10 years ago he was married. They had a little girl. And that relationship lasted about 6 years. His wife actually left in the middle of the night. She waited for him to go to a meeting. She planned her escape. She felt the marriage to be so abusive and so confining. Now I didn't learn about this, of course, until much later.

So we saw each other casually for about 6 months, and then he started talking about, have I ever thought about getting married again, and I said, well, I had but you know it's difficult for a lot of the work that I do. I'd been practicing at relationships as per the therapy. You see, he was safe up to that point, because he was really commuting. So up until the point when he started talking about marriage, I felt like it was a safe relationship.

There were things that I'd noticed about him that were like little red flags. When I entered the relationship with Mike I had a great deal of self-confidence. The successes with the therapy, especially the phone call with the man who had been harassing me, gave me tremendous self-confidence. I was like so terrified of making that phone call. I felt that if I could survive making that phone call with that kind of terror—and it was just making a phone call, for God's sake—I could survive anything. I felt I was successful.

So Mike happens to be very authoritative. He's real clear about what he wants and what he doesn't want, and I discovered early on that if I didn't do what he wanted me to do he'd, like, have a problem with that. He'd get angry sometimes, or he'd just kind of roll up his sleeves—and he's brilliant, this man's brilliant—and he would just go to work at convincing me that his way was much better than my way.

So it would get to the point every time where I would say to myself, well, it doesn't feel right, but it's okay, it's okay. I hadn't been in a relationship in a long time and wasn't used to it, so I would take myself out of it, so by the time he started talking about marriage, I said, "Well, for us it's out of the question, because you live in Lancaster County and I live up here and I'm not moving, I'm not going anywhere." So he said, "Well, I own my business, I can take it anywhere." The long and short of it was that we ended up getting married less than a year later.

After that, from the time that we were engaged to the time we got married, I began to notice a relative change in the way that he related to me and to some of the things that were going on, and my part of it was, not once during that time did I stand up and say, "Excuse me, but this isn't going to work for me, this just doesn't feel right, it's not going to work." So I never did that, everything that bothered him I would make it be okay, it was just too difficult. . . .

I see this statement as a major indictment of our therapy. It was for this very type of situation that we were working—where she would feel righteous indignation and act to correct the injustice.

Betsy: The other thing that should have been a huge red flag to me at the time was the relief that—you know, all the while that we were dating we had, like, the talk about sex. Now, I'm a real woman, it's not like I'm a total virgin . . . and he says that he didn't value his wife, that the minute you start having sex with someone the relationship that you're forming starts being about that and you stop getting to know each other and all the rest. Well, I kind of agreed with that, you know, sometimes it does happen, so he said that he'd be happy to wait until we were sure that we were getting married. The really annoying part was that at the time I was looking [good], I was losing weight, I was swimming 45–50 minutes a day.

Once we got married, within a 3-week period this man did a complete about-face. We got back from our honeymoon and—he didn't even want to make love on the honeymoon, which was almost a mercy, if you can imagine it, and I'm thinking, now, Mike, what's going on here? The honeymoon—we waited this whole time but I actually enjoyed the wait, but now we have got to know each other, but he's like, forget that, so I thought, oh boy, something's really strange. But the last night it worked out all right. I was relieved, I felt this is going to be okay, it just seemed to me that it was going to be okay, but I

> was afraid that he was so revolted by my body that he didn't
> want me, all this kind of stuff, you know.

Betsy felt profoundly rejected by her husband's lack of interest in her sexually. I believe the rejection was all the more painful because she had been working on her body and her sense of well-being, and her self-esteem had increased greatly in our work together. Time would show, however, that this was just the beginning of the challenges she was about to face.

Betsy: But we got back and within 3 weeks he started talking and he said the cats have got to go. I said, "Mike, these are my pets, you've been with these pets for like a year and half now, and now they bother you and now all of a sudden you are allergic?" I said, "Well, first of all, there's all kinds of things you can do. If you are allergic to the dander we can clean the house. . . . I had to find good cat homes for them. To me it was a tremendous sense of betrayal right out of the gate. He wouldn't take no; either they or he goes. When we were going out, he was making about $70,000 a year and he was talking about retiring. He's 45 years old and he says he wants to retire. But it never occurred to me that a month after we got married he'd quit his job. So that was it, he quit, he's done.

Then there were two or three other things. One of them was we had gone to visit his daughter, who had just turned 11. She and I get along really well. It's a good relationship as far as I'm concerned. And she wanted to go on a picnic, and so he took us up on this high mountain in Lancaster County and decided that we would walk down to a gorge. When we got down there he said, "How about it if we walk to the end of the gorge and then I'll call a friend up to pick us up and take us back to the car." I said, "Well, how long is it?" and he said, "It's about 2 or 3 hours and a half." I said, "Look, I don't think I am in that good a shape to do this. This is rocky, boulder terrain," but you know, he got real upset.

But it turned out to be almost one of those survival things, we almost had to call the paramedics in, and I blew my knee and almost couldn't get out on my own. Three hours turned into like 9 hours, and it was getting dark, we'd left around 10 in the morning, there it was, 9:00 at night, and we were nowhere near close to getting out and he said, "I've done this by myself." Finally he got us away from the gorge up onto a ridge where we followed the power line in. But it was—we had to be picked up, I mean, I just couldn't do it. At that point I thought, boy, you have to learn how to take care of yourself, because you cannot trust him to do it, he does not know how.

For the next year and a half our marriage, I'm embarrassed to say, it was not a relationship. He would want something a certain way; if I objected in any way at all, he would say I wasn't listening, that I was being aggressive, that I was going on, that I didn't want a relationship, that he was leaving. I never saw that a lot of what was going on I was responsible for, for just not standing up for myself. That all it would take was just for me to say, "Stop, please, we can't go on like this."

So she's caught up in a closed system with this man who does what he can to make her increasingly dependent on him. Indeed, abusive situations like this are fed by isolation, to the point where she distances herself by going on sabbatical, where she meets a counselor who helps to give her a perspective on her situation.

Betsy: And so it happened in 1998 I went away for an 8-week sabbatical. I was in trouble; I didn't know how much I was in trouble until I got away. When I got away the relief was so great that I thought, what is wrong with this picture, what's going on? So I got into some counseling and the counselor said, "You do know that this is an abusive relationship, it's abusive," and I said, "No, no, it's not abusive. He's brilliant, he just wants things the way he wants them," and then she said, "Does he treat you in public the way he treats you in private at home?" and I said, "Well, no, of course not," and then light bulbs began to go off. And then I thought, you know what, he does know, or he would be just doing it everywhere. So that was kind of a trigger point for me, and at that point I began to rally.

I just remembered, you know, the whole thing, that when we [you and I] were seeing each other [in therapy] it was so hard for me to do and it took so much courage to challenge people like Edward. I realized that once again I had to re-create in my life. . . . Do it or die. . . . You know, my belief in God is the only thing that kept me from committing suicide. Every day I was thinking about how to do it so that people—loved ones—would not be hurt, so that my family wouldn't know that it was suicide, going through cases, getting up, going to work because work was the only place that I felt in any way safe.

Coming back from the sabbatical—I wasn't home a lot during the sabbatical—I said, "Things have got to change. I'm not going to do this anymore. This is not good for either one of us, it's certainly isn't good for me. During the 4 weeks prior to the sabbatical, I gained 64 pounds.

Dr. Fishman: So angry all the time.

Betsy: Oh, tremendous, tremendous and not having any sense of being able to express it, and when I got back from sabbatical and visited some counseling groups, then I started expressing some anger in counseling in a real healthy way. When we were in counseling, "he was fine, I was the one that was all messed up." When I got back from sabbatical, I continued counseling, and at one point within 3 weeks he decided that he was going to leave, and I said, "You know what, Mike, please don't let the door hit you on the rear, by all means go. Grab your things, pack your things up, you cannot be happy unless I do what you want me to do and I can't do that, it's just not going to happen. Yes, this is the way it is, this is work in progress, this is the way it is, either you like it or you don't like it, but this is the way it is."

Of course he didn't leave. So that was the beginning of me being really able to start dealing with whatever it was that I had never dealt with in my entire life very well and just figuring out what feels well, what feels good, so I'm very strong right now.

As one would expect, with a man who is overinflated and insecure, he backs off when she stands up to him. Their relationship changes as she begins the process of regaining the sense of self she had in our therapy.

Betsy: Our marriage is still rocky at times, but it is like a thousand percent better than it was. I was not planning on moving back, and then in December he said, "If you come back, I'll make an agreement with you—if you come back and at any time I mistreat you or treat you in any way that you feel is disrespectful, you can leave again and file for divorce," and I thought that was going in the right direction, so I moved back home and he was really making an effort.

I feel much more in control of the relationship and of myself. Last month he wanted to vacation in California. Then he said that I couldn't take 2 weeks, I'd need to take 4, and I said I couldn't take 4 weeks off from my ministry with less than a month's notice. There was no way I could do that; I'd just got back from 10 days in Montreal, I won't go. And so I again said, "I'm not going, I can't do this, there's no way." So a week ago I'm on the phone with his mom and she said, "So you guys are coming when?" and I said, "Well, Mike's going, but I'm not going." Well, he's sitting right there and he slams his book down and he say's something like, "Well, that's fine, because I'm not going if you're not going" and walked out.

Dr. Fishman:	Are you losing weight?
Betsy:	Yes, I have lost 32 pounds.
Dr. Fishman:	Great.
Betsy:	Yeah. And I've got a ways to go even before I get back to where I was.
Dr. Fishman:	How will you do that?
Betsy:	With Weight Watchers®.

I wonder why this approach is effective at this point of her life; it was not at all salutary prior to our treatment. Was it our work? Or the fact that she is now married? Or is it effective because she and the other members can commiserate about their impossible *spouses*? It may be that it is now effective because she has a much richer social network. Or all of the above factors, for these are not necessarily mutually exclusive.

Dr. Fishman: Is he still close to his mother?

Men like this are always close to one parent or the other—usually their mothers. Somebody in their world has to support Olympic narcissism like this. As a manifestation of his overinvolvement with her, Mike had a stormy relationship with his mother. Expecting the same closeness and all-forgiving maternal nurturance from Betsy, he arranged to be adopted by her in antics such as quitting work after the honeymoon.

Betsy: Yeah, yeah, his relationship with his mother has healed a lot. But he really—one of the things that almost—having called the wedding off, we got real close, and I thought, this is how he treats his mother, this is how he treats his vehicle, how is he going to treat you, Betsy? It was like this huge thing, and I kept telling him, he was saying things like "You remind me of my mother in some ways," and it was, like, Wow! so this is like scary, because he didn't have at the time very much respect for his mother. They are just exactly alike, these two people are like opposite sides of the same coin, just exactly alike, and boy do they get on each other's nerves, and I don't know what he said to her, he doesn't tell her he loves her, appreciates her, just kind of tolerates her, doesn't. . . . If she calls, he monitors all the phone calls, he doesn't like to pick up and find out it's his mother, he likes to be in control.

They sound like embattled lovers.

Dr. Fishman:	When you think of our work, what do you think made a difference?
Betsy:	The martial arts. I cannot tell you what a difference that has made. Now, I'm seeing it just in little areas where I have found myself very uncomfortable with something, and I would remember how I'd do it, be able to do that. The knowledge that I could take care of myself if pushed was very helpful and continues to be.
	The other thing was, the three or four times I needed to take a stand for myself when I was with you, it so scared me I felt like I couldn't survive. That was like a wake-up call for me. Had Mike done some of the things before we were married that he started doing [afterward], I would not have married him. I think I've never in my life known how to stand up for myself, never, and that was just the beginning. It was like, I don't know what we would have had to do, if I could have seen you while I was seeing Mike, what the changes would have been related to some of the things he was asking.
	I think it would have been very different, because I think that with the things he'd do or say I'd think, wait a minute, wait a minute, how do you feel about that . . . the way I think we would probably have addressed it right then and there, but at the time I didn't, I just—it was too uncomfortable, so I didn't do it.

There is a consistent pattern in some of the cases: We stopped treatment too soon.

Betsy:	And the group part of it—I think that the group sessions at the end with Joy and Betty were important.
Dr. Fishman:	What other parts of the therapy were important?
Betsy:	It was different than anything I'd ever done before, because we were dealing with life as it was happening. And usually when a person goes to a psychologist, even a crisis counselor, it's like you sit there and you tell a story like I've been doing here, but I was in it at the moment and we were dealing with it. It was like, we're going to make a phone call right now. You know, you just get really—I felt no, no, we can't do this, we

can't do this, I won't survive . . . so it was like we would walk me through it . . . [laughs] and how good I felt afterwards, how absolutely relieved and good I felt afterwards. I had actually done this thing. . . .

Dr. Fishman: How about more specifically your relationship with your husband, Mike?

Betsy: Oh yeah, oh yeah, that . . . during my relationship with Mike, when it finally got to the point where I got away actually on sabbatical, I traveled the whole time, and during that journey . . . some of the things that I was remembering about our therapy, how it actually feels, it feels like you cannot survive to stand up. . . . Where does that come from? So what's going to happen if you disagree, the earth is not going to stop rotating.

Dr. Fishman: Anything else you have learned?

Betsy: [That] we don't know why we human beings seem so fragile on the surface. . . .

DISCUSSION

One model that I think is important in understanding the treatment of eating disorders is that of Robert Putnam on communities. According to Putnam, one of the most severe problems in America today is the attenuation of social bonds, which he explores in his book *Bowling Alone* (2000). According to Putnam, the concept of social capital has been "independently invented at least six times" (p. 19), but it was James S. Coleman who "put the term firmly and finally on the intellectual agenda" (pp. 19–20) and developed the social capital framework. Formal sociological research has shown that communities with less social capital—the social resources that can be drawn on by the individuals in a community—have more teenage pregnancy, lower educational performance, more child suicide, and more prenatal mortality. According to Putnam, states that have high scores on his Social Capital Index, meaning states "whose residents trust other people, join organizations, volunteer, vote and socialize with friends—are the same states where children flourish: where babies are born healthy and where teenagers tend not to become parents, drop out of school, get involved in violent crime, or die prematurely due to suicide or homicide" (Putnam, 2000, p. 296). Indeed, he believes that "bonding social capital constitutes a kind of sociological superglue, whereas bridging social capital provides a sociological WD-40" (p. 23). The concept of social capital has become increasingly important to our field. Indeed, the interest and acceptance of this idea is considerable. For example, an Internet search of the term "social capital" yielded 30,000 hits.

The goal of our therapy was the restoration of a viable community for Betsy. To use another of Putnam's terms, we, with Betsy's lead of course, needed to deal with the social glue in her life. Whereas Betsy was alienated from her community and from rewarding relationships, she was all too connected with problematic relationships such as with Edward, her sexual harasser. The goal of therapy thus involved realigning her social connections to render her social milieu coherent and enable her to recover social capital that was truly supportive for her. Betsy was successful in this work while we were working together. After her marriage, it took her some time to resurrect what she had learned in therapy, but ultimately she did so. Indeed, we can hear from the follow-up how profound and empowering the intervention was for her.

When I present this case, I am sometimes criticized. The intervention is seen as coaching; Betsy is not going through the experience of her own volition, and it will make her more dependent and do little to enhance her ego development. I do not accept this criticism. The co-therapist and I did support Betsy; indeed, we did coach her. What we did was to create a safe context in which she could connect with those parts of herself that were dormant. Within this context, she could challenge and confront in ways she hadn't done previously. She had trust in us and accepted the reality that we created: That the way out of her eating disorder was to become a person who did not shrink from conflict.

On the other hand, Betsy had no family to support the changes. To the extent that the coaching may have created a dependency, I suspect that my absence after therapy was deeply felt. (I had moved out of the area and was not available.) It may well be that in my absence she did not have the support she needed to challenge her husband, especially at the beginning of their marriage when he betrayed her repeatedly.

As I review the videotape of our intervention session, it is clear that we are not just coaching but allowing her to stretch. There are profound silences as Betsy reaches into herself for the courage to challenge her harasser. It is a clear indication of how she was profoundly searching.

Betsy's case, as we have noted, is a systemic phenomenon. To the extent that she was isolated and manifested her misery by eating too much, she isolated herself further. And in her isolation she had less support and social confirmation, especially in challenging situations. Indeed, in those situations where it is important to redress perceived wrongs, it is much more difficult to do so alone.

How does the clinician assess change in eating disorder clients? One important indication of change is the ability to maintain appropriate barriers in relationships; the patient does not allow herself to be robbed of her autonomy. She recognizes when the barriers are being intruded upon and is ready to address the conflict. In order to have intimacy, one must have a voice in modulating the relationship, to make it to one's liking.

It is always difficult to know when the system is strong enough that therapy can be terminated. Betsy's marriage shortly after the end of therapy and her allowing herself to be rendered voiceless is troubling, to say the least. It was unfortunate that I was not available to be a resource to her during this early period in her marriage. I prefer to see myself as part of an ongoing treatment system, somewhat like a general practitioner in that I am available to the patient and family when new difficulties come up.

Finally, why was this therapy successful to the extent that it was? Certainly my relationship with Betsy was very positive. I had come highly recommended by Joy, the patient described in chapter 10, who had begun treatment about 6 months earlier and had experienced dramatic change. The therapeutic relationship is really the terra firma on which all successful therapy is based. Beyond that, I believe—and her words confirm—that working with the broader context served to be a profound experience for her. I believe that the parameter from the psychosomatic family model— conflict avoidance—was the correct isomorph to be used. It served as the process handle by which we were able to profoundly change the system. Did this work to significantly transform the presenting problem of compulsive overeating? By the end of our therapy, Betsy was well on the road. Then, when she found herself in this very difficult relationship, avoiding all conflicts, she again gained weight.

Finally, I think it is important to acknowledge Betsy's courage during this process. In a short period of time, she was challenging habits and fears that were so deep that they had some complicity in her morbid obesity. Throughout our work, and really from then on, to hear her say it, she was challenging herself, stretching to grow.

CHAPTER 10

Eating Disorders with Comorbid Diagnoses

Go to the heart of danger; there you will find safety.
—Larry Hartzell, Martial Artist

In chapter 1, I discussed the literature on the incidence of comorbidity between eating disorders and such diagnoses as depression and obsessive-compulsive disorder. I also expressed my strong reservations about the usefulness of such diagnoses in patients with eating disorders.

Psychiatry is an imprecise field, and psychiatric diagnoses are far from objective. It is a common experience for clinicians to examine the chart of a chronic patient and see a vast array of varying diagnoses that have been assigned, with a similarly vast array of medications prescribed, often duplicating or counteracting each other. Another danger is the proscriptive power of the diagnosis itself. To the extent that the patient believes the diagnosis, she sees herself as limited and does not stretch to grow and thus reifies the limitation. This, of course, is a contextual phenomenon; her significant others also believe the reality of the diagnosis and do not challenge her to grow. There is a circular process: "I am limited, I can't change." "She is limited, we can't expect change." "No one is pushing me to change; they think I can't do it, so I won't push myself." Social scientists say reality is confirmation by significant others. Thus the self-fulfilling prophecy confirms the diagnosis but traps the suffering patient.

This hall of mirrors quality of diagnostic categories is so profound that it behooves the clinician to challenge the diagnosis whenever possible. My perspective is that biology is only one component of a biopsychosocial evaluation. More relevant is the social context. In the intensive structural therapy (IST) model, stress is seen as instrumental in the emergence of symptoms; even if a biological substrate problem exists, it is the stress in the context that is bringing it forth. And practically speaking, it is the stress in the context that we can do something about, often in short order.

JOY: SHE WOULD NEVER BE "NORMAL"

My first contact with Joy was in the spring of 1991. She was requesting refills of her psychiatric medications. She had just been discharged from a partial hospitalization program, where she had been treated following her second inpatient psychiatric hospitalization that year. Each hospitalization had been precipitated by a serious suicide attempt.

The facility where I was working at the time was a small outpatient clinic that worked heavily with severely troubled patients referred by case management companies. A frenzied managed care company case manager had referred Joy to me when, late on a Friday afternoon, she had run out of medications. Suffering from bulimia, she was on seven medications, many in the same therapeutic and treatment category. Each of her psychiatrists, getting no results, had added yet another medication in the hope of ameliorating her suffering.

Joy dated her psychiatric difficulties to age 15, when her bulimia began. It waxed and waned in severity for the next 20 years. During this time, she was addicted to cocaine for a year, supporting her habit through prostitution.

Despite her difficulties, she married in her 20s, obtained a college degree, and had a son. Throughout this time, her bulimia and suicidality continued. Her psychiatric problems were aggravated when she and her husband embarked on a course of infertility treatments. The roller coaster of hope and disappointment and, even more significantly perhaps, the effects of the drugs, with symptoms of pregnancy and at times menopause, exacerbated her emotionality. She became increasingly depressed, resumed her old habits of cutting herself and head banging, and then became actively suicidal.

The afternoon of our first meeting, Joy presented as an attractive, thin but not emaciated 32-year-old who was visibly upset. Speaking with blunted affect, she described her present mental state. She felt good about her hospitalization and her stay at the partial hospitalization program, which she saw as something of a breakthrough. Now she understood the cause of her difficulties over these many years: She had borderline personality disorder. She understood that she would never be "normal" and would probably be on medications for the rest of her life.

When I attempted to explore her relationships, she resisted. She was concerned only about her disorder. As the earlier cases have demonstrated, however, it is the difficulties in the client's relational context that are maintaining the problem. And, indeed, Joy went on to comment, almost in passing, that if her marriage did not change in 2 weeks, she was going to kill herself. After considerable urging, she agreed to bring her husband to the next session.

The Second Session

With her husband—a heavyset, balding man with a soft voice—sitting to her left, Joy began the session in a manner that seemed comfortable to her; almost dreamily, she catalogued her psychiatric difficulties. She seemed oddly at ease at this task, or at least well trained in it. My goal was to get her to abjure this passive, hopeless, and self-destructive view for herself. She must become a catalyst for change within her system. She could not do it if she believed that she had an indelible flaw that predestined her for self-destruction.

Dr. Fishman: Tell me more. When you say you did all these unpredictable things in your life, I don't know how you'd describe them.

Joy: Like what?

Dr. Fishman: I don't know, you say your whole life there were various things you did that were very upsetting.

Joy: I tried to kill myself twice, or suicide attempts—I'm beginning to understand the difference. Once I think when I was 13, and once again I think when I was 14. I was a prostitute for a while when I lived in Chicago. I'm bulimic. I've been bulimic since I was 17.

Dr. Fishman: Are you still bulimic?

Joy: Yeah.

Dr. Fishman: When were you a prostitute? What was that all about?

Joy: Make money. Fast.

Dr. Fishman: Were you using drugs as well?

Joy: Yeah.

Dr. Fishman: What kind of drugs?

Joy: Cocaine. Not regularly. Just when I do a job, they always have it. I was raped two times, both of which I think were my fault.

Dr. Fishman: How's that?

Joy: I led them on.

Dr. Fishman: Where were your parents during all of this?

Joy: Home.

Dr. Fishman: I know, but why weren't they in your life?

Joy: 'Cause you don't tell your parents this stuff. 'Cause then they won't let you go out of the house.

Perhaps Joy is rationalizing here to avoid the conflict that would have arisen had she told her parents of her rape. On the other hand, her parents might not have been capable of dealing with this sort of news, and she may not have been avoiding conflict but rather saving everyone from profound upset beyond what they could handle.

There is also a pattern of isolation. A telltale sign is that her parents were not perceived as a protective force in her life. She doesn't even understand my question "Where were your parents?" by which I meant, "Why weren't they looking after you?" She simply says, "Home," showing that she is unable to see the parents as able to offer her protection or even to help her reactively.

Dr. Fishman: How old are you during all of this?

Joy: I was raped when I was 13. I'd never had sex before. The next time I think I was 16 or 17. But this is not the kind of thing you tell your parents. I had an abortion when I was 17. And I did tell my mother because I was too young; she had to sign for them to do it. And I was all scared, too. And she said she was so happy that I told her because she said most kids wouldn't tell their parents.

I mean, I know that part of my cutting myself and hurting myself and smashing my head into the wall is to get away. I just have this incredible desire to get away from reality, from what I'm feeling. So, that's why me more than anyone else in the world. I have this incredible need to get away from the pain. Me particularly, I guess. And that's why I ended up in the hospital and on medication.

Joy seems to equate the pain she is feeling with being with people. As I reflect on the session, I think she is making an association that serves to compound her despair: The fact that she isolates herself only exacerbates her distress. It is in context, in relationships with others, that we confirm who we are. The other self-defeating aspect of Joy's situation is that she avoids people rather than confronting them. To the extent that she does so, her relationships are characterized by less satisfactory experiences with others, only leading to further withdrawal.

Joy's concern with the uniqueness of her experience ("me, more than anyone else in the world") I see as a result of her isolation. To the extent that she does not share experiences, she does not understand that other people struggle. This way of viewing her concern, according to the search-for-strength perspective, offers a more workable approach than one that would highlight the paranoia implicit in the perspective.

Joy:	You know, that's how I wound up on medication, and that has something to do with, I'm sure, my relationship with my husband, Michael, and I'm not sure exactly what at this moment. But part of feeling alone when I'm with him . . . you know.
Joy:	[Later in the session] I have something wrong with me. I don't function normally, and for us to sit here and pretend that I do, and just talk about me and Michael and our relationship—I mean, that's fine, and I can even see that this is valuable in dealing with someone who's a borderline personality, because one of the things they recommend is that you do family work. I'm afraid that you're not going to pay enough attention to that, or something. . . .
Dr. Fishman:	I think you might be afraid that I'm not going to treat you like a patient. Everybody treats you like a patient; I want to treat you like a woman who doesn't have a full life but can have a full life, who doesn't have all these things wrong with her. I want to deal with the positive parts of yourself.

My goal in the therapy was to transform Joy's context, both internal—her tendency, when stressed by relationships, to retreat and become bulimic and self-destructive—and external—how she handled relationships and how she isolated herself. The bulimia was the result of dysfunction in these domains. When the external was transformed, the internal would be ameliorated. Of course, in the process of the internal self being transformed, her mental schemas would change, and as they did, she would impact on her relationships differently, and so on.

Dr. Fishman:	You've been focusing on the negative parts, and I'm not sure that's all that you need. Look at this room. It's a hall of mirrors. You can go back and forth in the mirrors forever. One mirror reflects the other, back and forth. If you believe firmly in your heart that you are flawed as a person, you will do everything you can to prove that hypothesis, because nobody wants to be wrong. If you believe, instead, that you have tremendous potential and there's lots that you've done in your life that's positive, that has nothing to do with "borderline," that's one of the things that should be worked on.

Dr. Fishman: [Slightly later] The idea is not to focus on your problems; it's to make it so that you are confident of yourself.

Joy: I'm just so confused.

Dr. Fishman: I understand. I feel for you, and the psychiatric field is unbelievably confusing. It's a mess.

Joy: [Crying] I mean, I want to believe what you're saying. . . . And maybe what we do here will make a difference finally, but nothing else has. My whole life, nothing else has.

It is important to note that I was emphatic when I said, "The field is unbelievably confusing. It's a mess." I was attempting to let her know that she had connected with me at the affective level. Without connecting with her pain, I would have been too rational and thus ineffectual. Her experience with many of the significant people in her life had been one of disconfirmation: She was declared either mentally ill (by the psychiatric establishment), too emotional (by her husband and the alliance of her husband and son, who saw her as emotionally out of control), or weak (by her own self-doubts, demons fed by her isolation).

I saw this as a special moment of linkage between the self of the therapist and the self of the patient. I was commiserating and empathic, both for the pain—for the years that she suffered these symptoms—and also for her confusion, created by my introducing an alternative therapeutic reality.

But here we also see the struggle between two models. I sensed her fear that I would not treat her like a patient. For a long time, her identity had been based on the opinion of others that she was flawed. She actually seemed to be afraid that I was *not* going to pay enough attention to that. I was struck by her utter despair and certain pushiness as she tried to obtain validation that she was, indeed, handicapped. I countered with another definition of self; I would not treat her in the way she was trying to compel me to. I could have said, "I think you are borderline, but there's help for borderline." Instead, I chose to abandon that label, which I think she used destructively, part of seeing herself as "unable." Acceptance of the label would have missed the opportunity to wean her from her pernicious sense of self.

This struggle was made more difficult by her isolation, and yet for that reason was all the more essential. Her influential context consisted of her mental health providers and her conflicted family. Indeed, the psychiatric establishment played a major role in the homeostatic maintenance of her system. In this rarified world, there was scant input to confirm her as a whole person, a nonpatient. Even her good friend was closely involved in her psychiatric struggle; she cared for Joy's child while Joy visited her many doctors and groups.

I attempted to provide a context that was as powerful as her present one. In this redefinition of the context, I sensed that this might have been the first time she could not manipulate people by declaring herself incapable or sick. Thus, the initial task of the therapy was to win the battle of the models, to get Joy to see herself as capable and able to address the dysfunctional relationships in her life. If she saw herself as ill, she could not fight; she would remain locked in the position of the patient. If she saw herself as a competent person, she could empower herself to transform the contexts that were rendering her symptomatic. The implicit precursor to this change was that Joy be willing to accept that her context was relevant in the maintenance of her difficulties and that it must be addressed and changed.

This was a turning point in therapy, the first of a number of therapeutically induced crises. I saw this crisis as addressing the inner directives that organized her self, her most profound inner talk—the way she addressed herself. I was trying to retrieve the positive opinion of self. But cognitive changes would not be enough. They would reframe the problems but would not have sufficient intensity to transform the system. Joy's problem was not simply how she saw herself, but rather how her social system supported this reality. Her systems had to change to support her changed concept of self. Armed with this changed definition of self, Joy could be supported (and challenged) to revise the dysfunctional relationships by changing her patterns of conflict avoidance and self-isolation.

As I reflect 11 years later on the treatment, I am struck with the complexity of this individual. The baseline was just total desperation—the sense of not having any more options, the total disintegration of the self. To me those were the major issues, and I had to center on the basic maneuver, which was to make her feel worthwhile, to make her feel that she had a right to *be*. That was accomplished, but at a price to her narcissism. Previously, it had to be her way. In the process of our work, I believe she learned that she could get devotion through sharing relationships. That introduced an important focus for the upcoming work.

Work with the Family Context

The third session included Joy's husband, Michael, and her 7-year-old son, Billy. It was clear to me that the therapy would have to address her identity as mother and the triangular relationship with her husband and her son. I had to support Joy in challenging patterns that had been oppressive to her, both to depathologize her from a weak, voiceless mental patient and to empower her to transform the relationships in her life.

Dr. Fishman:	[To Joy] Are you the only person in the house who helps with homework?
Joy:	Yeah. Michael doesn't know it exists.
Dr. Fishman:	I guess Michael has no formal education, is that right? [I know he has been a teacher; Michael laughs.]
Joy:	Yes. He doesn't take any responsibility, really. Some things can't change. [To son] Why don't you go out and play with some toys? Daddy and I want to talk to the doctor for a minute.
Billy:	I'm not going out there by myself. I'm scared.
Joy:	Just out into the lobby.
Billy:	[Energetically burrowing into his father's lap] I'm scared.

The lobby is only a few doors down. Of course, the boy's resistance may come from a sense that he cannot leave his parents alone, that they need him to diffuse their conflict. Is this the boy's role at home? Is he caught in a triangulation, impeding his parents' resolution of their conflicts and his own development?

Joy tries to take the boy out. He whimpers and she lets him go back to his chair.

Dr. Fishman:	[To Joy] You were saying that you always do too much.
Billy:	[Burying his face in his father, who is totally passive] Help me!
Michael:	What can I do?

The boy's enmeshed connection with his father is clear. He asks his father for help, and the father responds by commiserating with the child, not by supporting his wife. Even his helplessness suggests hopelessness against an irrational force. I see this as a further insult to Joy, an implication that she is not a reasonable being.

Billy:	[Looking beseechingly at his father] You can do nothing?
Michael:	Then wait for us out there.
Billy:	I don't want to. Daddy, I'm scared. Help me.

Joy gets up, obviously burdened, and dutifully leaves the room with the boy. She returns and almost comically the boy follows her back into the room. His reappearance further demonstrates his disrespect for his mother and her powerlessness.

I see the family problem emerge in the room. Not only are father and son inappropriately close, but this coalition also somehow leaves Joy to do most of the unpleasant tasks of parenting. In addition, she is disempowered in carrying out these tasks by the pernicious disrespect for her.

Behavior patterns like this are creating the stress that leads to the emergence of Joy's eating disorder symptoms. These dynamics diminish Joy's self-esteem and predispose her to isolate herself further—and to accept the unacceptable conditions of her life.

Dr. Fishman: [To Joy] This is a pattern you need to change? [Joy nods] I think you need to get Michael to take Billy out of the room. He needs to support you in this. You should not be doing all of the unpleasant tasks of parenting.

Michael: [Takes Billy out and returns] One of the things that concerns me is how scared he is. At the house, he won't go into the next room because he's afraid to leave us.

Dr. Fishman: As your marriage gets happier, he'll be more willing. [Husband nods.] He's concerned about you guys.

I am addressing the complementarity of the family: to the extent that his parents are embattled, the child must be close to them. Should they become less embattled, he will have less concern and will be able to distance from them. I emphasize the point that their son will be more normal if their marriage improves in order to increase the father's initiative with his wife. Because the father is so involved with his son, seeing that connection may make him more supportive of my therapeutic efforts.

Dr. Fishman: So what about Michael helping out? You were a teacher weren't you?

Michael: Unh-huh.

Dr. Fishman: And your background is in history, isn't it?

Joy: I was a teacher, too, a history teacher and a math teacher.

Dr. Fishman: Well, if you don't use your mouth and your voice to get something to change. . . .

Joy: I guess I feel there's not that many things I do with Billy. Homework is one thing I do with him, and I'm screwing it up, obviously. He doesn't think I'm doing it right. His homework is bad because I'm doing it with him, and . . . I just don't know what to do with that.

Dr. Fishman: Well, can't you and Michael do different subjects?

Joy: He's only in first grade. He comes home with spelling homework, and he comes home with math homework.

Dr. Fishman: When you say that Michael's just not that involved with raising the youngster. . . .

Joy: Well, I think he's very involved in playing with Billy. I'm always the heavy.

Dr. Fishman: So really, what we're talking about is sharing that burden, not the difference between arithmetic and spelling and stuff like that.

Joy: [To husband] Do you know what that means? Do you understand what he's saying?

Michael: Oh, absolutely.

Joy's question implies that she thinks her husband is stupid. My reading on this is that she had, until now, given up trying to get Michael to hear her entreaties.

Joy: I do too.

Dr. Fishman: This is an extended honeymoon he has with this young man.

Michael: But we have a big disagreement about what's required. And how to do it. That's the problem. Joy draws lines in the sand and says don't go across this line or else. And I don't agree with that line, you know.

Dr. Fishman: You think it's too rigid. Or arbitrary.

Michael: It's always arbitrary. She'll make a stand on a point that I don't agree we should make a stand on.

Dr. Fishman: [To Joy] So why don't you defend yourself?

Joy: I don't know, it's not worth it. I . . . I . . . I don't know how to do this. I feel like I draw lines when they're necessary, and I try not to, because I don't believe in that either. I think there should be as much playtime in this life as possible and that we shouldn't be drawing lines and that organization is only to allow for more playtime.

Michael: [Laughing] That's simply not true. You and Billy have power struggles. You want him to do it *now* because you said so, and you want me to get involved, and I'm not interested. If it's something like we agree on a bedtime and it's 8:30 and that's the time, I have no trouble enforcing that. But it's when all of a sudden you've decided this is the way it's going to be; I don't back you on that. I don't, and that's probably not a good thing. I don't know how to deal with it. But I'll be happy to help with homework, as far as that goes.

Joy: Good. The first thing you could do is to know that he has homework and to look for it, to know that a child needs to have homework done, to be bathed, to be fed, all those things that come with having a child. All those awful things that come require time schedules.

Joy competently gets her husband to agree to cooperate to a much greater extent with the domestic chores. At the same time, her husband challenges Joy to be more responsible. In the past, it was difficult for him to do so. Her diagnosis functioned as a kind of medically sanctioned shield that encouraged conflict avoidance; it kept the system stuck and the marital relationship unauthentic. The spouses could not confront each other and deal honestly with differences. Buying into Joy's pathology, her husband could not encourage her to act and live more normally, and she lived in a kind of bubble. He often would not try to stop her from making choices that he knew were reinforcing negative attributes.

During the 6-month treatment, there were weekly sessions with the family. As Joy changed, the therapy dealt not only with the problems with which they had presented but also with the emerging problems of a changing system. For example, Joy's place in the family changed from the sick, disqualified family member to a competent person who was to be respected.

The Introduction of Martial Arts

As with Betsy, described in the last chapter, I decided to introduce martial arts as a new context that could bring forth different, more functional facets of Joy's self. Joy kept avoiding issues by calling herself too weak to address them, and she often referred to her lack of power. I believed it essential to provide a context that would counter this organizing core, for her sense of weakness was reinforcing her pattern of conflict avoidance. To the extent that she felt weak, she would avoid conflict, and this conflict avoidance led to indignation, bulimia, and depression. I had challenged her idea that she was "only a borderline" and thus frail and damaged. I told her we would work to counter this feeling that she was weak. What better way to deal with weakness than try to turn the weakness into strength?

In a sense, bringing in a martial artist is almost like bringing in a rehab specialist as a complementary therapist. The main arena continues to be family therapy. I was not simply referring her—it would be absurd to pin the whole therapy on martial arts or tae kwon do—but was seeking to maximize the leverage of family therapy. By introducing a specific context,

that of strength building, I was attempting to give her a corrective relationship so that she would have the confidence to address and resolve her other
relationships.

   This was the first time I had used this intervention, and I brought the
martial arts instructor into the therapy room itself after the third therapy
session. A burly man in his early thirties wearing a military camouflage
suit, he began by describing his model of martial arts.

Instructor:	You don't have to do anything but stand here. It's patented. Six million Chinese aren't wrong. I need your upper body built up, from your chest to your arms. I'm going to move everything upward and change your attitude about things.
Joy:	Push-ups and stuff?
Instructor:	Oh, yes.
Joy:	[Laughing] I can do two, so. . . .
Instructor:	Hey, no problem.
Dr. Fishman:	Would it be possible for you to begin the first lesson here in the room?

The instructor nodded. The chairs were pulled aside, and Joy and her family lined up, facing the instructor. As Joy, her husband, and their son began
the exercises, the teacher gently challenged the three, especially Joy, to
push themselves beyond their stopping point.

   After this session, Joy had a course of lessons at the instructor's studio.
She had to stop after she had a strained back, but at a follow-up interview
3 years later, she described the martial arts as pivotal in enabling her to
challenge her husband and to have the confidence to deal with her other
troublesome relationships.

Psychotropic Medications and the Medical Context

Medication in a treatment regime is considered a standard of care in the
medical community in this country, and in our pro-medication culture
there is considerable value in its placebo effect, if nothing else. My own
perspective is to use medication as conservatively as possible, usually to
stabilize a situation when I do not feel I can transform the context with
therapy alone.

   When Joy started therapy with me, the regimen of medications she was
on was extremely troubling to me. There were overlapping drugs in the
same categories, as well as drugs that were contradicting each other, and

Joy had been complaining of memory difficulties and hair loss. I had begun to decrease the medications so that, should she need medications, it would at least be a regimen that made sense. When she had been off antidepressants for about a week, her eyes looked brighter and she reported that her memory had improved.

Dr. Fishman: So, how are you doing otherwise?

Joy: Better than I expected. I'm a little confused about my women's group, what my purpose is there. I was doing great till I got there, and I just don't understand . . . I have to reestablish what I'm doing and try to figure out if it's something that's working for me.

Dr. Fishman: What did you talk about in women's group?

Joy: I talked about the karate and stuff, about fear. . . .

Dr. Fishman: Were they supportive of the karate?

Joy: Yes, they were, actually, very. I talked about going off the medication, and the nurse was concerned and said she thought it was a bad idea. I just stood up for myself and said, "I know what I'm doing." And I'll know if it's not going right, I said, "Listen, my hair's falling out, I feel terrible, I don't remember anything."

This triangulation of patients between mental health professionals is endemic. I might have asked Joy to choose one program or another, but I did not believe I had the credibility at that point to ask her to make the choice. Ideally, one should work with other professionals to provide congruent treatment. In this case, however, the differences were irreconcilable, and I thought it would be better to let the consumer choose.

The Work Context

Structural therapy is sometimes accused of being unrelated to the deepest inner directives that are accessible under hypnosis and perhaps in individual therapy. Joy's therapy makes clear that we *are* addressing her subjective experience. Deeply embedded fears yield when the therapist organizes other contexts that validate the new facets of self.

One of Joy's major fears concerned her ability to function outside the home. Her recent work experience had mostly been volunteer work. In IST the clinician considers the nature of the workplace and tries to determine whether it will undermine or foster the development of a new self-esteem. Would Joy's volunteer work at a social service agency give her increased self-confidence so that she could more forcefully advocate for herself? I thought not. She worked alone in a small office, doing repetitive tasks that provided no opportunity for intensive skill growth. Joy was an educated woman, with a college degree. She would do better in a setting where she could enhance her social relationships and develop new skills.

Furthermore, I felt that a paid work situation would be a more confirming context, enhancing her sense of well-being in several ways. Obviously, it would give her more financial stability and autonomy; it is easier to speak up if you have financial independence. It would also be a more supportive context. Francesco Maturana (personal communication, 1981) once said to me, "One reason people go to work is for love." The love he meant is the love that people feel for one another in the workplace and that gives them the confidence to address conflictual situations.

During a session in the second month of treatment, we were discussing the couple's financial situation.

Dr. Fishman: What's a relevant issue?

Joy: Save money.

Dr. Fishman: Let's not talk about saving money, because saving money is passive.

Joy: I know what I need. I need a job.

Dr. Fishman: I think you need a place where you can go every day, not necessarily the whole day. [To husband] Do you encourage Joy to get a job?

Michael: Oh, absolutely. . . . But I don't confront her, I haven't for years.

Dr. Fishman: To the extent that you don't confront her. . . .

Joy: [To Michael] I wish you would.

Dr. Fishman: [To Michael] Don't back down. [To Joy] I think getting a job would be a wonderful thing, because it will be more social, somewhere where you'll have a better sense of accomplishment. You'd be normal.

They discussed options. Joy was incredulous when I suggested that she have a job by the next week. I did this to create a crisis, to force the issue so that new patterns could emerge. I was also anticipating passivity and stalling, which I countered by requesting immediate change. They negotiated and said, "Well, in a week and a half."

I also wanted to see how the husband would react, because he had come to subscribe to the idea that his wife was a chronic borderline, a cripple, who could not be pushed. I encouraged Michael to both support and challenge his wife. To the extent that he challenged her to get out and do more, he implicitly confirmed her and gave her a vote of confidence.

In this session, I was seeking a vision of the rewards that could come from being in a competent working position. At one point I told her to visualize herself in a situation of competence and to anticipate the thrill of not being passive but proactive. Like reading biographies, imagining these scenes gives people a sense that they can have alternative scenarios for their lives. I was impressed by her readiness: She would nod and indeed would seem to see herself as competent. She then would discuss pertinent associations to work, and how much she enjoyed it.

This process I call "accessing" the competent self. With each context introduced, I was searching for her competent self. Let me emphasize, however, that visualization is a small and even trivial part of the accessing process. The competent self is attained through changing the contexts of a person's life. Beyond that, the self is transformed when the patient herself or himself is empowered to affect these contexts. Joy, for example, was able to get her husband to share in the housework and prevailed on the social service agency to pay her a salary for the work she was doing. These more intensive contexts further confirmed her as a person.

In response to the therapist's urging, Joy and her husband decided to start a business venture together. He played the piano and she sang. They went to nursing homes and performed for the elderly residents.

The Context of Friends

The work of therapy also included work with Joy's friends, her peer system. Part of what Joy had been suffering from was isolation. She did have some friends, but they were friends who were always focusing on her mental problems, fancying themselves amateur psychotherapists. The one more positive friendship was with Betsy. Betsy offered warm and cheerful camaraderie as well as the opportunity to volunteer at a social service agency, which she hoped would enhance Joy's self-esteem as well as expand her social circle. We had a session with Betsy, at which Joy was able to address the way the volunteer work was not meeting her needs and persuade Betsy to give her a paid position. As I said earlier, this was only partially successful; she needed a more extensive social system in terms of her isolation.

Bringing peers into the therapy session can be invaluable in revealing what therapy is about. Joy's therapy included a session with the friend who took care of Billy when Joy went to her various treatments. At one point the friend said, with a sweet smile, "I'm good enough to take care of your kid, but not good enough to be your friend?" The session went on to deal with the artificiality of their relationship. Each woman had resentments toward the other that they had never confronted. It was difficult for Joy to address her friend with these issues, because she was beholden to her for caring for her son. Nevertheless, she was able to confront her friend (and vice versa) so that they could have a more honest and less stressful relationship.

Conclusion of Therapy

The therapy continued for 5 months, two or three times a month. Joy was weaned off medication. At one point, Joy told me that she and her husband had decided to adopt a baby and asked if I thought she could handle it. I said, "Definitely." I thought she and her husband could handle the inevitable stress, and I said I would be glad to support their application. Joy called me the next day, saying she had decided to quit her group therapy and the partial hospitalization program, because when she asked for a letter of support for the adoption agency, they refused. They said she could not possible handle the stress. At that moment, she decided they were too negative and were holding her back.

When therapy was terminated, Joy and her family were stable. They stated they were content with one another and appeared to be so. Joy was working at the social service agency in a more responsible position. Their son was doing well. And although her husband was unhappy with his boss, he was becoming increasingly essential to the organization. I gave the family my usual refrain: I work like a family doctor in the sense that, after I help people through a difficulty, I try to be available should they need additional therapy.

THE FIRST 3 YEARS AFTER TREATMENT

Shortly after the end of treatment, Joy and her husband adopted two children from Russia, sisters aged 6 and 3. The children spoke no English, and their new parents spoke little Russian. Joy and Michael expected problems, and although the children did not seem quite right, they thought things would work out in time. After 3 months, however, they learned that both children had fetal alcohol syndrome. Both were severely disabled, and it was suspected that they had been sexually abused. The couple was coping with this enormous problem just as their son, Billy, was entering adolescence.

I saw the family sporadically over the next 3 years as Joy and Michael struggled with these extremely hyperactive youngsters. Although the older was controlled with Ritalin to some extent, they were both immensely difficult. At one point the pressure was exacerbated by Joy's contracting a severe case of Lyme disease. A few months afterward, her husband left his position at a large corporation and became a consultant. His extensive travels for his job required him to be away from home 3 nights a week. His absence increased the stress on Joy; she had the responsibility for three children, two hyperactive and seriously handicapped and one about to enter adolescence.

Joy and her husband coped with the stresses courageously. Their marriage was taxed to the limit at times, but they stayed together, and Joy's bulimia and suicidality never returned. Clearly, the fact that Joy had remained asymptomatic during these immensely stressful years meant that the changes were profound. Joy had become a business person, opening a clothing store.

Why was the therapy successful thus far? One cannot say that the change was due simply to the fact that she no longer was being treated for infertility. These changes were both internal and external. Joy credited a conscious decision to confront her husband and her context, rather than become sick again. Her distress had been transformed: She saw the difficulties as stemming from her context, not from a flaw in her mental architecture. But we clinicians are always reserved in our self-congratulations. At this point, we were only 3 years after her treatment.

THE 10-YEAR FOLLOW-UP

Ten years after the initial course of treatment, I invited Joy to come in for a follow-up interview. Since the last time I had seen her, 7 years before, a tremendous amount had happened in Joy's life. The care of the impaired children the couple had adopted had eventually placed more stress on the marriage than they could handle, and Joy and Michael had divorced. Each had found a different spouse who was more useful in the care of the girls. Michael had married the Irish au pair when she was under pressure to leave the country. After several brief relationships, Joy was now living with a construction worker who had a very large, helpful family. Patrick was a no-nonsense man who the girls, perhaps because of his size, tended to listen to. Joy had opened two clothing stores, and while she had had to close one, she had proved successful as an entrepreneur.

The Joy who comes into my office is now middle-aged, 30 pounds heavier than 10 years ago.

Joy: I was wondering if I was ever going to see you again!

Dr. Fishman: So it's been—how long?

Joy: I was wondering that. Did I have my girls yet? I have had my girls about 6 years. They were the beginning of the end of the marriage.

Dr. Fishman: They are a challenge.

Joy: To this day, they continue to be a challenge.

Dr. Fishman: How old are they?

Joy: Nine and 11. The 9-year-old is about this big (points to about 4 feet). We see a neurologist [for her]. It struck me recently—we were all sitting there, her father, his au pair, we were all there, three grown adults—and none of us can handle this kid! No question, it is not even close. You know, the reason I adopted them is I thought, how difficult could it be? I have done many difficult things in my life. I went to Mississippi and taught art, to kids who had never had art before; they would rather pull a knife on you than listen to you. Inner city in D.C., the same thing; I turned it around—but I cannot manage this child. She just, like, gets me. It's a control issue for me, it is a control issue for Michael. You cannot control her—there is absolutely no way. We have actually gotten to the think about little baby handcuffs, something to keep her in bed at night so we can sleep at night. She has no conscience.

Dr. Fishman: She goes to school?

Joy: She is doing better in school. We keep messing with the medications to get her to the point where she will not be knocked out but yet she can focus. She is learning to read; she is learning to read faster than her older sister. One day she is not, the next day she is. She seems bright to me, but the neurologist said that she probably had an IQ lower than 75. But I don't know what IQ is based on.

Dr. Fishman: They can be pretty arbitrary tests.

Joy: She is very smart; she will have a conversation with you long before her older sister [will]. She will notice things and ask questions. She has everybody figured out. I sleep on the couch; she can slither right past me and go right to the kitchen

and get to the sharp knives. She knows us. She is amazing—
she knows us.

I am struck by how difficult this child must be. Joy's having to sleep on the couch is a severe hardship. It is a testament to her commitment to keep the child at home and out of an institution.

Joy: We tell her to do something, she says, "No." We can yell at her, hit her—she just says, "No." I have never seen a child do that. Most children are afraid of adults on some level, they will listen and get intimidated. She has no fear of consequences— a child who has no conscience and doesn't fear consequences. I think this is the worst thing that ever happened to me. And the best thing. I don't believe that anything is an accident: It has to be. I don't believe that anything can be the worst thing. Everything happens with a reason. I talk to God every day: "Were you drunk?" People say how do you do it? I say I cannot do it.

I have pang of guilt; I wonder if she is getting the help she needs to handle this child. Could not an intervention from a family therapist help create a system that is more effective, more coherent? Is this an avenue that can be explored? As I reviewed this interview 8 months later, I was sorry I did not suggest more resources to her, other than accessing the county system, which she was already doing. On the other hand, in this elegantly balanced system that had been created around these youngsters, would she have seen me, one of her biggest supporters, as criticizing her? It could even have unbalanced the system by shaking her confidence, had I implicitly questioned what she was doing.

Joy: Given that I had a control issue—bulimia and all that stuff—it is kind of ironic that I wind up with a child like this.

Dr. Fishman: Let's do some follow-up. Let's start with the symptoms.

Joy: That's over. Completely, really. The thought occurs to me every now and again, but once in a blue moon, and then I think, "Why would I want to do that?" I weigh 30 pounds more and it doesn't bother me.

Dr. Fishman: You were depressed. I was reviewing the video—you were depressed and suicidal.

Joy: I would like to see that [video].

Dr. Fishman:	You might not necessarily want to revisit that part of your life. You were on huge amounts of medications.
Joy:	Just driving here I was revisiting that. I was shaking when I got here. As a matter of fact I am battling that as we sit here. I just stopped and picked up a prescription for Effexor®. And I kind of keep trying to go off that stuff; I was on Prozac for years and years. And then it didn't seem like it was working, when I was throwing people out of my life. I keep throwing this guy out of my life and then inviting him back in. He is the one who said, "The Prozac makes you nuts, makes you too impulsive." I stopped taking it, and I wasn't really okay. Then I went to this Effexor stuff, which I like okay. My doctor told me it makes me normal, it makes me slow down, stay calm and think. The medication helps me manage it. It's such a subtle thing, to go off the edge. I am afraid of that. I say to Patrick, "I don't know how to know." It has been in my life that you wake up one day and not be okay.

Medication can be very helpful when people are in unrelenting situations. There is no structural intervention that can reduce or transform the stress resulting from having these very difficult children. The medication helps with the anxiety and depression resulting from the intractability of her plight.

Joy:	I think I could probably live without it, but I feel the job I'm doing as well as I am, dealing with my children, who push me right to the edge. . . .
Dr. Fishman:	It works for you; it's a crutch.

I regret saying that, but she puts me in my place.

Joy:	I don't agree with "crutch," I really think that's not what it is for me. "Enable" would be better. It enables me to do things I wouldn't be able to do; it allows me to achieve more things in my life. I could go without it, and I would be a different person. I would probably have my daughter in an institution a long time ago. I wouldn't continue to try to give her a normal family life, which is what I try to do. I wouldn't have expanded my business, I wouldn't have had the energy. I would believe the thoughts in my head, that I can't do this, that I don't want to, what's the point, I'm too tired.

Dr. Fishman: At our last meeting your marriage was starting to unravel. Let's talk about that point.

Joy: I was young, determined, willful, didn't know how to get what I wanted but I knew what I wanted. I think if I were back with my husband I would have him in the palm of my hand, because I have learned—I have learned about men, getting what I need, giving what other people need. Patrick brought this up the other day. "I can understand why your marriage fell apart. You didn't give him what he wanted and you didn't ask for what you needed. You were very needy." I became very needy. I can get that way now, but I hate it. I was going through a lot. I got Lyme disease. When I got home from Russia with them, Michael wasn't there for me. I was exhausted; I insisted we hire someone. He stopped coming home. He said that he had to make more money for the kids. Michael had to marry the au pair to keep her here in the States; there was no one to take care of the kids. I said, "Doesn't she bore the life out of you?" He said, "No, she is just the same all the time—very reliable."

The fact that the couple had divorced raises questions at the level of theory. As a family therapist, was I not committed to the health of the couple *per se*? Not necessarily—the stakes were too high. My commitment was to this patient, an extremely complex and difficult soul who thought that the only way to be is *not* to be. Blocking her self-destructive anger was a priority. Ironically, on the other hand, I think the couple was working very effectively. They were functioning as a very good, non-married parental unit. They had enlarged their system to include two other people who were their helpers, in an almost managerial way. In terms of their untenable situation with these kids, and especially given their limited financial resources, their divorce, in one sense, was a "divorce of convenience." The new arrangement was allowing her and the kids to remain stable.

Joy: [referring to Michael, her ex-husband] Now we have a great relationship. He didn't believe in me; now he does. I asked him, "Why didn't you believe in me? I was an incredible person." He still doesn't know. He still doesn't admit it. Now I am really sensitive. My boyfriend, he says one negative thing about me, I will tell him, "Don't you ever threaten me!"

I think this is a very different person from 10 years ago. She is constantly vigilant, monitoring her boundaries. She has learned to address the conflicts immediately.

Joy:	Patrick is a good learner. . . . And he really loves me. He has ADD [Attention Deficit Disorder], he can't read, but he is so good with my kids. I was saying to a friend, he is the perfect father for the children. I had a baby-sitting emergency, he got off work early, he picked them up. He calls me on the cell phone—I am down at Motor Vehicles—I ask, "How are the girls?" "Oh, they are fine. Now we are going out to get something to eat." I would never do that; I can't manage going anywhere with them. I think my daughter has reconciled herself with how big Patrick is, that she has to listen on some level. His family is very nice to me. He has taught me how important family is. I love going there, being part of his family. I never got that before.

Her partner has the added advantage of a large family, who add to her sense of community and confirm her as a person. Her demons fester in loneliness. It appears that this relationship provides support in a way that she did not have when our therapy began. In those days, most of her non-family friends were professional helpers. They were paid to focus on her deficits, which, indeed, perhaps exacerbated them. Her partner's family sees her not as a patient but as just another family member. Thus, since our treatment she has created a drastically different context for herself, a context that supports a much more competent self. This new context has played an important role in the changes I see in Joy.

Joy's work context had changed as well. She had opened two stores selling clothing but was in the process of closing one.

Dr. Fishman:	How is the other store doing?
Joy:	Excellent—but I am going to have to recover. I am financially broke and financially drained [laughing].
Dr. Fishman:	What are the issues? What worked? One thing that may have worked profoundly is the new job, being a businesswoman?

To me as the therapist, this was a continuation of an important intervention. One central focus of our therapeutic work was diminishing Joy's isolation and finding a context for confirmation of the self. I encouraged work as one such context, and by the end of our therapy Joy and her husband were entertaining at nursing homes and Joy was being paid for her work at the church.

Now, in her stores, Joy could be nearly autonomous. And she was a pretty driven, competitive person. Dealing with contractors and others in her business, she could use the same energy and competitiveness that had bristled in her confining marriage.

Joy had seen a number of therapists in the years since our last meeting, in part to satisfy her friends, who were self-styled (though untrained) therapy experts and therapy consumers. When the stresses of her situation left her in tears, her friends would insist that she needed more help, that she was denying serious psychiatric problems. For a time she allowed her powerful friends to steer her into serial therapeutic relationships, in order to keep their friendship and counsel.

Joy's last therapist had told her that she should stop seeing Patrick, because he was addicted to cocaine.

Joy: She thought if I used the drugs I would get seriously addicted. But that's not the case. When Patrick uses, I say, okay, I'll use with him, but I can take it or leave it. I use it rarely. I don't know if he's ever going to stop doing it. But he taught me to be affectionate with my kids. I wasn't like that before. He is very tactile. I come home from work, he rubs my feet. He hugs my kids, he tickles them. [If] he gets himself arrested and winds up in jail—oops! But I don't think he will. I think he has gotten clear where he is going. He said, "Joy, I've had this problem for years, but now I have something I want to live for."

Eventually Joy strengthened her resistance and declared, "No, I'm done [with therapy]. What I need I have."

Joy: I am not in denial; I don't need any more work [therapy.] Anything else I do in my life will reflect what I have learned. I will get better every day. The only proof is that it worked [the therapy]. And the others did not work. I am no longer a bulimic—I haven't been for many years. I am no longer suicidal—I haven't been for many years. While my life has stresses, so does everybody's. All my life I was the yellow canary [a metaphor we had used in our work]. I dropped dead so the guys don't have to. Obviously there are times when I am upset about something—when I would have symptoms of "mental illness," like sitting in a rocking chair and crying. My friends would say, "You need a psychiatrist." I would say, "That is not something I would deal with with my psychiatrist. I can handle it."

While her friends tried to make her over into a perfect personality, she came to accept herself, to respect her own style. She forgave herself her faults. She made her own stability out of a very unstable style. But the only way to tame an unregulated person is to accept her wildness. She did just that, and her strengthened resolve was rewarded, I believe, in her role as entrepreneur. It appears that her passion and energy, her wildness, even a bit unregulated, fit the needs of her business environment.

I asked Joy what she remembered of the therapy.

Joy: I remember we would sit here and we would talk about the relationships in my life. If there were any problems, you would have me bring them here. With anything I couldn't resolve, okay, get them here, move through this one, move through that one. And it did help. It was very different. You never wanted to talk about classic psychology at all. You didn't want to hear about any names of what was wrong with me; you didn't want to hear if I had borderline personality disorder or if I was schizophrenic or manic-depressive. My friends all thought you were wrong. I had trouble believing it, but by the end I totally believed you. You always said, "There is nothing wrong with you; you are sensitive." I remember one time you said to Michael, "How tall are you?" He said, "6'1"." You said, "You are 6'1" and your wife is sensitive. That's the way things are. You don't have to attach anything to it, you just have to be responsive to her.

Dr. Fishman: It's a good quality.

Joy: Most of the time in my life it is a very good quality.

Dr. Fishman: So, what worked in the therapy?

Joy: I think what worked is how much you believed in me. I think that's the best part. You said to me, "Joy, you are a strong woman. I know you can do this." And also, you did not tell me what to do. You believed in me enough to believe that I could figure it out. You never told me to get rid of a person in my life. You never told me I should spend more time with that person. You never told me I should stop throwing up. You left it up to me; I got a lot of strength from that. A lot of times I thought you were crazy. Didn't you get that I was mentally ill, that I had been voted to be in an institution the rest of my life? Which is what they were telling me: "You will never be able to raise children; in fact, the child you have will be taken away from you." That's what the opinion was. I thought, I've got to trust this guy. I had to trust you.

There is always the generic question, when we are doing therapy, of whether our individual techniques make a difference or whether it is only the gestalt of the therapeutic relationship that does the trick. Joy commented on the enduring value of the use of the enactment technique.

Joy:	When [my friend severely criticized me], I thought of Michael. In the session, when Michael would attack me, you would ask me, "Are you going to defend yourself?" I would say, "No, what is the point." I thought if somebody really thinks that about me, then what is the point. [Later] I think learning to confront stuff is the most valuable change.
Dr. Fishman:	That's what you did.
Joy:	In fact, I get to the end of the day and marvel at how many confrontations I make—like, call the insurance company and tell them they fucked up—if they are going to represent small businesses, they have to do it differently—then call the guy who sold me the policy. Well, that is what you taught me!

I had challenged and coached Joy to address and resolve numerous conflictual relationships. As I recollect the treatment, when we dealt with conflict avoidance, I didn't say, "Face conflict." I would say, "Get strong, so you can face conflict." I think that had theoretical import, because the patient needs to be equipped to face conflict, and certain experiences, like martial arts, will enhance confidence and strength.

Part of the contribution of this material should be the realization that differentiated and partial therapies can be used to build up the self of the person who has to face conflict, when the conflict avoidance is based on fear and feelings of weakness. In some ways, this is a different therapy. What Joy's treatment represents is family therapy that is not what people think of as family therapy. Here, I worked to organize contexts to chisel out certain skills, certain strengths that were missing. It's a model of rehabilitation, in fact, based on a philosophy of building competencies. You cannot ask someone to walk before all parts of the leg are working. You can't get people to try a certain task unless certain preliminary skills are set. In this model, we deal with the more dysfunctional parts. We do not assume that everything needs rehabilitation.

Interestingly, one thing that did not work for Joy was group therapy, which is widely accepted as essential for eating disorder (ED) programs. She found it too competitive, with people in a race to show who could be more symptomatic.

Joy:	The kiss of death for someone with an ED is talking about it. Put me in a room full of bulimics and I'll be throwing up by the next night. It's a control issue. If a person with bulimia can do it better than the person over here can, they will try, because that is their personality, to have more control.

CHAPTER 11

Therapeutic Impasse: "Where the Rubber Hits the Sky"

Words are powerful; ideas that follow from them are more powerful. There are certain ideas upon which the treatment in this book is based. Central is the necessity of addressing each person as part of a coherent system. I remember seeing a Sierra Club poster many years ago: a beautiful mountain valley in springtime, brilliantly colored wild flowers abounding. The caption read, "I bent down to pick a flower, and realized it was attached to the universe."

The therapy in this book works because the patients and their families are treated systemically: The professionals, the family members, and community resources work together, and the treatment addresses the factors in the system—at both the micro level (the family) and the macro level (the broader context)—that are creating stress for the patient. When therapy does not work, one reason is the absence of a coordinated treatment system. The case that follows is representative of the experience of numerous patients caught in a mental health system that fails to address the broader context that is keeping the patient symptomatic.

Reviewing the videotape years later, I am struck by Bree's appearance. A tall woman, with light blond hair and pale blue eyes, she is very anorexic and emaciated. What is most striking about her is her fragility. In the first segment below, she talks about her living situation with her husband. A week before there had been a session with Bree and her parents, in which everybody talked about how socially isolated she was.

The immediate crisis between her and her husband occurred the day before. At the session the previous week, her husband had criticized her because she wasn't sociable enough. This past weekend, her husband castigated her when she innocently brought a male friend home (with her children and parents in the house). What we see in this segment is the rigidity of the system: how critical her husband was of her. There is a fine line for her to walk, and it is a moving line that changes without her knowledge. Commensurate with that is the conflict avoidance; she never challenges the pattern but only protests occasionally.

Dr. Fishman: Well, how was the weekend?

Bree: Saturday wasn't bad. Yesterday was a total nightmare. Arnie and I just didn't get along, that's an understatement.

Dr. Fishman: Really?

Bree: Yeah.

Dr. Fishman: You were at each other's throats?

Bree: Well, no, it didn't start out that way. It's just that old inconsistency thing; he just can't be consistent with me. I told him that I had somebody stopping over and he was totally cool with it. It was a guy, a friend who as a matter of fact helped me change my tire and everything a couple of weeks ago when I had a flat tire. And you know, I'm talking about having someone stop by, a guy stop by when my parents are there, my kids are there, and Arnie is gonna be there, so I'm not up to anything, it's pretty obvious.

This is a guy who I happen to have a bit of compassion for because he just lost his wife not long ago to cystic fibrosis and I think he just needs a friend and I need a friend, and we make each other laugh, so it seemed to me that it was okay. So Arnie was good with it. Arnie went out to play basketball with his friend and came back drunk . . . [pauses, shaking her head with pursed lips] and decided he didn't like it that the guy was over visiting, even though the guy . . . [shakes her head and raises her hand, exasperated]. It was, like, I just couldn't deal with it. How come it was all right in the morning and it wasn't all right in the afternoon? And he caused a big scene: "Come here, I want to talk to you, I don't want some guy hanging around" (taking on Arnie's voice sarcastically). It was like . . . and that was, like, just the tip of the iceberg, you know, because then, basically he told me, although I tried not to take everything he said that seriously because I knew he was drunk, but he told me that he thinks he's a saint for staying married to me.

And I said to him, "Well, there's a lot of people who think that I'm not that bad for staying with you." And he said, "Like who? Give me three names of three people" [taking on his voice again]. So I did. And then he said that he couldn't trust me any-more because I hadn't told him that. So I'm no longer to be trusted. [Raises her open hands in the air] I can't win, you know.

This then brings in the broader context, where we have each of them talking to the other about their relationship. This is a frequent practice for troubled couples—they complain to their friends about their spouses and set in motion a vicious cycle that profoundly destabilizes their relationship. They are unhappy, so they complain to their friends, who side with them and inflame them further. Of course, their spouses, who have not heard the complaint, don't have the opportunity to change, and they complain all the more to their friends. This pattern can lead to an exacerbation of the anger each feels for the other. The result can be a symmetrical sequence that can get out of control, as in fact happened the following week.

Dr. Fishman: Where was everybody else when this happened?
Bree: They were all downstairs. I was in the bathroom all weekend [laughs] painting it.
Dr. Fishman: Oh yeah, how's it looking?
Bree: It's done.
Dr. Fishman: Is it?
Bree: Yeah.

I am trying to create a context of confirmation for Bree. This is the therapeutic technique of searching for strength. This chronically passive woman has done something proactive: She has painted the bathroom. I see this as a small but valuable step toward our therapeutic goal: for Bree to activate to challenge the relationships that are maintaining her symptoms.

Dr. Fishman: Pictures tonight? [Photos of the painted room]
Bree: Well, no, I took pictures, but they are not developed yet. Actually I didn't take the "after" pictures yet.
Dr. Fishman: Okay.
Bree: But it's done.
Dr. Fishman: So maybe Wednesday we'll get the pictures?
Bree: I'll try . . . you can trust me, believe me, no matter what Arnie says. . .
Dr. Fishman: I trust you. I think you're a very honest person.

Bree:	Well, Arnie doesn't think so, I mean I don't know if maybe . . . then I tried to bust him on the inconsistency. I said the main conflict I have with you is your inconsistency drives me up the wall. I need to know where I stand with you all the time, or at least most of the time, but never know what to expect. I mean, I didn't expect him to come home from playing basketball drunk, to begin with. Now if he said to me, "We're going out to play basketball, then we're going out to have a few beers," I might've had some notion of what to expect. And the fact that it's okay that Lee comes over and then it's not okay anymore, and he can't get past that. Then I also told him, "You know, it lowers my self-esteem because you don't think that people could just like me. You don't think that it could be just that somebody likes me just to like me, somebody thinks I'm an okay person just to hang around with." [He thinks] somebody thinks I'm fun, they all want something from me. [He thinks] of course this guy wants to have sex with me, that's why he's coming over, you know. Same thing with Alice. He thinks Alice is interested in me or something, that's why she's my friend. Nobody can just like me for myself. And that makes me feel like shit. [Lowers her head.]

A generic issue with Bree, one that continues for many years, is that she has a great capacity for being attracted to the downtrodden—Lee, who has lost his wife, her friend Alice, who is crippled. She surrounds herself with people who need her greatly. The flipside, however, is that she doesn't know how to have a more reciprocal relationship. She finds herself exploited by these relationships. (Some years later she got involved with a man who was in prison. Their entire relationship consisted of his calling her collect to talk about his life. He told her he was in prison for government-related espionage that he could never tell her about.)

Bree:	But . . . all rules were out the door. Anything we had worked toward just seemed to go down the tubes in one afternoon. He said he doesn't want to be married to someone who is suicidal.
Dr. Fishman:	Now where is he today?
Bree:	Work.
Dr. Fishman:	He couldn't make it today?
Bree:	[Shakes her head "no."] He couldn't make it today. He knew he couldn't make it, but he made this appointment anyway. . . .

There is an interesting dynamic here: He doesn't want to be married to someone who is suicidal, yet he doesn't make it to the psychotherapy sessions to help her out of the suicidality. Of course, there may have been things that impinged at work, but he had missed a number of sessions. And his wife thinks that he had no intention of coming to the session, that he knew he had a conflict when he made the appointment.

Dr. Fishman: So how did it end?

Bree: It never ends with him. There's never a final ending put on anything. I tried to . . . because I like to know where I stand, you know . . . I tried to get some kind of a closure on the argument or disagreement or whatever. I told him about the guy, I said if it bothers you forget it, we won't have him over anymore, it's as simple as that. It's not worth it to me, it's not like this great, you know, thing. But that wasn't good enough for him. Then I started getting mad at myself and thinking why should I give in like that? There's no reason why he shouldn't be able to come over, you know. In the grand scheme of things, why not? And then he sits there and says I'm not socializing. He tells you, he tells my parents, I'm not socializing. So I told him I can only socialize with the ones you handpick for me, right? I can't socialize with the ones that I pick. There's no . . . [shaking her head] So I can't be trusted, nobody likes me, and I mean. . . .

Dr. Fishman: Not only that, you're a loose woman.

Bree: Oh yeah, well [smiles] maybe I am, I don't know.

Dr. Fishman: Well, that's what he's implying.

A week or two after that, Bree came into a session with a black eye. I asked her what the problem was, and she said her husband beat her up. I then suggested that she call him and bring him into the session. He refused to come. She wanted to go to the police, and I supported her in empowering herself in a dangerous situation. In terms of our therapeutic work, I saw her going to the police as addressing conflict directly—something new for her. The police intervened, and her husband was jailed briefly. That was the beginning of their divorce.

As we worked in our therapy, Bree became increasingly stable. She started college. Much to her amazement, she got straight As. Her children did well, and she was able to have an almost amicable relationship with her ex-husband. Her social life and her relationships with men added stability. Men were not abusive to her, nor did the relationships cause her great emotional distress. At the conclusion of our work, it was still not clear how the system was maintained. Why did Bree seem to always find herself in problematic relationships? Was this pattern maintained in the context of her parents' marriage? Did their system need her to perpetually present problems to them? Her parents were practiced at bailing her out. Was that act the pattern that stabilized their marriage?

As I was leaving the city to begin a fellowship, I attempted to address this system. I had a number of sessions with Bree and her parents. They were long-suffering, totally devoted to their daughter. They were the homeostatic maintainers, always bailing out their daughter.

Had I stayed in town and had our work progressed to the point that Bree was stabilized over some considerable length of time, she might have left therapy living a fulfilling life without the constant need to have a crisis in her life. Unfortunately, what happened was a very different course, a sequence of therapies with a number of different psychiatrists and a dizzying array of diagnoses, including dissociative identity disorder and borderline personality disorder.

THE 3-YEAR FOLLOW-UP

Three years after the end of therapy, I asked Bree to come in for a follow-up session.

Dr. Fishman: Thank you for coming. I am writing up my cases, and I would like to follow up and get a sense of what worked, and what didn't work.

Bree: That doesn't surprise me about you—that you want to help other people. Some things never change.

Dr. Fishman: I hope that's true. So, let me get a sense of where things are.

Bree: Well, I'm not anorexic.

Dr. Fishman: Clearly. You look very well.

Bree: Yeah. I'm a little overweight, actually.

Dr. Fishman: You're okay with that?

Bree: No, I'm not okay with that. I'm not okay. I haven't had anything to eat in a day, but I put on a bunch of weight.

Dr. Fishman: We last met about 3 years ago.

Dr. Fishman: You were involved in a relationship that was pretty heavy-duty. . . .

Bree: I am still involved in it, and it's still heavy-duty. It's still like an albatross around my neck, you know what I mean? Not a good thing.

Dr. Fishman: But you can't get out?

Bree:	Seems like it. Seems like neither one of us can. Neither one of us can leave the other one alone.
Dr. Fishman:	All right. We met in '97. You were not anorectic at that time?
Bree:	No, but I went on to become anorectic again.
Dr. Fishman:	What happened?
Bree:	I left you. I went to see Dr. Baxter. No offense or anything like that. [I had referred her to him.]
Bree:	It was just that at that time, we didn't accomplish a damn thing, and it culminated in me taking an overdose.
Dr. Fishman:	What was that about? What were you so upset about? Do you recall?
Bree:	No, because it wasn't planned. It was very impulsive, which I have a lot more insight into now than I did before. One of the reasons why I really got my back up with him was that Dr. Baxter sent me to a psychiatrist who clearly sexually harassed me. I went back and told Dr. Baxter, and did a reality check, and asked him if he thought it was sexual harassment. He said, "Absolutely! I am so sorry. I will never refer another patient there. I am sorry you had to go through that. Yada yada yada." Then, after I overdosed, he was on his way out of town, he called you, and you weren't available. He wanted someone to see me when I got out of the hospital. Everyone was like, "No, don't keep her in the hospital. She gets worse in the hospital." So, he was okay releasing me to my parents. The only contingency was I had to go see that doctor. The one that we agreed had sexually harassed me. So, I just wrote *Dr. Baxter* a letter and told him I was discontinuing treatment. Then he sent me some bills that didn't make any sense to me. That escalated into him getting a judgment against me. I hope he's really happy about that, because I asked him every single time I left his office, "Do I owe you anything? I can't afford to run up a bill." After I discontinued treatment, it was like he was mad, and had a little hissyfit, and decided to send me a bill for thousands of dollars, which he knew I couldn't pay. He knew I was going through bankruptcy at the time. He held back—I can't believe that he would do it—but he held back his bill until all the bankruptcy went through, so I couldn't write it off on the bankruptcy. So I don't have warm feelings about him.

The therapist seeing Bree has been one more episode of betrayal. On the basis of confidential information, he waited until she went through bankruptcy and then sent her a bill. This scurrilous petty larceny is typical of her pattern of being betrayed as she proceeds through life. A savvier, more self-empowered person might have sued him for malpractice for his breach of confidence.

Once when I was presenting this case, one of my colleagues asked how I knew that Bree was telling the truth. I said that after years of experience, one functions on the basis of gestalts. You learn to constantly scan for consistency. After many hours of meeting with Bree, I am convinced that she is an outstandingly honest person. Indeed, one of her impediments is that she is so straightforward, almost to the point of naïveté. So when she describes the psychiatrist's behavior, I believe that she's telling the truth.

Dr. Fishman: I'm sorry about that. I had no idea.

Bree: Things happen. So, I decided I'm not going to therapy anymore. I'm not taking any more medicine. I went cold turkey on everything. That worked for . . . it worked but . . . it seemed to be the ticket . . . but then I began to get very anorexic again, very depressed. So, I started going to my family doctor, and I started seeing a therapist there. I saw him for about 2 years.

Dr. Fishman: What medication were you on?

Bree: First, I went in there and said, "No medication."

Dr. Fishman: Is this '98?

Bree: Yeah, I guess so. The only thing I would let him prescribe, just to make him feel better, was Atarax®. I was adamant that I wanted no medications whatsoever. I don't know. Somewhere along the line I was seeing this therapist, Betty. I think she was just basically doing stabilization management. She wasn't doing anything to help me, but she thought that I had DID—dissociative identity disorder. She left for another job, so . . . what did I do . . . My family doctor started writing me scrips again for antidepressants—Klonopin®? Let's see. I'm blanking out. I've always known that I have DID, ever since I was a kid. I'd walk into the classroom and I wouldn't know anybody in there. I wouldn't know why I was there. I knew something was wrong. I wrote my mother and father a letter, when I was 14, that said, "There's something wrong with me. I'm not like everybody else. I find myself in situations. . . . I don't understand why I'm in them." My mom just says, "You're dramatic. You have a vivid imagination." She blew me off. It just cracks me up because . . . I mean, you know, I come walking in here with my kids and everything, but we are clearly a family in crisis.

SIX-YEAR FOLLOW-UP

Six years from the time I first saw Bree, I called her for a follow-up. I hadn't heard much from her during those years. Occasionally when I was in town I would see her for a follow-up session. There was always a tale of woe—she continually had unsatisfying relationships that were filled with *Sturm und Drang*. Indeed her life was never quite settled, and most significantly, she was always being treated within a different mental health therapeutic regime. Each one she'd hoped, or been told, would provide the ultimate answer to her problems.

Bree begins the session reassuring me nothing has changed in terms of her presentation of self to the world. She is still struggling; other people are one up, Bree is consistently one down.

Bree: Last Thanksgiving I was hospitalized at the clinic for 10 days. My parents were at my home. I broke both my heels. I jumped down a flight of stairs. Anne dared me to do it. I don't know what I was thinking. Especially after having been anorectic for several years, and my bones. . . . I broke both my heels. So, my parents had to come out, and I so could not stand being around them that I had to be hospitalized during that time. Then, I've been seeing one of Dr. Abel's colleagues.

More reassurance that nothing has changed. First, she does something profoundly self-destructive by jumping down a flight of stairs at the dare of her 16-year-old daughter. I find this remarkable. Does her system require her to be the eternal patient? When things are relatively quiescent, she activates the problem to return things to the miserable status quo. The other thing that has not changed is that she has yet one more confirmed diagnosis—now it is DID. From my vantage point, diagnoses are tools that are supposed to lead the way toward people becoming more functional, living happier lives. One more questionable appellation clearly only keeps Bree in the quagmire of being a patient for life.

Bree: I've been seeing her for about a year, and she's been treating me for DID, but it was going really slowly because I am very resistant, because I've been in denial about it forever. No matter what, I've been in denial. I never wanted to tell anybody that I had DID or MPD or whatever because it was the way I coped. I didn't want to change. I was very resistant to it. I remain a little bit resistant, but I got a lot better at [the clinic].

> They had an unbelievable trauma disorders unit there. I got a lot of work done while I was there.

This is a woman who is a great consumer of psychiatric services. She has difficulty getting along with her parents, so she spends a week in a psychiatric hospital. Most people go stay with friends or try to resolve it independently. Later in our meeting she begins to describe another inpatient stay at another psychiatric hospital in another community. She is talking about a special program that she was in. Note that her work is going slowly because she is resistant—it is her fault. She doesn't consider that the therapist might be incompetent!

Dr. Fishman: What did they do?

Bree: They worked with all parts. They taught me internal communication. They taught me containment skills, grounding skills. Their therapy is very intensive. All the groups were not as important as the one-to-one therapy. They got me to remember some of my past. I came home with such a good, hopeful feeling, that now, I knew I was on the right track.

Her statements are a great condemnation of individual therapy. There she was spending hours going through the various solipsistic self-enhancement programs learning about herself, away from her children and community, delaying her true developmental tasks such as getting a job, finding an appropriate relationship, and being there for her troubled daughter. It is difficult enough to change one's social system. It's even more difficult when you're out of town.

In fact, it is clear that she was divided regarding her obligations. Indeed, she appeared to feel an obligation to the treatment team at the hospital, saying at one point, "I knew how to better work with my therapist, how she could better help me, and how I could be a better patient." At the hospital in New York, she was learning to be a better patient. Meanwhile, 150 miles away, all hell was breaking loose at home.

Bree: The very next day, after I got home, I had to hospitalize my daughter.

Dr. Fishman: For what reason?

Bree: Suicidal. She was cutting. She was doing drugs, and it was one of the hardest things I've ever had to do, was to put her in a place that I never wanted to be in, you know? I just never . . . more than anything. . . . I never wanted her to turn out like me. I'm not saying she will, but it's just. . . .

Dr. Fishman: It scared you.

Bree: Yes. I have an adolescent part that likes her a lot, and doesn't know where to draw the line between mom and friend. It's gotten out of hand. We were smoking pot together. My therapist is trying to help me with that. I was trying to get help for that at the hospital. I thought I had everything under control, but then just the other night my daughter got arrested—possession of marijuana in my home—while I was there.

I am becoming increasingly outraged. This woman is a hostage of the mental health system: "I have a part of myself that is still adolescent." A very convenient part—she takes no responsibility, and the system confirms her lack of responsibility. Clearly there is an alliance between the mental health system and this woman, and perhaps her parents. No wonder her daughter is having trouble; her mother is not doing what parents need to do for adolescents. No wonder her daughter is depressed; her mother has abdicated her responsibilities as a parent.

There's another reason for the girl's depression. and that is that she's very worried about her mother. She hears that her mother is damaged. Her daughter is a very loving young lady, increasingly relegated to the role of mothering her mother. This role alternates with the two of them being sisters who smoke pot together.

Dr. Fishman: How did they get in?

Bree: They knocked on the door, and I let them in. She had a few people over. I let them smoke pot in the house, and I opened the front door. Everyone ran out the back door. She came in and said, "It's all mine." They arrested her. I was like, "Well, couldn't I take the charges for her or anything?" They said, "No, she's already confessed to it. Every bit of marijuana in this house." There wasn't much—just a little bit in the ashtrays and stuff like that—but she got arrested for possession. Her relationship with her father is horrible. She hates him, and I think that drives a lot of her problems. Other than that, she's too entangled and too enmeshed with me and my problems.

Now we hear about the daughter and how she is very involved with her mother. The daughter is in individual therapy, so she has someone who is hearing her side of the problem. But the therapist is not working directly toward transforming this dysfunctional social system; in fact, her efforts appear to be working in the opposite direction, driving everybody to their corners.

It is a pity that none of the professionals took a broader lens and saw that the unit of intervention was the struggling, profoundly unhappy family. That the girl's father—and her mother, for that matter—wasn't involved in the treatment is tragic.

Dr. Fishman: Who is she in therapy with?

Bree: She was in therapy with someone locally. After the hospital, she said she didn't want to see that person anymore, because Arnie had found that therapist for her, for them to work on their relationship, but when the therapist talked to him, the therapist said, "She's got other problems right now, more pressing than her relationship with her father; her depression."

It appears that the therapist has a medical model perspective; the depression, like pneumonia, is within this girl, and she needs to have a pharmaceutical intervention and have someone to talk to. We do know what transpired after that: the girl's suicide attempt. No one would deny that this girl experiences the dysphoria of depression, but seeing the problem as emanating from within the young person effectively puts blinders on the clinician, who fails to appreciate the painful circumstances of her life.

The girl is estranged from her father. One would expect that, because she's so allied with Bree, who is furious with her former husband. So we get a better sense of what's going on with this girl—that is she is being actively triangulated between her parents. Not only does she not have a parental supervisory function from her mother, she is caught between her mother and her father. It appears to be Mom and the girl against Dad.

The treatment system is extremely inefficient and counterproductive. The therapists on each side have been recruited to be seconds in the battle. Their influence serves only to support each spouse in a symmetrical escalation, increasing the animosity and making the system even more troubled.

It is apparent from Bree's description that the professionals are not concerned about the triangulation that is clearly making things worse, especially for the girl. Interestingly, the brother has a good relationship with their father. It does not appear that he's being triangulated. One might suspect that the brother is the father's clandestine agent against the mother, but I don't think so. I suspect that he's taking a position of doing what he can to keep his head down and out of the fray.

The bottom line is that in all the huge number of hours and dollars the family is expending on the treatment system, no one seems to be even addressing this profound source of inner stress and instability for the girl—her triangulation between her parents and her recruitment to be mother's best friend.

Bree:	So, [the therapist] didn't want to see [Anne's] father anymore. She just wanted to see Anne. Then she sent her to a psychiatrist. He put her on two medications—an antidepressant and a benzodiazepine. That really annoyed me. I asked him not to give her any benzo's, under any circumstances, and when I was in the hospital, he gave her one and she abused it. I talked to him. I said, "Kids these days are abusing Klonopin, and Xanax®, and I really don't want you to write a prescription for her for that." She wrote a prescription for a benzo!

An epigram for this chapter might be the famous line from the Walt Kelly *Pogo* cartoon "We have met the enemy and he is us." Here we see another skirmish, this time between Bree and the psychiatrist who is treating her daughter. Bree, her daughter, and her mother are all seeing the same psychiatrist, and the doctor put this girl, who is already using drugs, on benzodiazepines, which are addicting.

Dr. Fishman:	Did you ever call him and tell him?
Bree:	No, I've never confronted him about the fact that he sexually harasses me every time I go there.
Dr. Fishman:	Why do you go there?
Bree:	A part of me likes the fact that I can get him to write a prescription for anything I want.

The price she is paying by going to this doctor is high: Not only is he giving her whatever drugs she wants, but he is undermining her self-esteem through the sexual harassment. If the goal of therapy is to help people function autonomously, the work with this psychiatrist is clearly counterproductive. It only further undermines her self-confidence and makes it all the more difficult for her to function in the community.

Dr. Fishman:	What medications are you on now?
Bree:	Now, I'm on two antidepressants and ritalin [amphetamine]. . . . So, that's where I'm at right now—trying to work with Anne's therapist, and trying to get things back to where they belong, and also trying to not forget about me in there, too, because since I got home from the hospital I've been consumed by this thing with Anne. I haven't been taking care of myself very well, so. . . .
Dr. Fishman:	How do you spend your time? Are you working? You were at school, a little while ago.

Bree: Yeah, I was in school, and then I kept getting this feeling like I need to be home, I need to be home, I need to be home—like a panic attack almost. I just had to drop out, and I've never gone back. I make $50 a week under the table making phone calls for this business, and I just started doing that. I'm sure it won't last long. I think I'm gonna be forced to get a job—at least part-time. I have so many stressors that it's unbelievable that I'm even walking around.

Dr. Fishman: How are you economically?

Bree: Above my means. I've always lived that way. It comes from Arnie—child support. It comes from social security disability for myself and children. And you remember Tony—prison Tony? Sometimes I get money from him. . . .

For many years Bree had a relationship with a man who was in prison, apparently serving a very long sentence. The relationship apparently continues to be important in her life. I see this relationship as another way in which Bree continues not to have true intimacy in her life.

Bree: So that's how I live. When I get really crushed I call my brother, and I ask him for some help.

Dr. Fishman: I met him and I met your parents?

Bree: Yeah.

Dr. Fishman: How is your son?

Bree: That's what was just on my mind. I was just gonna say that I try to make sure he doesn't get lost in the shuffle. He has a decent relationship with his father. He sees his father, and he knows that I have a lot of problems, and he knows that Anne's been going through a rough time, and it's strange, with Anne. She gets very good grades in school, despite all of the other stuff.

The striking thing about her daughter is that in the out-of-home context she does very well; she is at an exemplary student at school. This suggests that she essentially functions well, that she does not have profound dysfunctionality that pervades every area of her life. It is only in the tumultuous triangulating home situation that she is driven beyond distraction to suicidality.

Bree: The scary part is Anne's therapist gave her a DES scale [Dissociative Experiences Scale]—it's to measure dissociation.

> Apparently, she dissociates quite a bit, so she was recommended to Dr. Chapman by Dr. Jones to see if she needed an evaluation.

Now the daughter is pledging the club of the mental patients sorority. The individual therapist is now referring Anne to yet another mental health practitioner.

Bree:	She got another test, the SCID [Structured Clinical Interview for *DSM-IV*], to see if she was really dissociating, or if she just wanted to be like me. That's the other thing that bothers me. She seems to want to be just like me. She's always saying, "I'm just like my mom."
Dr. Fishman:	What is your relationship like with Arnie at this point?

I try to evaluate her present context, that is, her present relationships such as that with her ex-husband.

Bree:	I don't have any respect for him. I try to be cordial. I say "cordial," but . . . he still threatens. I kind of let that roll off my back. I don't let it affect me as much as I used to.
Dr. Fishman:	Between him and Anne, what is the difficulty?
Bree:	I really don't know. It's not like she just dislikes him. She vehemently hates him. There isn't anything positive she can say about him. It's just scary.

From my vantage point, I see that Anne has taken sides; she is in her mother's camp.

Bree:	I say, "He's your father. Don't you feel any kind of . . ." My son latches on to Arnie and they do guy things, and they never . . . they did things that didn't include Anne as her interests changed, as she grew up. She doesn't want to go to ball games anymore with them. She wanted to do different things, and he didn't go with the flow. He didn't change, despite the fact that he has a daughter. Now he tells me that both kids are completely screwed up, and they're walking down the wrong path in life, and it's all my fault, I should have given them up years ago. He could have done a better job of raising them than I have.

I have seen systems where a parent such as the father is so involved proving his estranged spouse wrong, he doesn't want the kids to do well.

To the extent they do well, it proves the wife right. Whether this applies to Arnie or not, I don't know; I've not seen him for many years. Regardless, there appears to be profound triangulation visited upon the children.

Dr. Fishman: Does he tell that to the kids?

Bree: No, I don't think so.

Dr. Fishman: Are you suicidal at this point?

Bree: Oh yeah, absolutely. I found it hard just to get through the night.

There is a wry quip that this reminds me of—"Aside from that, Mrs. Lincoln, how was the play?" I am flummoxed. All of these good intentions from, I'm sure, very conscientious practitioners, and she's still suicidal. I am shocked that they are not searching for consultations, and also I am saddened that after all these years, Bree is not a more savvy consumer of therapy. Shouldn't that be a message to the clinicians, that the model of therapy they're using and even their assessment are incorrect if, after all of this, she's still suicidal? I suspect she's suicidal because her life is miserably unfulfilling.

Indeed, the psychiatric perspective posits that when someone is suicidal it is because of profound psychiatric maladies such as depression. Colleagues of mine in Beijing investigated an epidemic of young women who were committing suicide (Pearson et al., 2002). Their article found that these women did not have preexisting psychiatric illness, and they had ample access to psychiatry. They were impulsively suicidal (using pesticides) because of the hopelessness of their situations living with their husbands in their husbands' homes. In the same way, from my perspective, Bree is suicidal in spite of all the therapy she is receiving because the therapy is not making her life more fulfilling. She appeared quite hopeless.

Dr. Fishman: Let's talk about your relationship with the man you're seeing, if you don't mind. Please don't tell me about it if you're not comfortable with this, because this is not a clinical meeting. Of course, this is only for my research.

I have virtually always found in my clinical experience that depression, like politics, is local. I've come to assume that if someone is depressed—or, putting the diagnosis aside, miserably unhappy—it is often those people that are close to them, the influential context, that is responsible for the maintenance of the depression. To repeat what I said in chapter 6, an article in the *Journal of the American Medical Association* examined factors predisposing people for unremitting depression. Some of the factors were previous depression, low socioeconomic status, and history of drug and alcohol abuse (Keller et al, 1994). One other factor that predisposes people to unremitting depression, depression that doesn't improve with treatment, was an intact marriage—in other words, being caught in a system that isn't changing (Keller et al., 1994).

Bree:	We've broken up and gotten back together a million times. Just when I think he's the most rotten person in the world, he'll—like, when I went to the hospital he took care of everything. He drove me down there, he picked me up, he did stuff for my parents. My waterbed leaks, he took care of that. He took the kids out to dinner one night to give them a break from my parents, and my parents a break from them. He visited me, and sent me packages. He couldn't have been more supportive. Now, since I've been home, I've only seen him once. We talk on the phone every single day. He's paying me $50 to make like two phone calls a day. So, I guess he's paying me $50 an hour. Actually, it's helpful because it helps me to structure my day, even in the smallest way.

An interesting relationship from my vantage point. As I observe Bree, this is a man who was there in the crunch, who was there when she was an inpatient, was there as long as she was not present. But for the last month he has been uninterested in socializing with her. He is available to give her work to help her financially, but if this month is any indication, he is not there to be a truly intimate partner.

Bree:	*Today, I go to therapy. I have four sessions a week, but I do it in 2 days, because the distance is so great.*

So what does she do with her time? She is a professional psychiatric consumer: She has four psychotherapy sessions a week, and it's a considerable drive from her house. Each round trip is 3 hours.

Dr. Fishman:	How do you pay for the therapy?
Bree:	I don't, most of the time. When I saw Dr. Abel, he asked me how much I could afford per week, and I told him $15 was about the most I could afford per day. So he sent that information on to the person he was referring me to, and she takes what she can get from Medicare. When I can pay her $15, I do. When I can't, she's okay with it.

Is this more exploitation of Bree? The therapist is paid by Medicare, because Bree is chronically disabled. I suspect that Bree is what's called a control case for a psychotherapist in training. If so, the clinician desperately needs Bree to continue as a patient. To fulfill her training requirements, she must have a certain number of patients who stay the course of therapy. This, of course, is a conflict of interest for the clinician. It is in her interest to keep Bree in treatment, but in Bree's interest to go on with her life instead of so much time in therapy.

I am struck by the continuing isomorphic pattern of Bree finding herself in situations where she is triangulated. It brings us back again to the true individual therapeutic work with Bree that we started, which was to support and empower her to challenge these systems in which she, for the lack of a better word, is victimized.

Dr. Fishman: In our work together—do you remember?

Bree: Mm-hmm. Most of it. Parts of it.

Dr. Fishman: I'm going to ask you about what was successful and what wasn't successful. What could have been done better, and what was done okay.

Bree: What could have been done better was more on my end than yours. What could have been done better was for me to be more honest with you and to tell you that I have a dissociating problem. I find things that I don't remember buying, and I'm spaced out so much of the time that it's hard to even really carry on a conversation at times, because I'm in and out, you know? When I came to you and said, "Everybody thinks I have a dissociative disorder" and you said, "I don't think so," that was exactly what I wanted to hear. You were my hero. It was like, "Dr. Fishman says I don't have a dissociative disorder, so that means I don't have one," even though I knew inside that I did, and I knew that it needed attention, because if it didn't, it was gonna keep cropping up, and it has. I tried to ignore it, and it's the kind of thing that just doesn't go away.

Reality is confirmation by significant others. Her present reality is that she has a dissociative disorder. When we were working she was functioning quite well in terms of relationships, was going to school, and was much more content. She was functioning competently in the real world, regardless of whether she was absent-minded or had a penchant for what could be called going to a fugue situation. Instead, we focused her on the positive parts of her life. Clearly the fugue situation is exacerbated by stress. If we decrease the stress, we have a much better chance of having a woman who will function well in the future. We see now that after years of focusing on her DID diagnosis, she was again suicidal the previous evening, struggling with a troubled relationship, no job, little money, and an out-of-control teenager. She had spent most of her life as a patient.

Bree: You definitely did encourage me to stand up to Arnie, and get out of that marriage, because that was a bad situation altogether. I think the fact that you were a bit strict and stern at times was good for me, as far as the eating disorder. You gave me a lot of hope. I'm sorry I haven't been able to live up to it, but at the time, I had a lot of hope that I could have a halfway decent life in spite of everything, and that hasn't been the case, actually.

Dr. Fishman: You haven't been very lucky with doctors either. I guess that the other doctor was not as helpful to you as I had hoped. I had thought that we would follow the same tradition, but he did no better than I did. There's no quality control.

I had ended my treatment with Bree, as I mentioned earlier, because I left the field after receiving a fellowship. I sent her to a colleague of mine whom I had partially trained, and it was a disaster.

Bree: When Arnie tells me that I did a lousy job raising the kids, I said maybe that's true, but I think that, at every juncture along the road, I did the best that I could at that time. The one thing that just can't be bought is the amount of love that there is in this house. I mean, we have a lot of problems, and a lot of things are going to hell in a handbasket, but there's tons of love, and that's gotta count for something.

Again another example of Bree's buying someone else's reality, when her husband chides her for doing a poor job raising the kids. Wasn't he involved? Has he no responsibility?

Dr. Fishman: You bet. A lot. A tremendous amount.
Bree: I really didn't fully understand the impact that my leaving for 9 weeks would have on them. It was too much for Anne.

This, of course, is one of the great indictments of individual therapy and especially of institutionalization. That is, the effect on the family is not sufficiently taken into account. In addition to the stigmatization, there is the fact that for 9 weeks she was away from her family. Such a lengthy absence would have a profound effect on any family, let alone a single parent family.

DISCUSSION

Reviewing this follow-up takes my breath away. When I was obliged to terminate my therapy with Bree, she was in school, her kids were doing well, her relationship with her ex-husband was not embattled, and, most importantly, she was neither anorectic nor suicidal. Now, 6 years after she and I began therapy, she has a completely tumultuous relationship, no job, and both she and her daughter are suicidal. Her anorexia is under control, but that is the only good news.

In my view, she has been crippled by the system. None of the therapists are dealing with the core conflicts, the chronic animosity between Bree and her husband in which her children are profoundly triangulated, especially the daughter, who is caught in the unremitting war. In fact, there are four therapists here—the son's, the daughter's, Bree's, and the psychiatrist. No one apparently has found it indicated for all involved to coordinate efforts for the good of the family. Moreover, there appears to be a serious conflict of interest here: Bree appears to be a control case for some sort of psychotherapeutic training, put on a schedule that fulfills training requirements for the therapist rather than her own needs,

A bittersweet afternote on Bree's story is that it was the untenable context in which Bree was living that predisposed her to those very symptoms that she was being treated for. Bree had been given the diagnosis of DID, dissociative identity disorder. T. M. Luhrmann has a very different perspective on this disorder than Bree's doctors: "Dissociation is a skill, and . . . can be learned. Some learn involuntarily, and their dissociation is pathological: unwanted, intrusive, uncontrollable. Others learn willingly, as a way of psychologically dropping out of the situation. . . . And the content is manipulable (2000, p. 18). The irony is, of course, that to the extent that Bree's unsatisfactory social situation is not addressed, she will be all the more inclined to flee into this dissociative context.

CHAPTER 12

Therapy for a Smaller Planet

Anei te Whanau (Here Is the Family)

We the family
the house of wellness
we stand as one
be strong

With love
We will overcome pain
We all believe
getting closer to wellness

Don't be afraid
You are a Chief/tainess
lifted up in the bosom
with the spirit

—Maori prayer

So here I am in New Zealand, looking out the window at Auckland, a city of 65 volcanoes, about as far as I can get from the United States. My present job is Clinical Director for Maori Mental Health Care for a large part of the Auckland area. The Maori are the indigenous people of New Zealand who, despite colonization, have maintained their culture. When I arrive at work each morning, a *karakia* is held where ancient prayers are recited. What is most interesting and refreshing to me is the Maori focus on *whanau* (family). There is a tremendous resistance to see people individually. When Maori introduce themselves to others, they state where their tribe came from, where their family came from, their family geneology, and the name of the mountain and river in the region where they came from. Having grown up in Chicago, I found this a difficult exercise, as there are no mountains and only one river, the Chicago River. (Indeed, the Maori, who hold great reverence for unspoiled nature, would be aghast to learn that for many years the legendary Mayor Daley dyed the river green for St. Patrick's Day.) New Zealand has a tiny population (4 million people), but it has severe multiple social problems, such as the highest per capita teenage suicide rate in the developed world. I came to New Zealand to work on a project using intensive structural therapy (IST) to help address this problem.

When I began this book, I was a chief medical officer of a large Medicaid behavioral health HMO, which was a subsidiary of the Philadelphia Department of Health. Our goal in founding this organization was to do managed care right, such that for once the economically disadvantaged citizens of a community could receive truly effective care—care that was consumer centered, accessible, and that advocated for the consumers and their families. I accepted this position because I felt working within larger systems I could improve the care provided, especially for children and adolescents.

At the outset, even before we had opened our doors, I had some warning signs. To make a transition from the existing insurance to new insurance, we requested transition forms from the provider. One such transition form stated the following: The patient was a 4-year-old girl who is on large doses of a powerful antipsychotic medication. The last line read, "Amy will be on this medication until she acknowledges legitimate authority." Here, the presenting symptoms were failure to follow instructions, not behaviors that could have been construed as representing a manifestation of a thought disorder. Only misbehavior was described, and there was no indication in the paper that they had considered for a moment any concerns for her developmental stages or that this girl was responding to a social environment that may have been stressing her.

My blood ran cold, but I thought perhaps this was an anomaly. I soon learned that the poor quality seen in this anecdote was not rare. In fact, it was common.

Our managed care company made some important contributions to the city's behavioral health delivery system. It provided improved access with a toll-free number, and consumers could choose which providers they wanted anywhere in the city. A consumer group within the company was available on the phone 24 hours a day, 7 days a week to help underprivileged individuals find the right providers. We developed a quality management system that provided fundamental oversight of care, such as ensuring that all workers who had contact with children had child abuse clearances from the state. The concept behind the company was that any savings would go back to the community in terms of model programs and prevention.

From my position as the senior psychiatric officer overseeing clinical care, I was increasingly concerned about the frontline services. The care we provided was very much structured like a donut—a good structure surrounding an empty middle. In terms of clinical accountability to the socially disenfranchised families and their kids, often it seemed sadly lacking.

My personal reaction was, in the words of the English philosopher Charles Handy in his book *The Age of Unreason,* that there was a "disappearance of difference." The kids were usually treated similarly to the 4-year-old girl, with the same myopic regimen—a profound inattention to context, resulting in an indifference to the specific pressures in the kids' lives. I recall one adolescent who tried to jump out of the window of his family's eight-story apartment. He was placed into a long-term residential system. When I investigated, I realized that no one had sought to find out what had precipitated his behavior. It turned out that his stepfather had just been released from prison and was terrorizing all the family members. The boy jumped out the window not because he was mentally ill, but perhaps because he was desperate. No medication, however powerful, can address this social situation. When the boy finally returned home, nothing would have changed.

In some ways, this book is old fashioned, because it focuses on psychotherapy. Take, for example, the lunch session. During the past 30 years (I conducted my first lunch session in 1974), I have seen many times the power of this intervention. This effectiveness has been confirmed by my colleagues and in the original psychosomatic research. In my experience, the lunch session, with its proscribed protocol for a behavioral paradigm and additional family therapy, is a very effective *psychotherapy* treatment for anorexia, a disease with the highest mortality of any psychiatric disease—not to mention, for those that survive, the high morbidity and tenacious chronicity.

In the original volume that described this work, *Psychosomatic Families* (1978), the last chapter was entitled "Psychotherapy for a Small Planet." They titled the chapter that because "in this quarter of the twentieth century, we are learning that resources are not infinite, that if man won his battle with nature, he would be, as E. F. Schumacher pointed out, on the losing side" (p. 329).

As I write, I am struck by the fact that what we have now is therapy for an even smaller planet—there are fewer resources to go around. These indeed are troubled times. People are increasingly aware of the "constraints of the eco-system," the daunting specter of global warming, global conflicts, and economic recessions from the major economies of the United

States, Germany, and Japan. The dream of our parents or grandparents of "one world" has now come back to haunt us, not as a great breakthrough of enhanced human consciousness and diminution of nationalism; quite the contrary, it is one world in terms of the pugilist terrorist acts, the borderlessness of terrorism. We see medical systems across the world straining at their seams. The inspirational proselytization of panaceas such as managed care now appear to many to be just so many more dashed hopes.

So what are some of the parts of this book that I believe will help to provide, in some small way, better, more effective care in this time of diminishing resources? What are some of the lessons from this book that might be helpful beyond the world of severe eating disorders? First, the positivistic belief in grounded observation, so central to the IST model. The psychosomatic work indeed was based in the tradition of grounded and rooted observation, originally described by Glaser and Strauss (1967). The examples of the lunch session in chapter 4 are probably the best examples in this book of following the minute-to-minute interactional patterns between the family members.

IST is a model that aims to streamline and focus on pivotal interactional dynamics within the family and the system in which it is embedded. These process interactional patterns that we focus on are on a sufficiently generic level so that, while they are addressed, the clinician is freed to appreciate and delve into family members' subjective experiences.

From time immemorial, bearing witness has been an essential part of the healing process. The power of this process is not to be underestimated. There is a hazard, however, for the therapist who is bearing witness to these subjective accountings to lose his or her objectivity. Absent objectivity, the clinician does not have the perspective to create change, and change, after all, is our charge. The beauty of tracking the process patterns, through the technique of enactment (Minuchin & Fishman, 1981), allows the clinician to step back from the content, from even the pain of the words, to track in a seminaturalistic way the family interactional patterns.

There is great power, in my experience, with this model beyond people who present with eating disorders. Crisis induction, working with key interactional processes, I've found to be invaluable in creating change with problems other than anorexia. The creation of a crisis, regardless of the presenting problem, allows the clinician and the family to work together to transform the problem with immediacy. The immediacy of a therapeutic crisis is important, because family patterns, especially in troubled families, tend to have their own inertia. It is the rigidity and the inflexibility of these systems that lead these families in circles. For example, every single Sunday, for her entire married life, Dorothy has been held hostage waiting for her parents to show up for breakfast. Nobody ever challenged this habit that made them all so uncomfortable. Now, that's rigidity!

The people in these pages are, for the most part, people sufficiently medically stable, as determined by their physician, to be treated as outpatients. As we have seen, most of these people are nevertheless fragile due to their severe symptoms.

There is an array of effective uses of this model for individuals whose symptoms are more severe and, at the other extreme, for people who are less symptomatic and healthier. For these situations, as well as for other presenting problems, there are components of this model that are effective. Some examples were in the realm of other psychosomatic diseases such as some asthmatics, and with programs that provide early intervention of troubled adolescents.

This psychotherapy model has been used with the most severe expressions of anorexia, with patients who are hospitalized. With the girl being closely monitored by the medical staff, we have taken advantage of the power of the family, especially the parents and their supports, as the treatment delivery system. The parents enforce the protocol, even the refeeding of the young person. The parents and their supports enforce the bed rest protocol. I have found this to be effective in terms of getting the young person's weight up, and transforming the family system while maintaining medical safety for the child.

Interestingly, at times the only difficulty I have found is with the medical staff. For example, things were proceeding, and the 15-year-old girl was beginning to eat and gain weight. The nurses at the local children's hospital became upset. They said that they had no idea of their role in the care of this child—"the family seemed to be doing all the work." I was summoned to a meeting with about 60 nurses, where I did my best to explain this model. One significantly helpful factor was the presence of the pediatrician with whom I was working. She and I explained the model to, I *believe*, the satisfaction of the nursing staff.

I have also found this model effective with mild anorexics. There are extrapolations to problems of lesser severity. For example, Raquel was a college student who suddenly developed anorexia. For the first time in her life, this young potential law student was losing weight dramatically. She had lost 20 pounds from her already lean body. I assessed her and the family and didn't see a psychosomatic family. As I further assessed her system, I saw the psychosomatic family system that was maintaining the eating disorder was her roommate situation, which was driving her to distraction. She had a roommate who was extremely intrusive, with conflict avoidance, rigidity, and overprotectiveness ubiquitous in the system. In fact, because of the intrusiveness, Raquel felt she was never able to develop a relationship with a member of the opposite sex: every time she began to date, all of her roommates were so critical of him and so intrusive that Raquel would lose interest in the relationship.

I worked with her to be sensitive to boundary intrusions. We then addressed her admitted terror of addressing conflict. With my coaching of this young woman to transform the system, her recent anorexia was ameliorated. At the 1-year follow-up Raquel was happy in law school, and the problem had vanished completely. In fact, she had even begun a relationship with someone near the end of our treatment. What follows are a few segments from a follow-up session the following year.

Dr. Fishman: Thanks very much for coming in. So how are things, and could you talk a bit about the initial problem that you came to see me with, some of our work and the follow-up from there?

Raquel: I had come to you because my parents had noticed there was a problem with my weight, and at the time I kind of knew that there was but didn't know what the real problem was. I came to you primarily because of my weight issue and really didn't have anything else that I thought it was about.

I think I was upset with my living situation, upset with school, there were a lot of . . . a little weak, a little depressed and I found that when I was here talking with you the focus wasn't on the food, it wasn't on what I was eating, it was on things going on in my life, kind of danger, warning signs that we talked about. And it was about friendships and being able to trust people, and being comfortable with people and through that, through modifying my friendships that weren't healthy or weren't good for me because of jealousy or just anger and selfishness and by changing those friendships it was helping me get more in control of what I really wanted, which was healthy relationships with people. . . .

Raquel's statement also is significant in the context of our work because at the initial stages of treatment there was a great deal of tension between Raquel, myself, and her parents regarding my treatment modality. Raquel's mother is a physician as is her father, and they felt very strongly that my focus should be on her weight and on nutrition, on her psychological preoccupation with food and self-starvation. My vantage point, of course, was that she should prepare to address the context and the relationship. Raquel's statement is a confirmation of the direction we took.

Raquel: As a result everything kind of fell into place, and I really didn't think about eating more or getting more fit or less sick physically—it just kind of happened and I don't really remember a time when I consciously said okay this is it, I'm going to change the way I'm viewing myself. It just, as I progressively got better and cut off the friendships that I thought were unhealthy, everything kind of progressed along with that.

Even with making new friends at school, I know where my boundaries are and I know what to look for and I know what the warning signs are. I think more now I try to protect myself rather than worry about how other people think of my friendships or me with other people. It's kind of more important for me now to be healthy with myself than not healthy with somebody else just because it's a friend or. . . . So yeah.

Dr. Fishman: Do you feel that you are more assertive in relationships? Because with those roommates you were somewhat subjected to some of the vagaries of their criticism. Are you better at setting boundaries and addressing the conflicts?

Raquel: [Nodding] I think it's more now that if I don't agree with something I won't just kind of quietly either not say something, which I think I had done, or go along with it to make other people happy. I definitely will say more what I think or how I feel, but I think also people ask me more because they do know that I will say something. Or maybe it's just because when I met the friends I have at school now they didn't know me as the person who just kind of gave in to things, which is why I think they ask for my opinion more often.

Dr. Fishman: Now when we met you were restricting your food, you were just really starving yourself to some extent. Has your weight changed since?

Raquel: Since my smallest, the thinnest I was, I've probably gone up about 20 pounds in the past year and a half.

Dr. Fishman: In terms of your relationship [with the man she met near the end of our therapy, a relationship they have maintained], when we started working, and this has to do with age also, you have matured, you were really not that connected to guys.

She had had difficulty finding a boy to go out with when our work began. She had gone through three and a half years of college without dating anyone. When I investigated the situation, it appeared that her roommates were extremely critical of all the boys she introduced to them. (She did say that she thought they were jealous of her because she was prettier—and thinner!—than the roommate she had the most trouble with.)

Dr. Fishman: Are you still with the same gentleman that you were?

Raquel: [Nods] It has been a year and a half. He is in Boston so it's a long distance thing. I'll go up there; he'll come to see me. It's rough at times, but I think we've kind of made the commitment that it's fine this way.

It is very interesting that she has created a context for herself to support her in handling relationships. We worked for about 3 months; during the last month, this relationship began. In many ways she recruited him to be her support as well as enhance her antennae in relationships with people. I don't get a sense of him seeing her as being a symptomatic "patient," but instead he seems a friend who helps her with vulnerabilities she may have with other friends.

Dr. Fishman: What did you weigh at your lowest?

Raquel: 106.

Dr. Fishman: You were 5'4"?

[Raquel nods.]

Dr. Fishman: You know I've seen much, much worse as you would imagine. I mean it's not really severe anorexia, but you were starving yourself and most importantly you were not happy, life was not fulfilling.

[Raquel is nodding.]

Dr. Fishman: What have you learned from the experience?

Raquel: Oh God, what have I learned? That I'm a very mental person. That if I really want to do something, whether it's not eating or becoming healthy, I can do it. I think I've learned the power of what somebody can do. Without having gotten through it, you can't fully understand the power that you have over yourself and that you can really do a lot of good and a lot of harm.
                   I feel like a different person. Sometimes, if I think about it, it's kind of bizarre. But you really did give me that ability almost to be a little bit more aggressive with how I dealt with it instead of running to my room and just saying, "okay guys stay out." It was a more hands-on approach to "I can't be in this friendship, I can't do this."

What we see here is an extrapolation with the work with the roommate in other relationships, especially with other young women. Apparently because of her striking appearance, there has always been a certain amount of jealously toward her. As a result of our work, clearly she is now able to have deeper friendships because she can regulate the process.

Through the therapy, there is a new isomorph that she has embraced and that is her own power as a person to address problematic, intrusive situations. As a result of her appearance, people often have agendas for her. Now it seems she is able to be freer to be close to people because she doesn't feel that she will be subsumed in the way she had been in the roommate situation.

As with Betsy in the chapter on compulsive overeating, specifically my coaching for her on dealing with her harasser, this was therapy that enabled the patient to change her relationships—not only the immediate relationships but also ensuing relationships. I have used the IST model many times in similar situations. I don't believe Raquel was a full-blown anorexic, but she was well on the road. The lesson for prevention is intervening at these early stages to deal with the key isomorph, and that isomorph is the conflict avoidance. With her roommates Raquel had created a psychosomatic family-type organization with the same patterns—the conflict avoidance, the enmeshment/intrusiveness, the overprotectiveness, and the rigidity.

I have found this model effective in numerous other contexts with other presenting problems. The characteristics of psychosomatic families are found in other situations as well, as with children placed by social services because of severe behavior problems. Their families tend to differ from eating disorder families in that they are often from the lower social economic strata of society. Nevertheless, in my experience, their families can resemble eating disorder families, with the same the parental split, conflict avoidance, rigidity, and the diffusion of conflict by a third—namely, by the behavior of the delinquent child.

Take an example from my recent work. When he came to see me he was 12 years old. He had been in treatment in the community for 5 years. Billy's behavior had become so out of control that his biological mother had moved out of the house, leaving Billy at home with his biological father and another sibling! The family was driven to such desperation that they spoke to their member of the New Zealand parliament, who wrote a letter to us and social services saying, in essence, "Can't anybody for God's sake do anything with this child?"

We developed the following intervention for Billy's family, based on the lunch session model. In the lunch session, the feeding of the child is the consequence around which the parents have to work together. With wayward children, today's parents rarely have any consequences that they can effectively use to change their child's behavior. By enlarging the family and treatment system to involve government child protection services, an additional resource is available to the parents for removing the young person from the home if he or she refuses follow the rules of the family.

In Billy's situation, the parents met with a therapist and were challenged to work together to address his behavior. In this process, I observed that one parent aligned with the boy, sabotaging the other parent's attempt to change Billy's behavior.

In this lengthy session, the parents ultimately decided on appropriate rules that they saw were necessary for the mother to maintain her sanity. The parents then attempted to negotiate with the boy but he refused: He said he would not follow their rules. At the end of the session, dramatically, social services drove Billy to a placement.

The system was set up as follows: If Billy was unwilling to follow the family rules, social services would keep him in a residential facility. When he was willing to follow the rules, he could go home. This created a profound crisis in the system. The parents had a sense of control, and Billy had a sense that he wasn't so powerful, which can terrify children and adolescents. The parents in the past had no leverage, so this intervention gave them some much needed power. Of course, as in the lunch session, the real work was structural, getting the parents to agree to work together.

This was a one-weekend intervention. The parents then canceled the next few sessions at the last minute. I called the parents; they didn't feel a need to come in. I called them 9 months later and asked how things were going. The mother said, "Things are fine. There are adolescent things that come up, but it's no big deal, we can easily handle them." Her son was doing better at school with his siblings and was participating on a sports team for the first time. And then she said, "Why didn't anyone do this 5 years ago?" Again, this is the model of creating a crisis, which is used as the fulcrum to change the system. And the important aspect of the model, of course, is that the essential caretaking system must reorganize so that the child is no longer triangulated between the parents.

Before we lost our funding, we conducted similar interventions with seven other families. When I left that clinic, five of the seven children were back at home, and the family systems were much better than they had ever been. Another child was living with a member of his extended family but was still functioning very well and had gone back to school for the first time in 3 years. The seventh child was still in active treatment.

WHAT ARE THE LESSONS OF PREVENTION FROM THESE PAGES?

One clear lesson to be learned from the cases discussed in this book is that the earlier kids are seen in treatment the better. That said, one should not give up hope with problems that have been chronic, even manifesting decades of chronicity. This has to do with prevention. As I've mentioned previously, the expectations of the clinician profoundly affect the course of the treatment. If we focus on the *DSM-IV* categories and their apparent immutability, we do not give hope for change, nor do we challenge people to push against those circumstances, which are maintaining the status quo that is keeping them symptomatic.

In the area of prevention, I was involved with Roberta Knowlton and Fred Andes in developing a prevention program for adolescents at risk of abusing drugs. As part of the school social programs in troubled areas in New Jersey, this program added a unique model of family intervention for these young people and their families. Based on IST principles, the therapy was augmented by a community resource person (CRP) from the child's community. This person accessed the essential resources in the community to help recontextualize the family, thus stabilizing the child's context. An evidence-based evaluation of the program found that the addition of the CRP significantly enhanced the effectiveness of the treatment (Fishman, Andes, & Knowlton, 2001).

What are the larger systemic lessons from these pages? We have seen that a coherent treatment system is invaluable in effectively treating people with difficult psychiatric problems. As I have mentioned, one important premise of this book is a very simple message: Old-fashioned talking therapy can be valuable. Psychotherapy, as described throughout this book, is a profoundly powerful tool for transforming eating disorders, a deadly, highly chronic set of diseases.

There are ideas in these pages that are contrary to much of the contemporary thinking taught in academic training programs, because of the focus on *conflict*. Indeed, the emergence of conflict is what transforms these systems. The time-honored "first do no harm" is interpreted by many to mean avoiding conflict, but I am urging the opposite: *We do the most harm by avoiding conflict.*

Another crucial point is the essentiality of the *system of care*. When Mary Jane England, M.D., was the president of the Washington Business Group on Health (as well as the president of the American Psychiatric Association), they challenged the wisdom of the time by parodying the slogan "It's the economy, stupid" with lapel pins that read "It's the system, stupid" (personal communication, 1995). It's *still* the system: While we are focusing on the family, we are also focusing on the system of care surrounding our patients. One essential issue addressed in each of the cases in this book was the clinical team establishing a congruent system of care. We see the importance of this fact in chapter 11 with failed systems of care.

I end this book with a sense of considerable concern regarding the future of psychiatry. T. M. Luhrmann, in her book *Of Two Minds: The Growing Disorder in American Psychiatry* (2000), says "a combination of socioeconomic forces and ideology is driving psychotherapy out of psychiatry. . . . If psychotherapy is axed from psychiatry by the bottom-line focus of managed care companies"—or by a myopic view of presumed psy-chopharmacologic needs of the patient—it would be "a terrible mistake" (p. 23). It would be bad for psychiatry. It would, in my estimation, be worse for our society, because "biomedicine encourages a way of thinking about mental illness that can strip humanity from its sufferers. And above all it would be bad for patients, who will be treated less well and less effec-tively if treated from a purely biomedical perspective" (Luhrmann, 2000, p. 23). The underlying lesson of this book, as I have said, is that psycho-therapy, which is increasingly discounted or marginalized in psychiatric care as well as general medical care, can potentially be profoundly power-ful. The thrust of virtually all of these cases was psychotherapy. Although there were ancillary treatments, they were for the most part supportive, not central.

An important corollary issue is whether psychiatry is so focused on the individual mind that it doesn't understand that the human mind is a cyber-netic mind, so social culture and context are crucial to understanding the individual and his or her context. To use a phrase from Gregory Bateson (1972), "the mental characteristics of the system are immanent, not in some part, but in the system as a whole" (p. 316). If psychiatry continues to train people just for the neurotransmitters and only focuses on the indi-vidual mind, the field will have lost its way. Take, for example, chapter 11 on troubled systems. A crucial issue was the failure of the professionals to create a coordinated treatment system. Many professionals today use treat-ment that has disconnected the biomedical from the social. Yet many diffi-culties that our patients experience originate in the social forces that create the stress in the patient's life. This stress is what leads to the exacerbation of the patient's problems.

If practitioner myopia continues to exacerbate, much will be lost and many people will be failed who are desperately seeking health. The chal-lenge to psychotherapy trainers, educators, and the next generation of practitioners is to confront the makers of policy and not allow short-term promises of biomedicine to weaken the profound biopsychosocial needs of our patients.

And, finally, I see this book as a challenge to the consumers and their families. They should insist on treatment that is effective, is evidence based, or at least has qualitative literature that accesses outcomes.

There is a profound paradigm shift that all involved need to espouse. The APA Guidelines in many ways determine the standard of care for eat-ing disorders; and throughout, the wording and the conceptualization view the problem as within the individual. If there is any lesson to be drawn from these pages, it is that these problems are the joint concern of the indi-vidual sufferer *and* his or her family. As a unit, they should seek care. As a unit, they should seek answers. As a unit, they should demand effective, family-based treatment.

Some people are critical of the phrase: "It takes a village to feed a child"; they say it ignores the primacy of the family. Similarly, the true lesson of this book is that it takes a family (*family* with a small *f*—the individual and her influential context) to effectively care for the fierce and enervating problem of eating disorders and to transform the problem for the long term.

Lunch Session Protocol

The therapeutic lunch session used for the sessions in chapters 6, 7, and 8 is based on the original work of Rosman, Minuchin, and Liebman (1975). In my experience, having used this technique myself for 30 years, the intervention becomes a fulcrum around which the family patterns are displayed and then changed. As I explained in the chapters, to the extent that the parents cooperate, their child eats. And it is very easy to see in the microanalysis, especially in chapter 5—when the parents act together, the child takes a bite of food. To the extent that the parents are split, however subtly (i.e., the mother says eat the sandwich, the father says don't make noise—the father is surreptitiously not supporting the mother), the child refuses to eat.

Most importantly, the clinician tracks the process during this session, modulating the intensity according to the therapeutic goal of getting the youngster to eat.

In presenting this protocol I use Lester Laborsky's format from *Principles of Psychoanalytic Psychotherapy* (1984) because it clearly spells out the steps of the intervention. It also can be a very useful tool when going back and analyzing the videotapes of sessions that do not go as well as would have been hoped.

As is clear in the chapters, the lunch session contextualizes the problem and often the youngster begins eating, but it does not represent system transformation. Ongoing family therapy is necessary. In many situations, if the patient is at a weight that must be increased, the lunch session is followed by a behavioral protocol. A schedule is drawn up with the input of the youngster's physician and the family that sets specific weight goals to be met by specific dates. If the patient does not bring her weight up to a particular goal by a specified date, she is prescribed bed rest and allowed to get up only to go to the bathroom. No reading or TV is allowed.

This paradigm is overseen and enforced by the parents (or by other members of the system during times when the parents are unavailable). Thereby, the protocol continues to maintain the pressure on them to change their relationship. They must work together and not triangulate their youngster.

What follows is a step-by-step protocol for the lunch session. I do not see this as an exhaustive description, but it should give the reader an overview of how this intervention is facilitated. This is the basic roadmap, if you will, for the clinician embarking on this intervention. I cannot overemphasize the importance of joining with the family members—giving them hope and confirming them as individuals—to demonstrate that you understand that this is a different approach, and likely one that they have never experienced.

Of course, this is done in the context of the overall treatment system. I customarily use this intervention at the second session. I ask the family to bring lunch. The content of the session is not the food that is before them per se. During these interviews the therapist maintains an essentially nonchalant attitude toward food. The content is pleasantries. As you see in examples, however, it is *process directed:* Should the young person not eat, the parents need to pull together and facilitate their child eating. The focus is no longer on the question of why the child won't eat, or on observing *how* she's eating; instead, eating is a natural function that is the backdrop to customary social interactions.

In my experience, the therapeutic emergence of conflict is curative in the psychosomatic system. Conflict, needless to say, is also stressful for the family and the child. The context created by the clinician is one of hope; the clinician should be clear that these interventions will be effective (in my experience they usually are effective) and also be empathetic to the family and child, acknowledging that this is a difficult treatment. The lunch session is in the tradition of countless other medical interventions that are uncomfortable yet effective.

I include the lunch session with some temerity. It is to be used by clinicians who have expertise in working with families, by therapists who have the experience to track the family process and know when to tell the family that they must "regroup tomorrow," and by professionals who know when they should bring in a consultant.

I am interested in the experience of clinicians using this protocol. I can be reached at www.intensivestructuraltherapy.org

ALGORITHM FOR EATING DISORDER TREATMENT: LUNCH SESSION COLLABORATIVE RESEARCH PROJECT

1. Protocol for Intake

a. The degree to which the clinician describes the program—that is, the importance of the family participation.

1	2	3	4	5
not at all	some	moderate	much	very much

b. The degree to which the therapist obtains signed releases.

1	2	3	4	5
not at all	some	moderate	much	very much

c. The degree to which the intake protocol includes clearance by pediatrician/family doctor.

1	2	3	4	5
not at all	some	moderate	much	very much

d. Degree of clarity of instructions to the family (procedures and documents).

1	2	3	4	5
not at all	some	moderate	much	very much

2. Stage 1: Lunch Session

a. Preparation

i. The clinician's context—degree of support from medical, administrative, other clinical staff (especially nurses).

1	2	3	4	5
not at all	some	moderate	much	very much

ii. Degree of recruitment of the essential family members—inclusion of the homeostatic maintainer.

1	2	3	4	5
not at all	some	moderate	much	very much

iii. Degree of usage of pre-tests for the family.

1	2	3	4	5
not at all	some	moderate	much	very much

b. The session

i. Degree of clinical assessment of the system.

1	2	3	4	5
not at all	some	moderate	much	very much

ii. Degree of creation of the therapeutic crisis.

1	2	3	4	5
not at all	some	moderate	much	very much

iii. Degree of choice of caretaker (often the less-involved parent).

1	2	3	4	5
not at all	some	moderate	much	very much

iv. Degree of recruitment of the other caretaker.

1	2	3	4	5
not at all	some	moderate	much	very much

c. Creating the therapeutic crisis

   i. Degree of focus on the eating.

1	2	3	4	5
not at all	some	moderate	much	very much

   ii. Degree of emphasis on the parents working together.

1	2	3	4	5
not at all	some	moderate	much	very much

   iii. Degree of clarification of unbalancing as necessary.

1	2	3	4	5
not at all	some	moderate	much	very much

d. Terminating the session

   i. Degree of emphasis on the parents' success or their working together.

1	2	3	4	5
not at all	some	moderate	much	very much

   ii. Degree of success in scheduling the session for the next day if the parents fail to work together.

1	2	3	4	5
not at all	some	moderate	much	very much

3. Stage 2: Behavioral Paradigm

a. Preparation

   i. Degree to which they have access to a doctor's scale.

1	2	3	4	5
not at all	some	moderate	much	very much

   ii. Degree of reinforcement of close collaboration with pediatrician/family doctor.

1	2	3	4	5
not at all	some	moderate	much	very much

b. Establishing the paradigm

   i. Emphasis on bed rest.

1	2	3	4	5
not at all	some	moderate	much	very much

   ii. Emphasis on no reading or entertainment, time to think about patient's future, etc.

1	2	3	4	5
not at all	some	moderate	much	very much

   iii. Emphasis on the necessity that one or both parents must be present to monitor the protocol.

1	2	3	4	5
not at all	some	moderate	much	very much

iv. Emphasis on the necessity that fixed caloric number must be arrived at with the help of the pediatrician/family doctor.

1	2	3	4	5
not at all	some	moderate	much	very much

v. Emphasis on the necessity that parents, with the help of the doctor, determine the daily weight gain target and the ultimate target weight.

1	2	3	4	5
not at all	some	moderate	much	very much

c. Monitoring the paradigm

i. Degree to which patient is weighed same time each day (with the same kind of clothing).

1	2	3	4	5
not at all	some	moderate	much	very much

ii. Degree to which there is agreed on weight gain/per unit time (often it is every 2 days) or complete bed rest.

1	2	3	4	5
not at all	some	moderate	much	very much

iii. Degree to which on days when weight is achieved the patient is free to resume normal life.

1	2	3	4	5
not at all	some	moderate	much	very much

d. Degree to which contract with the family is agreed upon to continue therapy after the ED remits (to stabilize new structure.)

1	2	3	4	5
not at all	some	moderate	much	very much

References

American Psychiatric Association. (1994). *Desk Reference to the Diagnostic Criteria from DSM-IV.* Washington, DC: Author.

American Psychiatric Association (2000a). *Diagnostic and Statistical Manual of Mental Disorders* (DSM-IV-TR) Washington, DC: Author.

American Psychiatric Association. (2000b). Practice guideline for the treatment of patients with eating disorders (revision). American Psychiatric Association Work Group on Eating Disorders. *American Journal of Psychiatry, 157*(1 suppl), 1–39.

Andersen, A. E. (2001). Eating and weight regulation. In *Virtual Hospital: Eating and weight disorders.* Retrieved August 19, 2003, from http://www.vh.org/adult/patient/psychiatry/eatingdisorders/regulation.html

Anderson, D. A., & Maloney, K. C. (2001). The efficacy of cognitive-behavioral therapy on the core symptoms of bulimia nervosa. *Clinical Psychology Review, 21*(7), 971–988.

Attia, E., Haiman, C., Walsh, B. T., & Flater, S. R. (1998). Does fluoxetine augment the inpatient treatment of anorexia nervosa. *The American Journal of Psychiatry, 155*(4), 548–551.

Bacaltchuk, J. & Hay, P. (2003). Antidepressants versus placebo for people with bulimia nervosa. *Cochrane Database of Systematic Review,* CD003391.

Bacaltchuk, J., Hay, P., & Trefiglio, R. (2003). Antidepressants versus psychological treatments and their combination for bulimia nervosa. *Cochrane Database of Systematic Reviews,* CD003385.

Bateson, G. (1972). *Steps to the ecology of mind.* New York: Ballantine Books.

Beumont, P. J., Russell, J. D., Touyz, S. W. Buckley, C., Lowinger, K., Talbot, P., & Johnson, G. F. S. (1997). Intensive nutritional counseling in bulimia nervosa: A role for supplementation with fluoxentine? *Australian and New Zealand Journal of Psychiatry, 31,* 514–524.

Becker, A. E. (1995). *Body, self, and society: The view from Fiji.* Philadelphia: University of Pennsylvania Press.

273

Bell, R. M. (1985). *Holy anorexia*. Chicago: Chicago University Press.

Bernstein, R. K. (2003). Dr. Richard Bernstein: A diabetic who took his health into his own hands. Retrieved September 15, 2003, from *Dr. Bernstein's diabetes solution* Web site: http://www.diabetes-solution. net/hands.htm

Blouin, J. H. (1994). Prognostic indicators in bulimia nervosa treated with cognitive behavioral group therapy. *International Journal of Eating Disorders, 15*, 113–124.

Braun, D. L., Sunday, S. R., & Halmi, K. A. (1994). Psychiatric comorbidity in patients with eating disorders. *Psychological Medicine, 24*, 859–867.

Bruch, H. (1978). *The Golden Cage: The enigma of anorexia nervosa.* New York: Vintage Books.

Brumberg, J. (2000). *Fasting girls: The history of anorexia nervosa.* New York: Vintage Books.

Bulik, C. M., Sullivan, P. F., Carter, F. A., McIntosh, V. V., & Joyce, P. R. (1999). Predictors of rapid and sustained response to cognitive-behavioral therapy for bulimia nervosa. *International Journal of Eating Disorders, 26*, 137–144.

Bulik, C. M., Sullivan, P. F., Wade, T. D., Kendler, K. S. (2000). Twin studies of eating disorders: A review. *International Journal of Eating Disorders, 27*, 1–20.

Collings, S., & King, M. (1994). Ten-year follow-up of 50 patients with bulimia nervosa. *British Journal of Psychiatry, 164*, 80–87.

Crisp, A. H., Norton, K., Gowers, S., Hale, W. C., Bowyer, C., Yeldham, D., Levett, G., & Bhat, A. (1991). A controlled study of the effect of therapies aimed at adolescent and family psychopathology in anorexia nervosa. *British Journal of Psychiatry, 159*, 325–333.

Dalviski, A., Rahbar, B., Meals, R. A. (1997). Russell's sign. Subtle hand changes in patient with bulimia nervosa. *Clinical Orthopedica*, Oct (343): 107–109.

Dare, C., & Eisler, I. (1997). Family therapy for anorexia nervosa. In D. M. Garner & P. E. Garfinkel (Eds.), *Handbook of treatment for eating disorders* (2nd ed., pp. 307–324). New York: Guilford.

Dare, C., Eisler, I., Russell, G. E. M., & Szmukler, G. I. (1990). The clinical and theoretical impact of a controlled trial of family therapy in anorexia nervosa. *Journal of Marital and Family Therapy, 16*, 39–57.

Dare, C., Eisler, I., Russell, G., Treasure, J., & Dodge, L. (2001). Psychological therapies for adults with anorexia nervosa: randomised controlled trial of out-patient treatments. *British Journal of Psychiatry, 178*, 216–221.

Devlin, M. J. (1996). Assessment and treatment of binge eating disorder. *Psychiatric Clinics of North America.* 19(4), 761–772.

Devlin, M. J., Yanovski, S. Z., & Wilson, G. T. (2000). Obesity: What mental health professionals need to know. *American Journal of Psychiatry, 157,* 854–866.

Dey, I. (1999). *Grounding grounded theory: Guidelines for qualitative inquiry.* San Diego: Academic Press.

de Zwaan, M. (2001). Binge eating disorder and obesity. *International Journal of Obesity and Related Metabolic Disorders, 25*(suppl 1), S51–55.

Eckert, E. D., Halmi, K. A., Marchi, P., Grove, W., & Crosby, R. (1995). Ten-year follow-up of anorexia nervosa: clinical course and outcome. *Psychological Medicine, 25,* 143–156.

Eisler, I., Dare, C., Russell, G. F. M., Szmukler, G., le Grange, D., Dodge, E. (1997). Family and individual therapy in anorexia nervosa: a 5-year follow-up. *Archives of General Psychiatry, 54,* 1025–1030.

Fairburn, C. G. (1985). Cognitive-behavioral treatment for bulimia. In D. M. Garner & P. E. Garfinkel (Eds.), *Handbook of psychotherapy for anorexia nervosa and bulimia* (pp. 160–192). New York: Guilford.

Fairburn, C., & Cooper, P. (1993). Eating disorders. In K. Hawton, P.M. Salkovskis, J. Kirk, & D. M. Clark (Eds.), *Cognitive behavior therapy for psychiatric problems: A practical guide.* (pp. 277–314). New York: Oxford University Press.

Fairburn, C. G., Cooper, Z., Doll, H. A., & Welch, S. L. (1999). Risk factors for anorexia nervosa: Three integrated case-control comparisons. *Archives of General Psychiatry, 56,* 468–476.

Fairburn, C. G., Cowen, P., & Harrison, P. (1999). Twin studies and the etiology of eating disorders. *International Journal of Eating Disorders, 26,* 349–358.

Fairburn, C. G., Doll, H. A., Welch, S. L., Hay, P. J., Davies, B. A., & O'Connor, M. E. (1998). Risk factors for binge eating disorder: A community-based, case-control study. *Archives of General Psychiatry, 55,* 425–432.

Fairburn, C. G., Marcus, M. D., & Wilson, G. T. (1993). Cognitive behavioral therapy for binge eating and bulimia nervosa: A comprehensive treatment manual. In C. G. Fairburn & G. T. Wilson (Eds.), *Binge eating: Nature, assessment and treatment.* New York: Guilford.

Fairburn, C. G., Norman, P. A., Welch, S. I., & Peveler, R. (1996). Cognitive behavioural therapy and focal interpersonal therapy increased long-term remission of eating disorders [abstract]. *Evidence-Based Medicine, 1*(2), 48.

Fallon, P., & Wonderlich, S. A. (1997). Sexual abuse and other forms of trauma. In D. M. Garner & P. E. Garfinkel (Eds.), *Handbook of treatment for eating disorders* (pp. 394–414). New York: Guilford.

Fichter, M. M., Leibl, K., Rief, W., Brunner, E., Schmidt-Auberger, S., & Engel, E. R. (1991). Fluoxetine versus placebo: a double-blind study with bulimic inpatients undergoing intensive psychotherapy. *Pharmacopsychiatry, 24*(1), 1–7.

Fichter, M. M., & Quadflieg, N. (1997). Six-year course of bulimia nervosa. *International Journal of Eating Disorders, 22*(4), 361–384.

Fishman, H. C. (1993). *Intensive structural therapy: Treating families in their social context.* New York: Basic Books.

Fishman, H. C. (1988). *Treating troubled adolescents: A family therapy approach.* New York: Basic Books.

Fishman, H. C., Andes, F., & Knowlton, R. (2001). Enhancing family therapy: The addition of a community resource specialist. *Journal of Marital and Family Therapy, 27*(1), 111–116.

Frattaroli, E. (2001). *Healing the soul in the age of the brain: Becoming conscious in an unconscious world.* New York: Penguin.

Garfinkel, P. E., & Walsh, B. T. (1997). Drug therapies. In D. M. Garner & P. E. Garfinkel (Eds.), *Handbook of treatment for eating disorders* (2nd ed., pp. 372–380). New York: Guilford.

Garner, D. M., & Needleman, L. D. (1997). In D. M. Garner & P. E. Garfinkel, (Eds.), *Handbook of treatment for eating disorders* (2nd ed., pp. 50–63). New York: Guilford.

Garner, D. M., Rockert, W., Davis, R., Garner, M. V., Olmsted, M. P., & Eagle M. (1993). Comparison between cognitive-behavioral and supportive-expressive therapy for bulimia nervosa. *American Journal of Psychiatry, 150*(1), 37–46.

Geist, R., Heinmaa, M., Stephens, D., Davis, R., & Katzman, D. K. (2000). Comparison of family therapy and family group psychoeducation in adolescents with anorexia nervosa. *Canadian Journal of Psychiatry, 45*(2), 173–178.

Gidwani, G. P., & Rome, E. S. (1997). Eating disorders. *Clinical Obstetrics and Gynecology, 40*(3), 601–615.

Gill, G. (1996). *Cecil textbook of medicine.* Philadelphia: W. B. Saunders.

Glaser, B. G., & Strauss, A. L. (1967). *Discovery of grounded theory: Strategies for qualitative research.* Chicago: Aldine.

Goldbloom, D. S., & Kennedy, S. H. (1995). Medical complications of anorexia nervosa. In K. D. Brownell & C. G. Fairburn (Eds.), *Eating disorders and obesity: A comprehensive handbook.* New York: Guilford.

Goldbloom, D. S., Olmstead, M., Davis, R., Clewes, J., Heinmaa, M., Rockert, W., et al. A randomized controlled trial of fluoxetine and cognitive behavioral therapy for bulimia nervosa: short-term outcome. *Behavior Research and Therapy, 35*(9), 803–811.

Goldstein, D. J., Wilson, M. G., Thompson, V. L., Potvin, J. H., Rampey, A. H., & The Fluoxetine Bulimia Nervosa Research Group. (1995). Long-term fluoxetine treatment of bulimia nervosa. *British Journal of Psychiatry, 166*(5), 660–666.

Gordon, R. A. (2000). Eating disorders: Anatomy of a social epidemic (2nd ed.). Oxford, Blackwell.

Gordon, R. A. (2001). Eating disorders East and West: A culture-bound syndrome unbound. In M. Nasser, M. A. Katzman, & R. A. Gordon (Eds.), *Eating disorders and cultures in transition.* Hove, East Sussex: Brunner-Routledge.

Gorwood, P., Bouvard, M., Mouren-Simeoni, M. C., Kipman, A., & Ades, J. (1998). Genetics and anorexia nervosa: A review of candidate genes. *Psychiatric Genetics, 8*(1), 1–12.

Gowers, S., Norton, K., Halek, C., & Crisp, A. H. (1994). Outcome of outpatient psychotherapy in a random allocation treatment study of anorexia nervosa. *International Journal of Eating Disorders, 15,* 165–177.

Gull, W. W. (1873). Anorexia hysterica (apepsia hysterica). *British Medical Journal, 2,* 527–528.

Haley, J. (1980). *Leaving home: The therapy of disturbed young people.* New York: McGraw-Hill.

Halmi, K., Mitchell, J., & Rigotti, N. (1995). Recognizing and treating eating disorders. *Contemporary Nurse Practitioner, 1*(1), 26–39.

Hamburg, P. (1996). How long is long-term therapy for anorexia nervosa? In J. Werne (Ed.), *Treating eating disorders* (pp. 71–99). San Francisco: Jossey-Bass.

Handy, C. B. (1989). *The age of unreason.* Boston: Harvard Business School Press.

Hay, P. J., & Bacaltchuk, J. (2002). Psychotherapy for bulimia nervosa and binging [Abstract]. *Cochrane Database of Systematic Reviews* 4.

Heilemann, M. V., Lee, K. A., & Kury, F. S. (2002). Strengths and vulnerabilities of women of Mexican descent in relation to depressive symptoms. *Nursing Research, 51*(3): 175–182.

Herscovici, C. R. (2002). Eating disorders in adolescence. In F. Kaslow (Series Ed.) & J. Magnavita (Vol. Ed.), *Comprehensive handbook of psychotherapy: Vol. 1. Psychodynamic/object relations* (pp. 133–159). New York: John Wiley.

Herzog, D. B., Keller, M. B., Sacks, N. R., Yeh, C. J., & Lavori, P. W. (1992). Psychiatric comorbidity in treatment-seeking anorexics and bulimics. *Journal of the American Academy of Child and Adolescent Psychiatry, 31*(5), 810–818.

Herzog, D. B., Sacks, N. R., Keller, M. B., Lavori, P. W., von Ranson, K. B., & Gray, H. M. (1993). Patterns and predictors of recovery in anorexia nervosa and bulimia nervosa. *Journal of the American Academy of Child and Adolescent Psychiatry, 32,* 835–842.

Holmes, T., & Rahe, R. (1967). The social readjustment rating scale. *Journal of Psychosomatic Research, 11,* 213–182.

Horesh, N., Apter, A., Lepkifker, E., Ratzoni, G., Weizmann, R., & Tyano, S. (1995). Life events and severe anorexia nervosa in adolescence. *Acta Psychiatrica Scandinavica, 91*(1), 5–9.

Horesh, N., Apter, A., Ishai, J., Danziger, Y., Miculincer, M., Stein, D., Lepkifker, E., & Minouni, M. (1996). Abnormal psychosocial situations and eating disorders in adolescence. *Journal of the American Academy of Child and Adolescent Psychiatry, 35,*(7), 921–927.

Howard, J. (1978). *Families.* New York: Simon & Schuster.

Hsu, L. K. G., Clement, L., Santhouse, R., & Ju, E. S. Y. (1991). Treatment of bulimia nervosa with lithium carbonate: A controlled study. *Journal of Nervous and Mental Disease, 179*(6), 351–355.

Hyman, B., & Williams, L. (2001). Resilience among women survivors of child sexual abuse. *Affilia-Journal of Women and Social Work, 16*(2), 198–219.

Johnson, W. G., Tsoh, J. Y., Varnado, P. J. (1996). Eating disorders: Efficacy of pharmacological and psychological interventions. *Clinical Psychology Review, 16*(6), 457–478.

Kaye, W., Strober, M., Stein, D., & Gendall, K. (1999). New directions in treatment research of anorexia nervosa and bulimia nervosa. *Biological Psychiatry, 45*(10), 1285–1292.

Keel, P. K., & Mitchell, J. E. (1997). Outcome in bulimia nervosa. *American Journal of Psychiatry, 154*(3), 313–321.

Keel, P. K., Mitchell, J. E., Miller, K. B., Davis, T. L., & Crow, S. J. (1999). Long-term outcome of bulimia nervosa. *Archives of General Psychiatry, 56,* 63–69.

Keller, M. B., Klerman, G. L., Lavori, P. W., Coryell, W., Endicott, J., & Taylor, J. (1984). Long-term outcome of episodes of major depression. Clinical and public health significance. *Journal of the American Medical Association, 252*(6), 788–792.

Kim, S. S. (2003). Role of fluoxetine in anorexia nervosa. *Annals of Pharmacotherapy, 37*(6), 890–892.

Kirsch, I., Moore, T. J., Scoboria, A., & Nicholls, S. S. (2002). The emperor's new drugs: An analysis of antidepressant medication data submitted to the U.S. Food and Drug Administration. Retrieved January 5, 2003. *Prevention and Treatment, 5,* http://www.journals.apa.org/prevention/volume5/pre0050023a.html

Klump, K. L., Wonderlich, S., Lehoux, P., Lilenfeld, L. R. R., Bulik, C. M. (2002). Does environment matter? A review of nonshared environment and eating disorders. *International Journal of Eating Disorders, 31,* 118–135.

Kotter, J. P. (2002). *The heart of change: Real-life stories of how people change their organizations.* Boston: Harvard Business School Press.

Kruger, S., & Kennedy, S. H. (2000). Psychopharmacotherapy of anorexia nervosa, bulimia nervosa and binge-eating disorder. *Journal of Psychiatry and Neuroscience, 25*(5), 497–508.

Laborsky, L. (1984). *Principles of psychoanalytic psychotherapy: A manual of psychoanalytic psychotherapy.* New York: Basic Books.

Laségue, C. (1873). On hysterical anorexia. *Medical Times and Gazette, 2,* 265–266, 367–369.

Lay, B., Jennen-Steinmetz, C., Reinhard, I., & Schmidt, M. H. (2002). Characteristics of inpatient weight gain in adolescent anorexia nervosa: relation to speed of relapse and re-admission. *European Eating Disorders Review, 10,* 22–40.

Lewandowski, L. M., Gebing, T. A., Anthony, J. L., & O'Brien, W. H. (1997). Meta-analysis of cognitive-behavioral treatment studies for bulimia. *Clinical Psychology Review, 17*(7), 703–718.

Lock, J., Le Grange, D., Agras, W. S., & Dare, C. (2001). *Treatment manual for anorexia nervosa: A family based approach.* New York: Guilford.

Lucas, A. R., Beard, C. M., O'Fallan, W. M., & Kurland, L. T. (1991). 50-year trends in the incidence of anorexia nervosa in Rochester, Minnesota: A population-based study. *American Journal of Psychiatry, 148*(7), 917–922.

Luhrmann, T. M. (2000). *Of two minds: The growing disorder in American psychiatry.* New York: Knopf.

Martin, F. E. (1985). The treatment and outcome of anorexia nervosa in adolescents: a prospective study and five year follow-up. *Journal of Psychiatric Research, 19,* 509–514.

Minuchin, S., & Fishman, H. C. (1981). *Family therapy techniques.* Cambridge, MA: Harvard University Press.

Minuchin, S., Rosman, B. L., & Baker, L. (1978). *Psychosomatic families: Anorexia nervosa in context.* Cambridge, MA: Harvard University Press.

Mitchell, K., & Carr, A. (2000). Anorexia and bulimia. In A. Carr (Ed.) *What works with children and adolescents? A critical review of psychological interventions with children, adolescents, and their families* (pp. 233–257). New York: Routledge.

Morgan, J. F. (2002). Review: Antidepressants increase remission and clinical improvement in bulimia nervosa. *ACP Journal Club, 136*(3): 106.

Morton, R. (1689). *Phthisiologica, seu exercitations de phthisi.* London: S. Smith.

Murphy, J. M., Laird, N. M., Monson, R. R., Sobol, A. M., & Leighton, A. H. (2000). Incidence of depression in the Stirling County Study: Historical and comparative perspectives. *Psychological Medicine, 30* (3), 505–514.

National Eating Disorders Association website. (2002). Retrieved June 15, 2002, from http:/www.nationaleatingdisorders.org

Noordenbos, G., Oldenhave, A., Muschter, J., & Terpstra, N. (2002). Characteristics and treatment of patients with chronic eating disorders. *Eating Disorders, 10,* 15–29.

O'Brien, K. M., & Vincent, N. K. (2003). Psychiatric comorbidity in anorexia and bulimia nervosa. Nature, prevalence and causal relationships. *Clinical Psychology Review, 23*(1), 57–74.

Parry-Jones, B. (1991). Historical terminology of eating disorders. *Psychological Medicine, 21,* 21–28.

Pearson, V., Phillips, M. R., He, F., & Ji, H. (2002). Attempted suicide among young rural women in the People's Republic of China: Possibilities for prevention. *Suicide and Life-Threatening Behavior, 32*(4), 359–369.

Peterson, C. B., & Mitchell, J. E. (1999). Psychosocial and pharmacological treatment of eating disorders: A review of research findings. *Journal of Clinical Psychology, 55*(6), 685–697.

Pike, K. M., Dohm, F., Striegel-Moore, R. H., Wilfley, D. E., & Fairburn, C. G. (2001). A comparison of black and white women with binge eating disorder. *American Journal of Psychiatry, 158*(9), 1455–1460.

Piran, N., Langdon, L., Kaplan, A., & Garfinkel, P. E. (1989). Evaluation of a day hospital program for eating disorders. *International Journal of Eating Disorders, 8*(5), 523–532.

Pi-Sunyer, F. X. (2000). Symposium on body weight regulation and obesity: Metabolic and clinical aspects: 1st plenary session: "obesity." Obesity: criteria and classification. *Proceedings of the Nutrition Society, 59*(4), 505–509.

Polivy, J., & Federoff, I. (1997). In Garner, D. M. & Garfinkel, P. E. (eds.). *Handbook of Treatment for Eating Disorders* (2nd ed., pp. 462–475). New York: Guilford.

Pope, H. G., & Hodson, J. L. (1992). Is childhood sexual abuse a risk factor for bulimia nervosa? *American Journal of Psychiatry, 149*(4), 455–463.

Putnam, R. D. (2000). *Bowling alone: The collapse and revival of American community.* New York: Simon & Schuster.

Rabkin, J. G., Wagner, G. J., & Del Bene, M. (2000). Resilience and distress among amyotrophic lateral sclerosis patients and caregivers. *Psychosomatic Medicine, 62*(2), 271–279.

Rastam, M. (1992). Anorexia nervosa in 51 Swedish adolescents: Premorbid problems and comorbidity. *Journal of the American Academy of Child and Adolescent Psychiatry, 31*(5), 819–829.

Ratnasuriya, R. H., Eisler, I., Szmukler, G. I., & Russell, G. F. M. (1991). Anorexia nervosa: Outcome and prognostic factors after 20 years. *British Journal of Psychiatry, 158,* 495–502.

Ricca, V., Mannucci, E., Zucchi, T., Rotella, C. M., & Faravelli, C. (2000). Cognitive-behavioural therapy for bulimia nervosa and binge eating disorder: A review. *Psychotherapy and Psychosomatics, 69*(6), 335–338.

Robin, A. L., Siegel, P. T., Koepke, T., Moye, A. W., & Tice, S. (1994). Family therapy versus individual therapy for adolescent females with anorexia nervosa. *Journal of Development and Behavioral Pediatrics, 15*(2), 111–116.

Robin, A. L., Seigel, P. T., Moye, A. W., Gilroy, M., Dennis, A. B., & Sikand, A. (1999). A controlled comparison of family versus individual therapy for adolescents with anorexia nervosa. *Journal of the American Academy of Child and Adolescent Psychiatry, 38*(12), 1482–1489.

Rosenvinge, J. H. (1990). Group therapy for anorexic and bulimic patients. Some aspects on the condition of group therapy and a critical review of some recent studies. *Acta Psychiatrica Scandinavica, 82*(Suppl. 361), 38–43.

Rosenvinge, J. H., Martinussen, M., & Ostensen, E. (2000). The comorbidity of eating disorders and personality disorders: A meta-analytic review of studies published between 1983 and 1998. *Eating and Weight Disorders, 5*(2), 52–61.

Rosman, B. L., Minuchin, S., & Liebman, R. (1975). Family lunch session: An introduction to family therapy in anorexia nervosa. *American Journal of Orthopsychiatry, 45*(5), 846–853.

Ross, C. A., & Pam, A. (1995). *Pseudoscience in biological psychiatry: Blaming the body.* New York: John Wiley.

Russell, G. F. M. (1979). Bulimia nervosa: An ominous variant of anorexia nervosa. *Psychological Medicine, 9,* 429–448.

Russell, G. F. M., Dare, C., Eisler, I., & Le Grange, P. D. F. (1992). Controlled trials of family treatments in anorexia nervosa. In K. A. Halmi (Ed.), *Psychobiology and treatment of anorexia nervosa and bulimia nervosa.* Washington, DC: American Psychiatric Press.

Russell, G. F. M., Szmukler, G. I., Dare, C., & Eisler, I. (1987). An evaluation of family therapy in anorexia nervosa and bulimia nervosa. *Archives of General Psychiatry, 44,* 1047–1056.

Sadock, B. J., & Sadock, V. A. (2003). *Synopsis of psychiatry: Behavioral sciences/clinical psychiatry* (9th ed.). Philadelphia: Lippincott Williams & Wilkins.

Selvini Palazzoli, M. (1974). *Self-starvation: From the intrapsychic to the transpersonal approach to anorexia nervosa.* London: Human Context.

Shapiro, F., & Maxfield, L. (2002). Eye movement desensitization and reprocessing (EMDR): Information processing in the treatment of trauma. *Journal of Clinical Psychology, 58,* 933–946.

Sigal, J. J., & Weinfeld, M. (2001). Do children cope better than adults with potentially traumatic stress? A 40-year follow-up of Holocaust survivors. *Psychiatry, 64*(1), 69–80.

Smith, C., Feldman, S., Nasserbakht, A., & Steiner, H. (1993). Psychological characteristics and DSM-III-R diagnoses at 6-year follow-up of adolescent anorexia nervosa. *Journal of the American Academy of Child and Adolescent Psychiatry, 32*(6), 1237–1245.

Snyder, R., & Hasbrouck, L. (1996). Feminist identity, gender traits, and symptoms of disturbed eating among college women. *Psychology of Women Quarterly, 20*(4), 593–598.

Spitzer, R. L., Devlin, M. J., Walsh, B. T., Hasin, D., Wing, R. R., Marcus, M. D., Stunkard, A., Wadden, T. A., Agras, W. S., Mitchell, J., & Nonas, C. (1992). Binge eating disorder: A multisite field trial for the diagnostic criteria. *International Journal of Eating Disorders, 11*(3), 191–203.

Steiner, H., & Lock, J. (1998). Anorexia nervosa and bulimia nervosa in children and adolescents: A review of the past 10 years. *Journal of the American Academy of Child and Adolescent Psychiatry, 37*(4), 352–359.

Steinhausen, H., Rauss-Mason, C., & Seidel, R. (1991). Follow-up studies of anorexia nervosa: a review of four decades of outcome research. *Psychological Medicine, 21,* 447–454.

Strober, M., Freeman, R., & Morrell, W. (1997). The long-term course of severe anorexia nervosa in adolescents: Survival analysis of recovery, relapse, and outcome predictors over 10–15 years in a prospective study. *International Journal of Eating Disorders, 22*(4), 339–360.

Telch, C. F., & Stice, E. (1998). Psychiatric comorbidity in women with binge eating disorder: Prevalence rates from a non-treatment-seeking sample. *Journal of Consulting and Clinical Psychology, 66*(5), 768–776.

Torrey, E. F., Bowler, A. E., & Taylor, E. H. (1994). *Schizophrenia and manic-depressive disorder: The biological roots of mental illness as revealed by the landmark study of identical twins.* New York: Basic Books.

Treasure, J., Todd, G., Brolly, M., Tiller, J., Nehmed, A., & Denman, F. (1995). A pilot study of a randomised trial of cognitive analytical therapy vs educational behavioral therapy for adult anorexia nervosa. *Behavior Research and Therapy, 33,* 363–367.

Vitiello, B., & Lederhendler, I. (2000). Research on eating disorders: Current status and future prospects. *Biological Psychiatry, 47*(9), 777–786.

Waller, G. (1999). Review: Medication and cognitive behaviour therapy control symptoms of bulimia nervosa. *Evidence-Based Medicine, 4,* 145.

Walsh, B. T., & Devlin, M. J. (1998). Eating disorders: Progress and problems. *Science, 280*(5368), 1387–1390.

Walsh, B. T., Wilson, G. T., Loeb, K. L., Devlin, M. J., Pike, K. M., Roose, S. P., et al. Medication and psychotherapy in the treatment of bulimia nervosa. *American Journal of Psychiatry, 154*(4), 523–531.

Watzlawick, P., Weakland, J., & Fisch, R. (1974). *Change: Principles of problem formation and problem resolution.* New York: W. W. Norton.

Wilfley, D. E., & Cohen, L. R. (1997). Psychological treatment of bulimia nervosa and binge eating disorder. *Psychopharmacology Bulletin, 33*(3), 437–454.

Wilson, S. A., Becker, L. A., Tinker, R. H. (1997). Fifteen-month follow-up of eye movement desensitization and reprocessing (EMDR) treatment for posttraumatic stress disorder and psychological trauma. *Journal of Consulting and Clinical Psychology, 65*(6), 1047–1056.

Wilson, T. G. (1996). Treatment of bulimia nervosa: When CBT fails. *Behaviour Research and Therapy, 34*(3), 197–212.

Wilson, T. G. (1999). Cognitive behavior therapy for eating disorders: progess and problems. *Behavior Research and Therapy, 37,* S79–S95.

Wilson, T. G., & Fairburn, C. G. (1993). Cognitive treatments for eating disorders. *Journal of Consulting and Clinical Psychology, 61*(2), 261–269.

Wolf, N. (2002). *The beauty myth.* New York: HarperCollins.

World Health Organization (1992). *The ICD-10 classification of mental and behavioural disorders. Clinical descriptions and diagnostic guidelines.* Geneva: Author.

Yanovski, S. Z., Nelson, J. E., Dubbert, B. K., & Spitzer, R. L. (1993). Association of binge eating disorder and psychiatric comorbidity in obese subjects. *American Journal of Psychiatry, 150*(10), 1472–1479.

Zimpfer, D. G. (1990). Group work for bulimia: A review of outcomes. *Journal for Specialists in Group Work, 15*(4), 239–251.

Index